Chapter 25: Wight's Loyalty

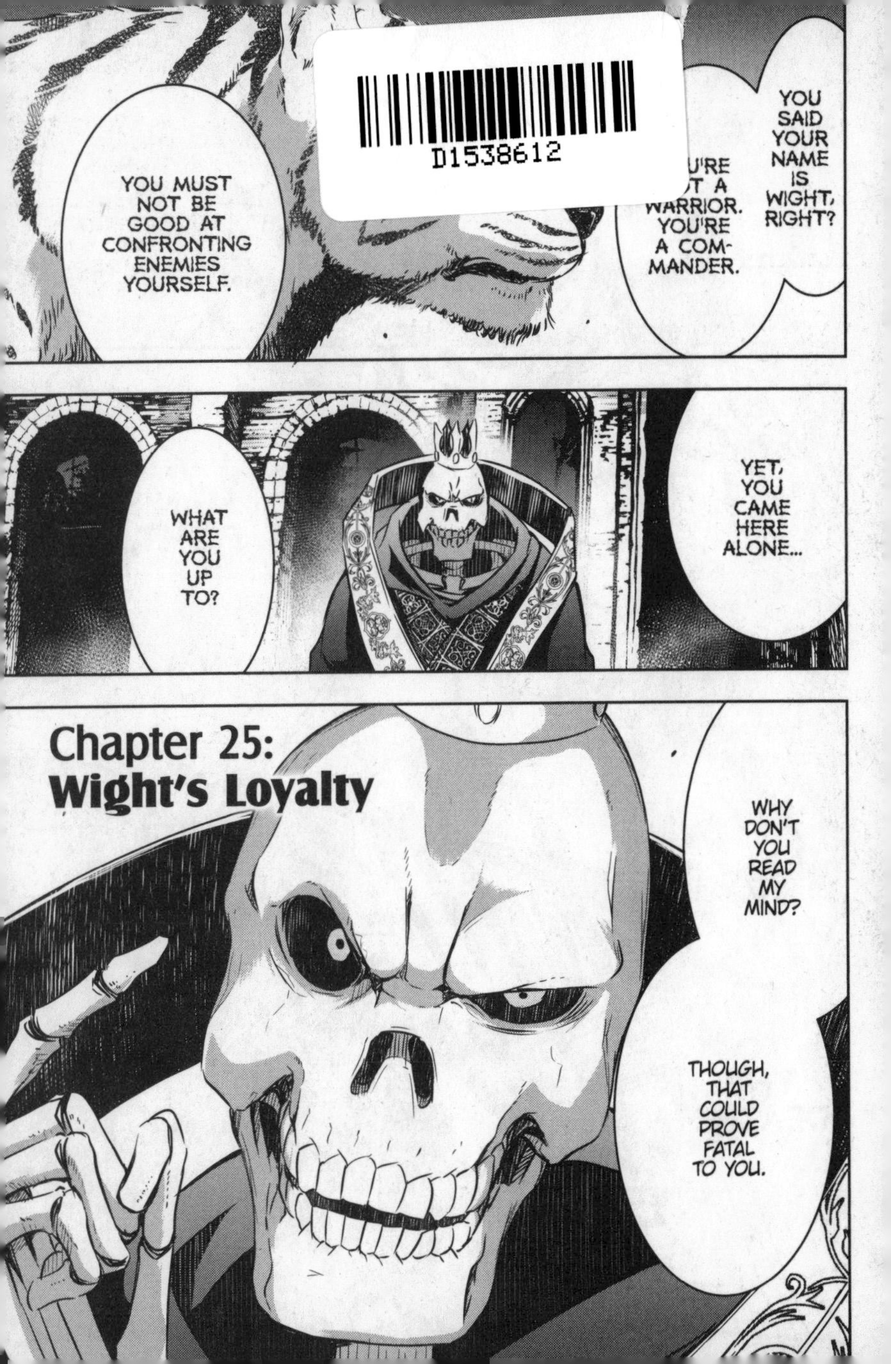
YOU SAID YOUR NAME IS WIGHT, RIGHT?
U'RE T A WARRIOR. YOU'RE A COM-MANDER.
YOU MUST NOT BE GOOD AT CONFRONTING ENEMIES YOURSELF.
YET, YOU CAME HERE ALONE...
WHAT ARE YOU UP TO?
WHY DON'T YOU READ MY MIND?
THOUGH, THAT COULD PROVE FATAL TO YOU.

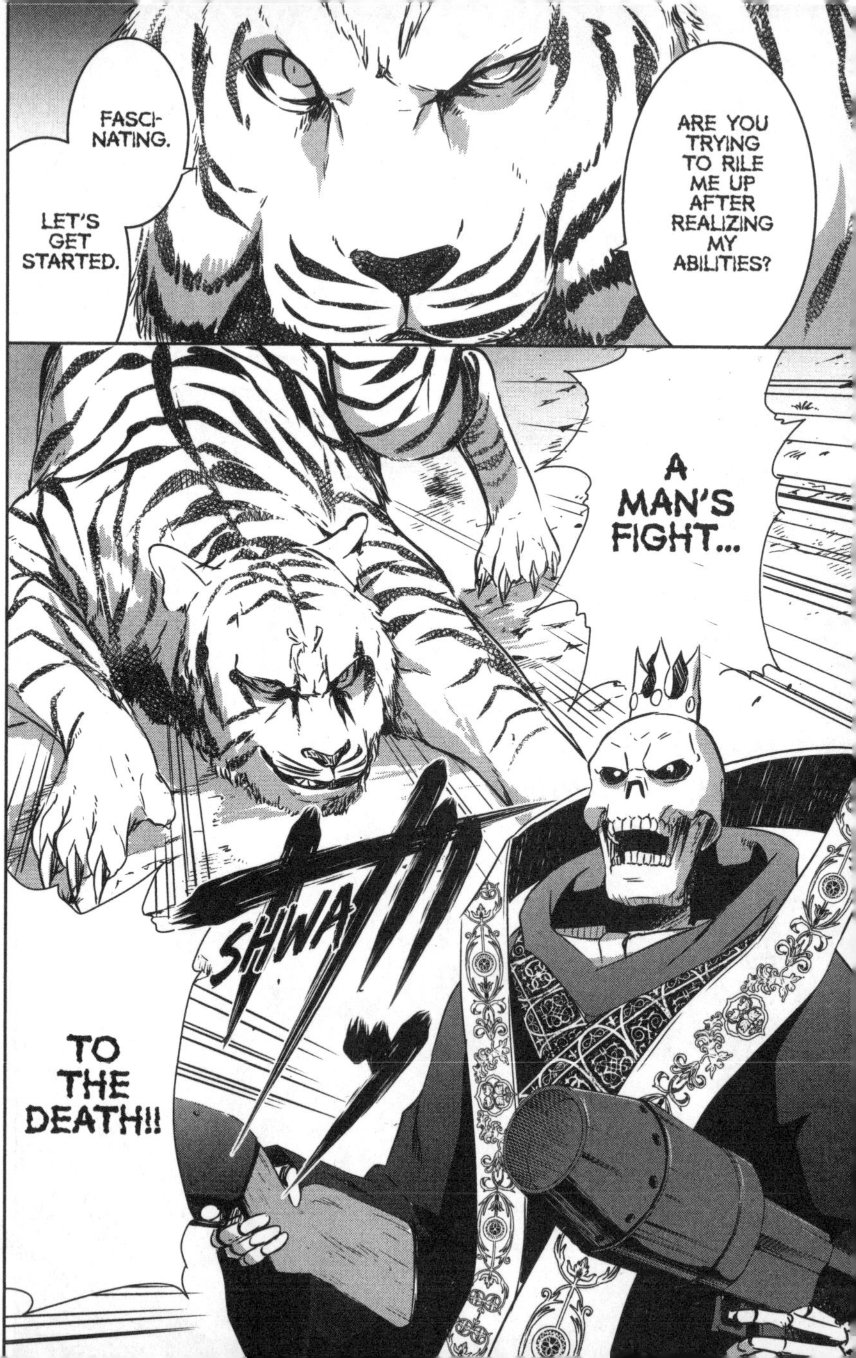

ARE YOU TRYING TO RILE ME UP AFTER REALIZING MY ABILITIES?
FASCINATING.
LET'S GET STARTED.
A MAN'S FIGHT...
SHWA
TO THE DEATH!!

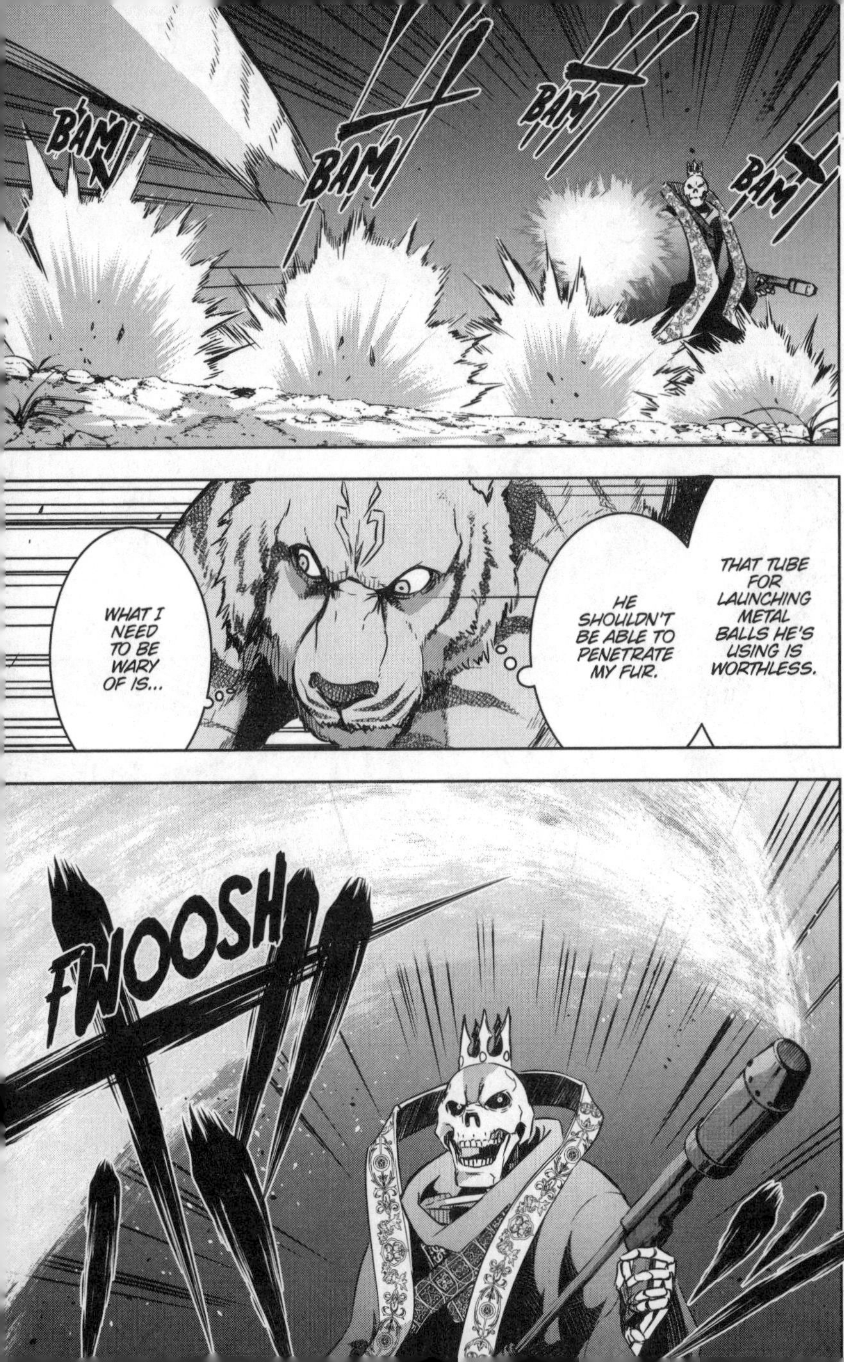
BAM
BAM
BAM
BAM
THAT TUBE FOR LAUNCHING METAL BALLS HE'S USING IS WORTHLESS.
HE SHOULDN'T BE ABLE TO PENETRATE MY FUR.
WHAT I NEED TO BE WARY OF IS...
FWOOSH

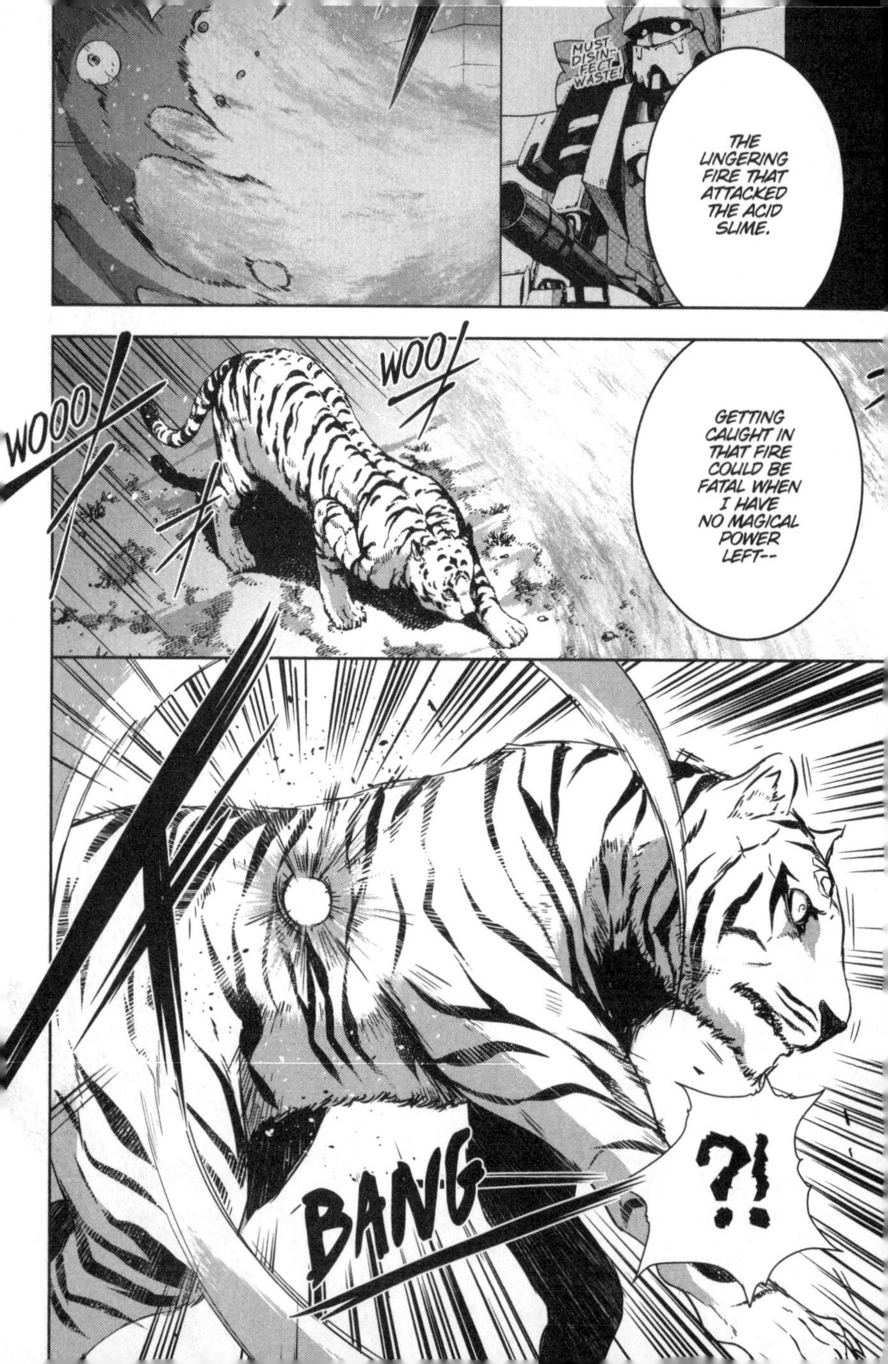

THE LINGERING FIRE THAT ATTACKED THE ACID SLIME.
MUST DISINFECT WASTE!
GETTING CAUGHT IN THAT FIRE COULD BE FATAL WHEN I HAVE NO MAGICAL POWER LEFT--
WOO
WOOO
?!
BANG

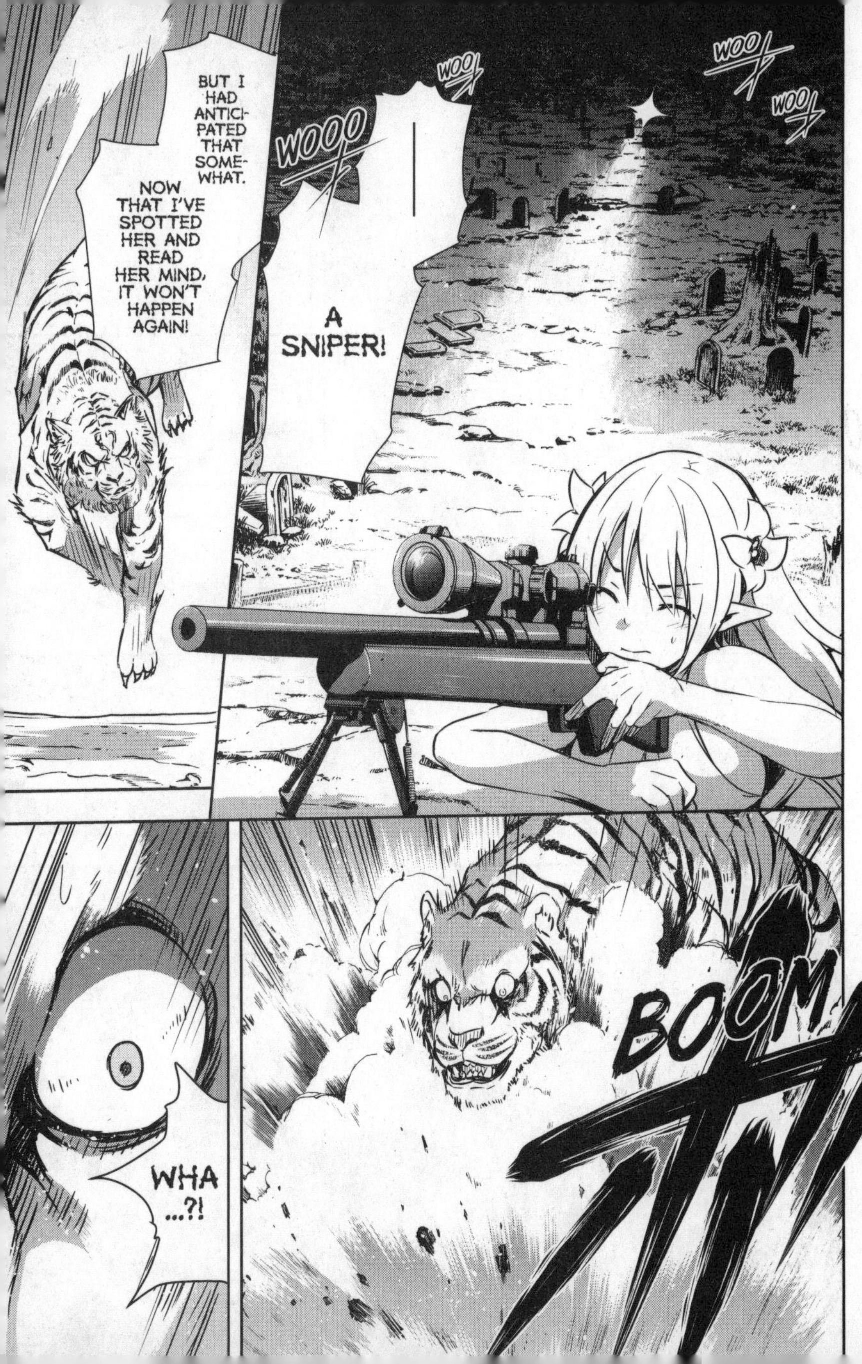
WOO
WOO
WOO
WOOO
A SNIPER!
BUT I HAD ANTICIPATED THAT SOMEWHAT.
NOW THAT I'VE SPOTTED HER AND READ HER MIND, IT WON'T HAPPEN AGAIN!
BOOM
WHA ...?!

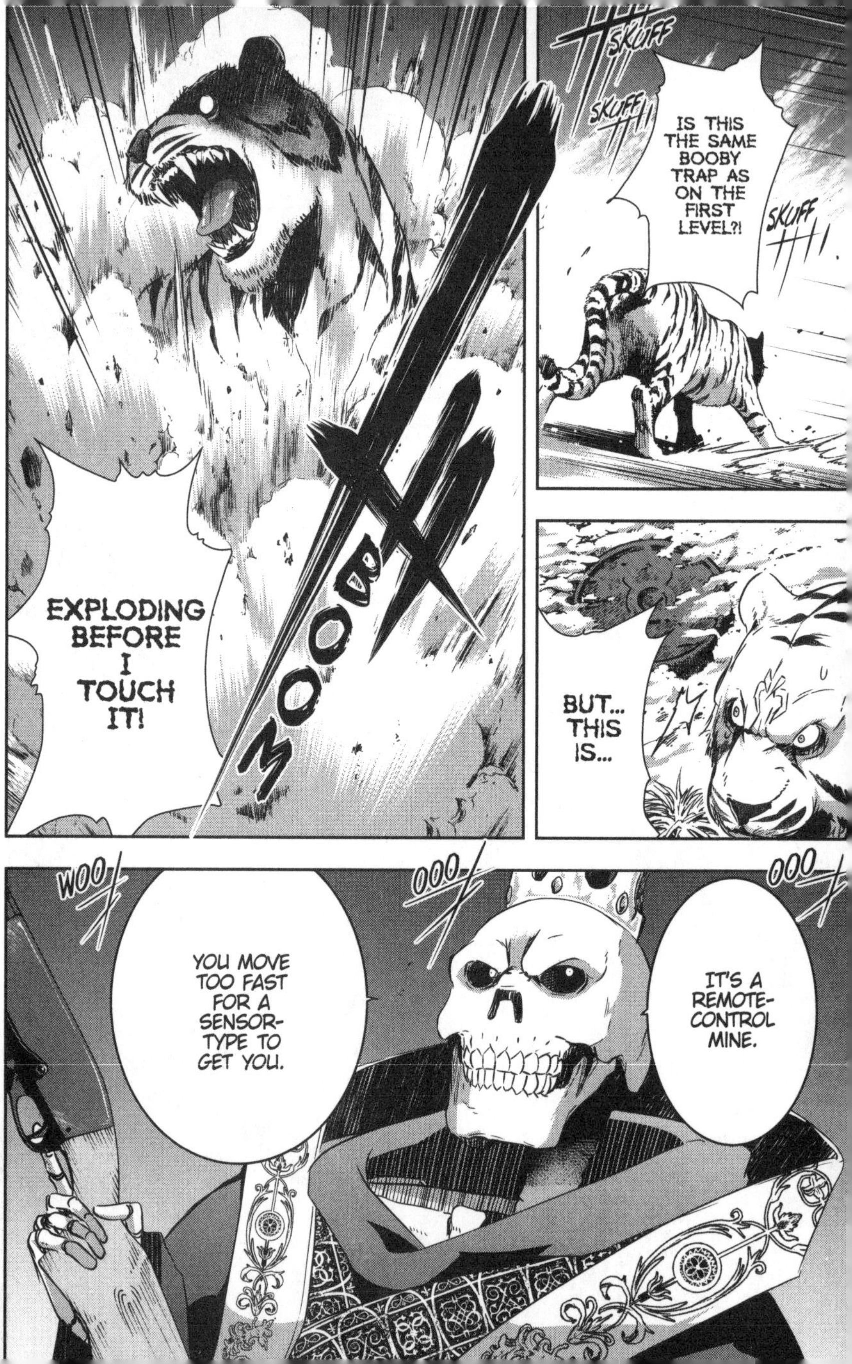
SKUFF
SKUFF
IS THIS THE SAME BOOBY TRAP AS ON THE FIRST LEVEL?!
SKUFF
BUT... THIS IS...
BOOOM
EXPLODING BEFORE I TOUCH IT!
OOO
IT'S A REMOTE-CONTROL MINE.
OOO
YOU MOVE TOO FAST FOR A SENSOR-TYPE TO GET YOU.
WOO

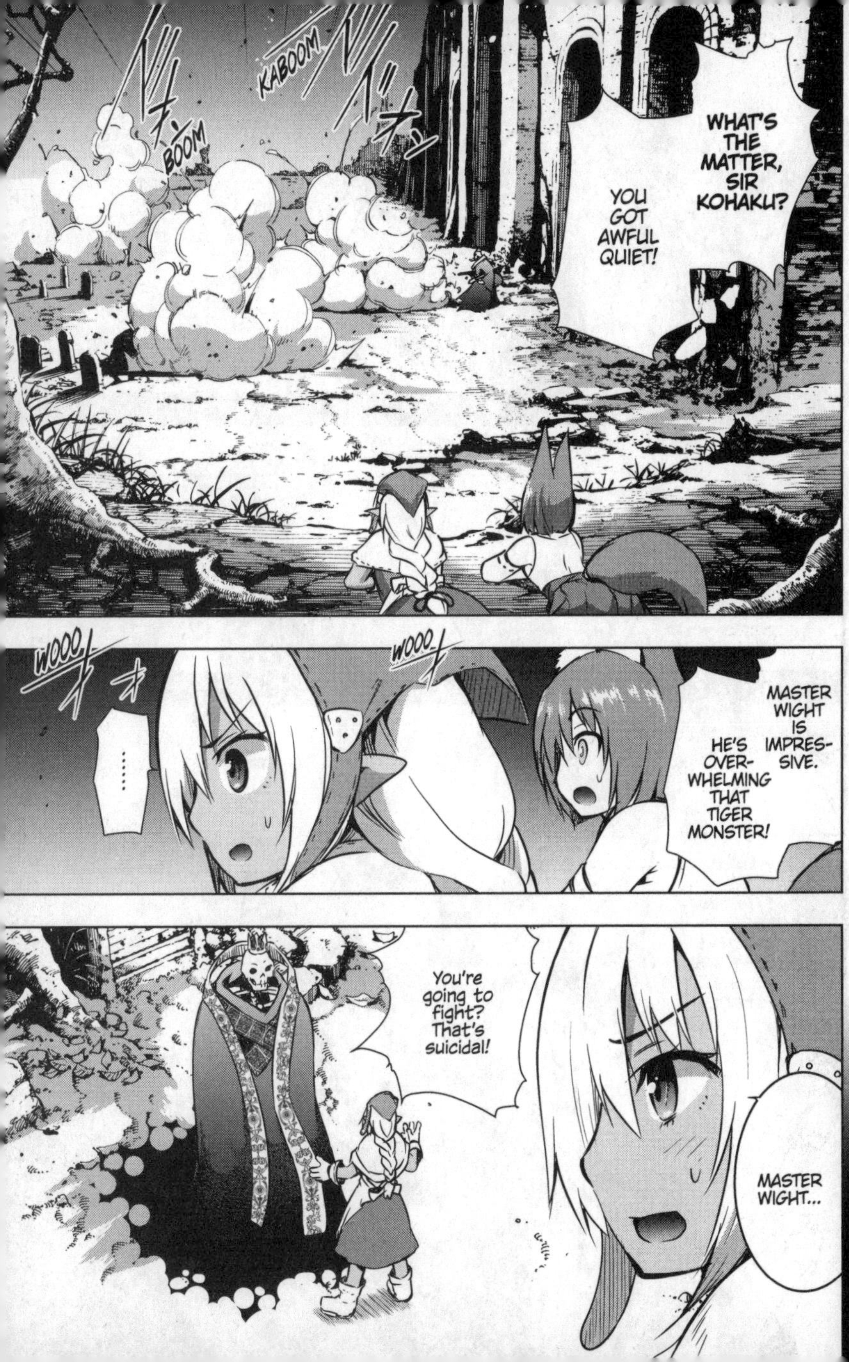
KABOOM
BOOM
WHAT'S THE MATTER, SIR KOHAKU?
YOU GOT AWFUL QUIET!
WOOO
WOOO
MASTER WIGHT IS IMPRESSIVE.
HE'S OVER-WHELMING THAT TIGER MONSTER!
......
MASTER WIGHT...
You're going to fight? That's suicidal!

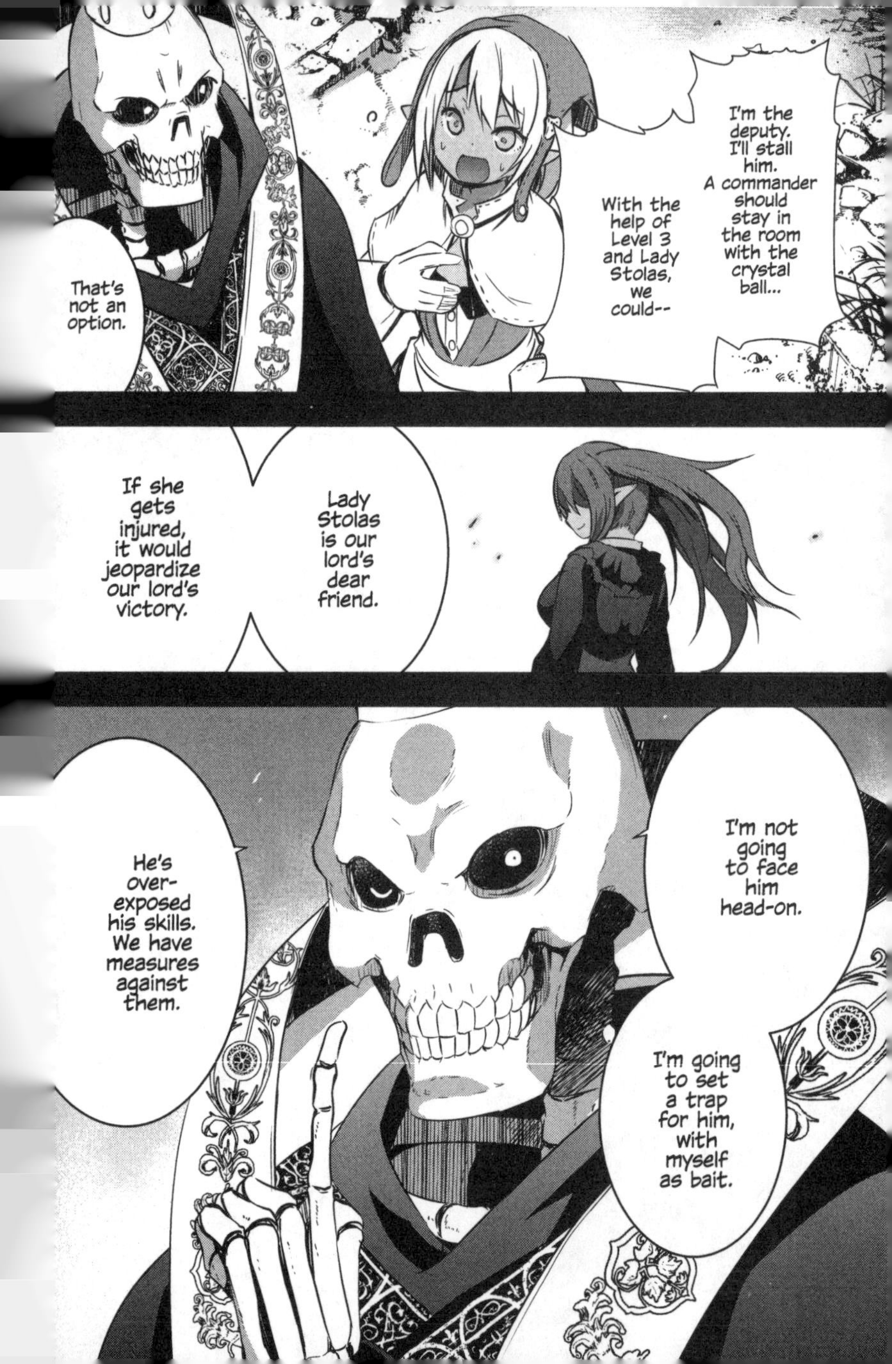
I'm the deputy. I'll stall him. A commander should stay in the room with the crystal ball...
With the help of Level 3 and Lady Stolas, we could--
That's not an option.
Lady Stolas is our lord's dear friend.
If she gets injured, it would jeopardize our lord's victory.
I'm not going to face him head-on.
I'm going to set a trap for him, with myself as bait.
He's over-exposed his skills. We have measures against them.

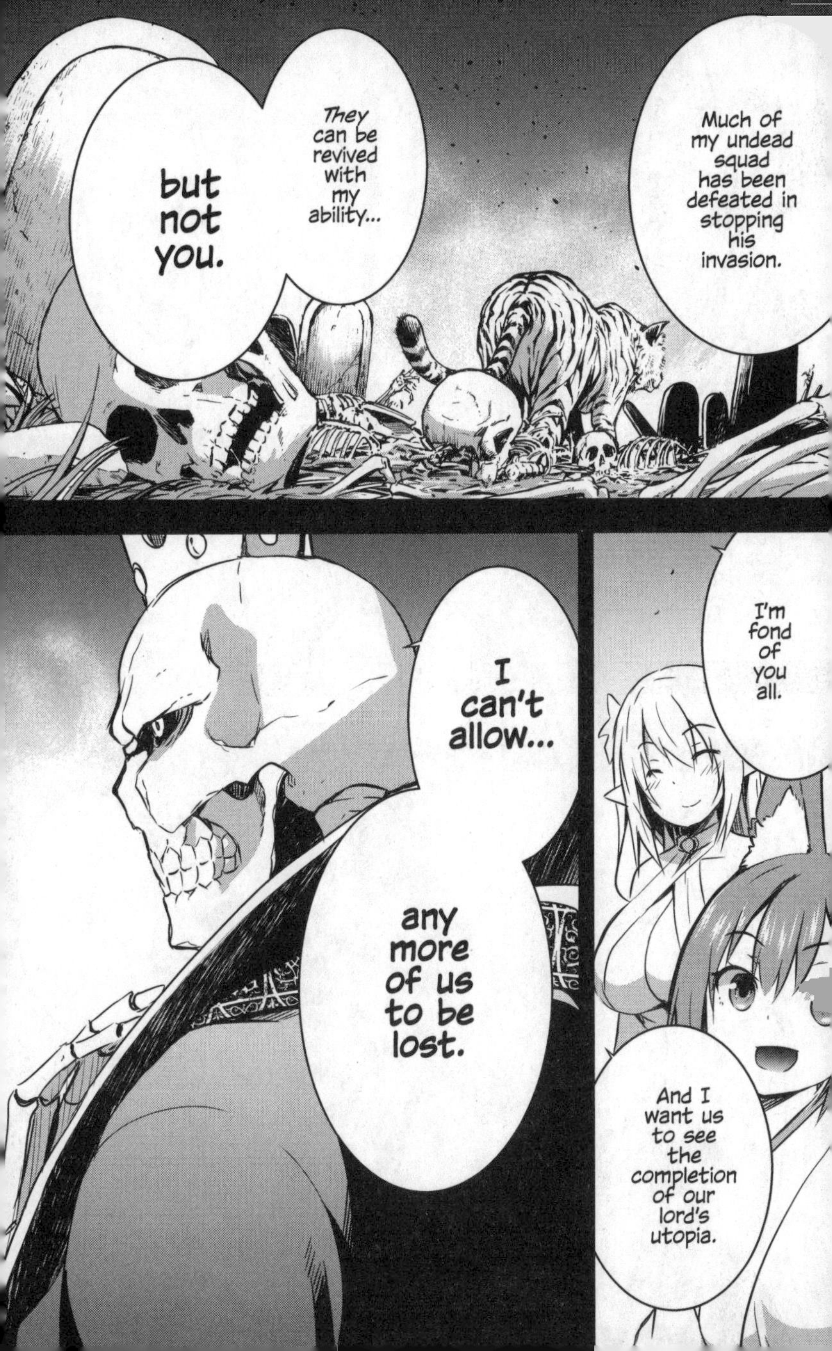
Much of my undead squad has been defeated in stopping his invasion.
They can be revived with my ability...
but not you.
I'm fond of you all.
And I want us to see the completion of our lord's utopia.
I can't allow...
any more of us to be lost.

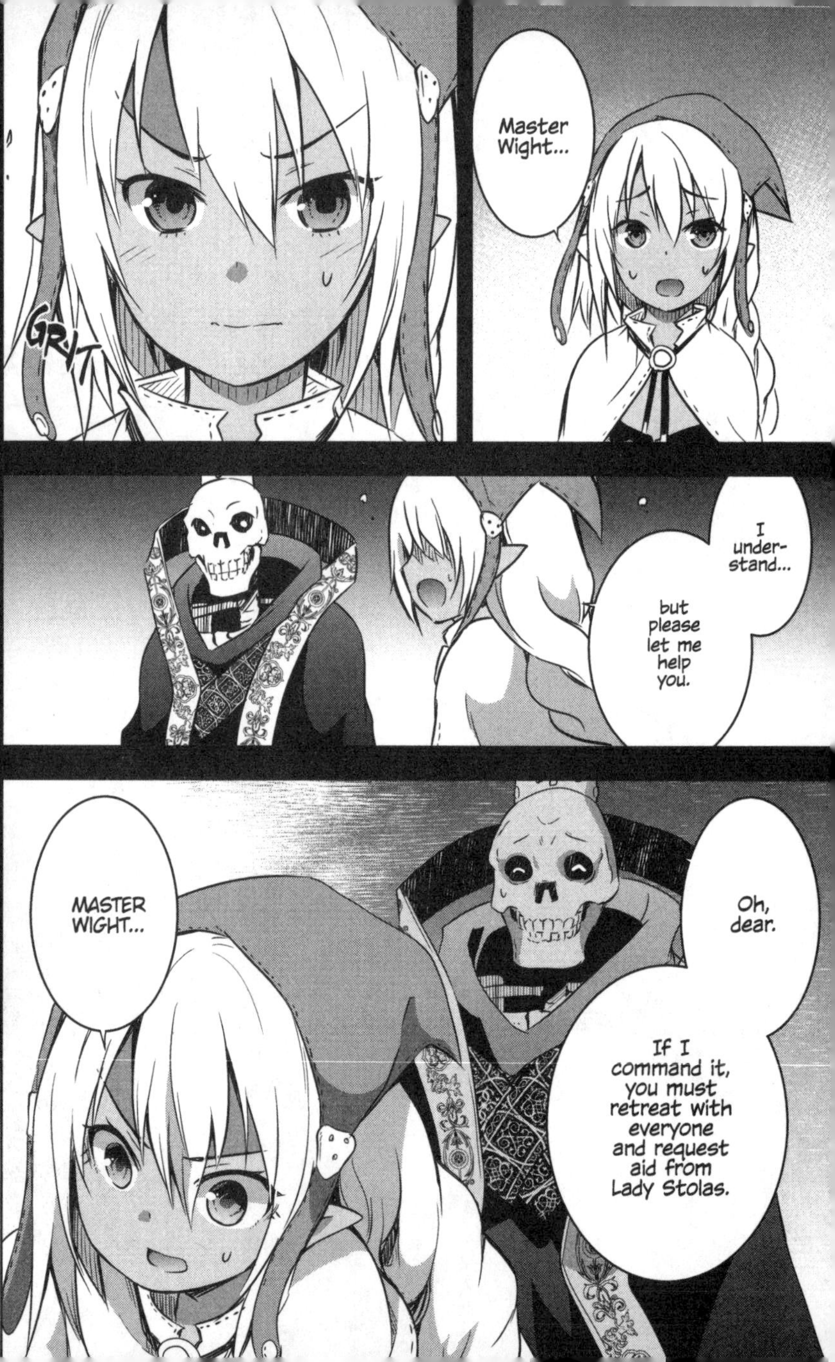
Master Wight...
GR-T
I under-stand...
but please let me help you.
Oh, dear.
If I command it, you must retreat with everyone and request aid from Lady Stolas.
MASTER WIGHT...

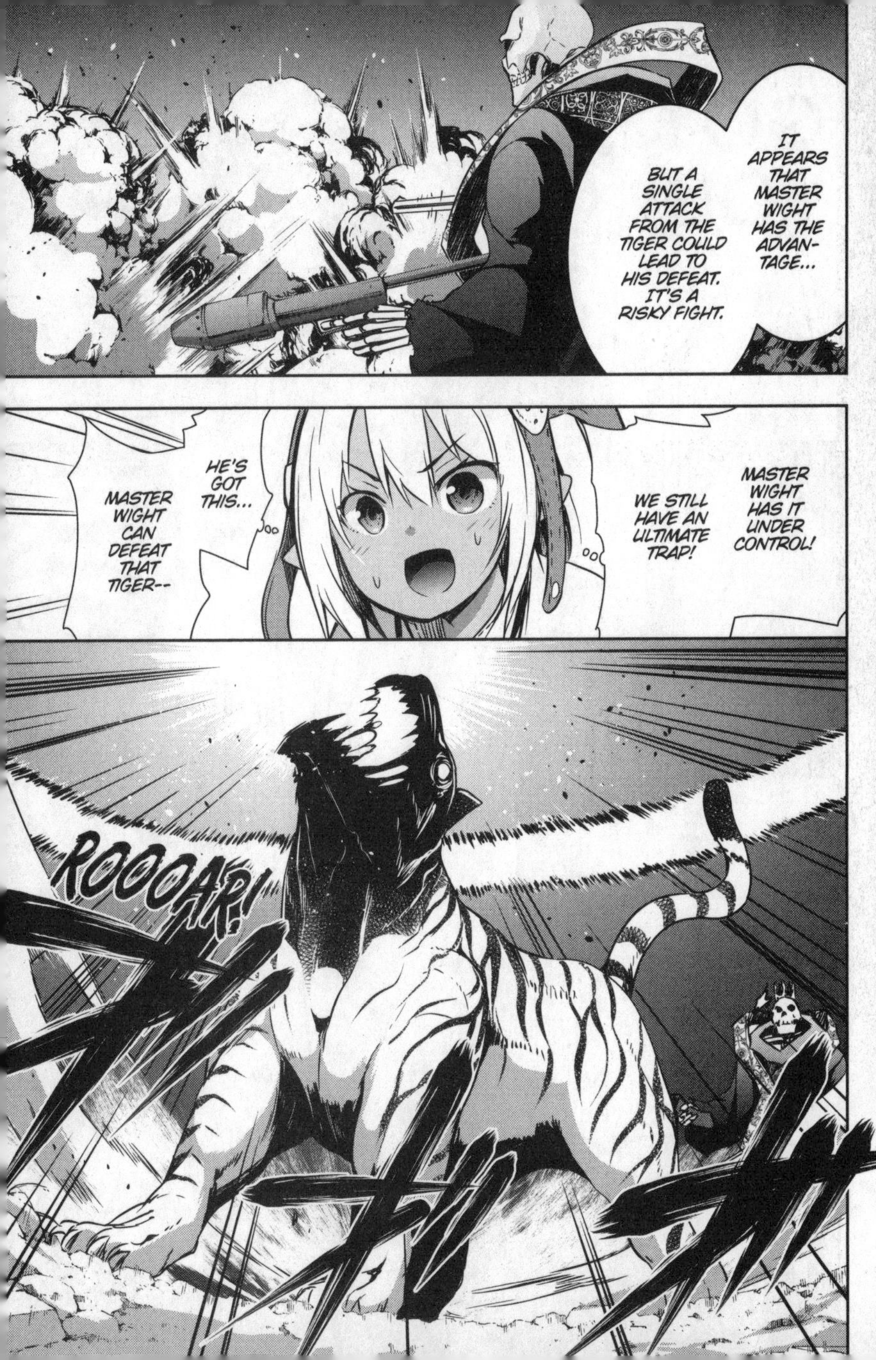
IT APPEARS THAT MASTER WIGHT HAS THE ADVANTAGE...
BUT A SINGLE ATTACK FROM THE TIGER COULD LEAD TO HIS DEFEAT. IT'S A RISKY FIGHT.
MASTER WIGHT HAS IT UNDER CONTROL!
WE STILL HAVE AN ULTIMATE TRAP!
HE'S GOT THIS...
MASTER WIGHT CAN DEFEAT THAT TIGER--
ROOOAR!

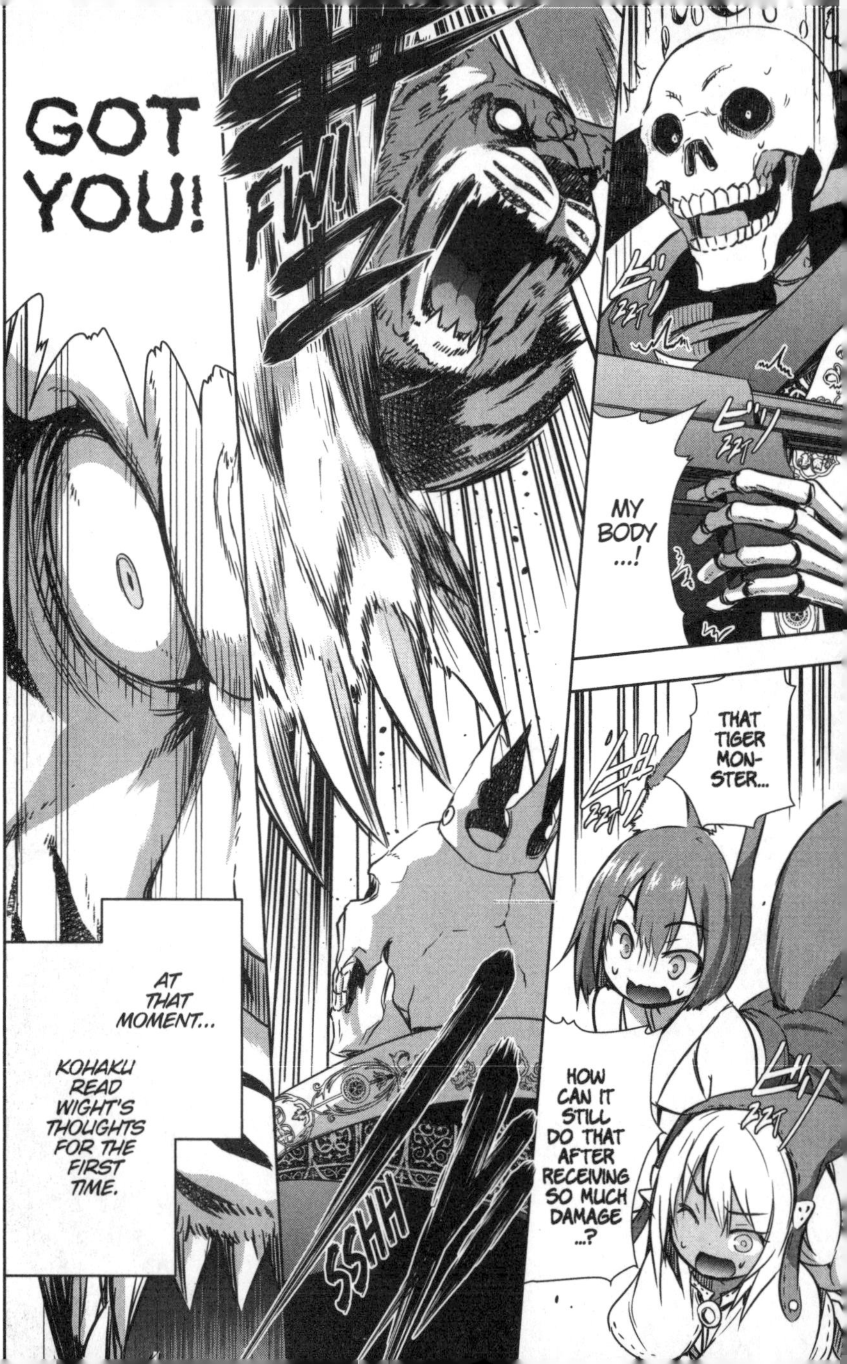
MY BODY ...!
THAT TIGER MON-STER...
HOW CAN IT STILL DO THAT AFTER RECEIVING SO MUCH DAMAGE ...?
FWI
GOT YOU!
AT THAT MOMENT...
KOHAKU READ WIGHT'S THOUGHTS FOR THE FIRST TIME.
SSHH

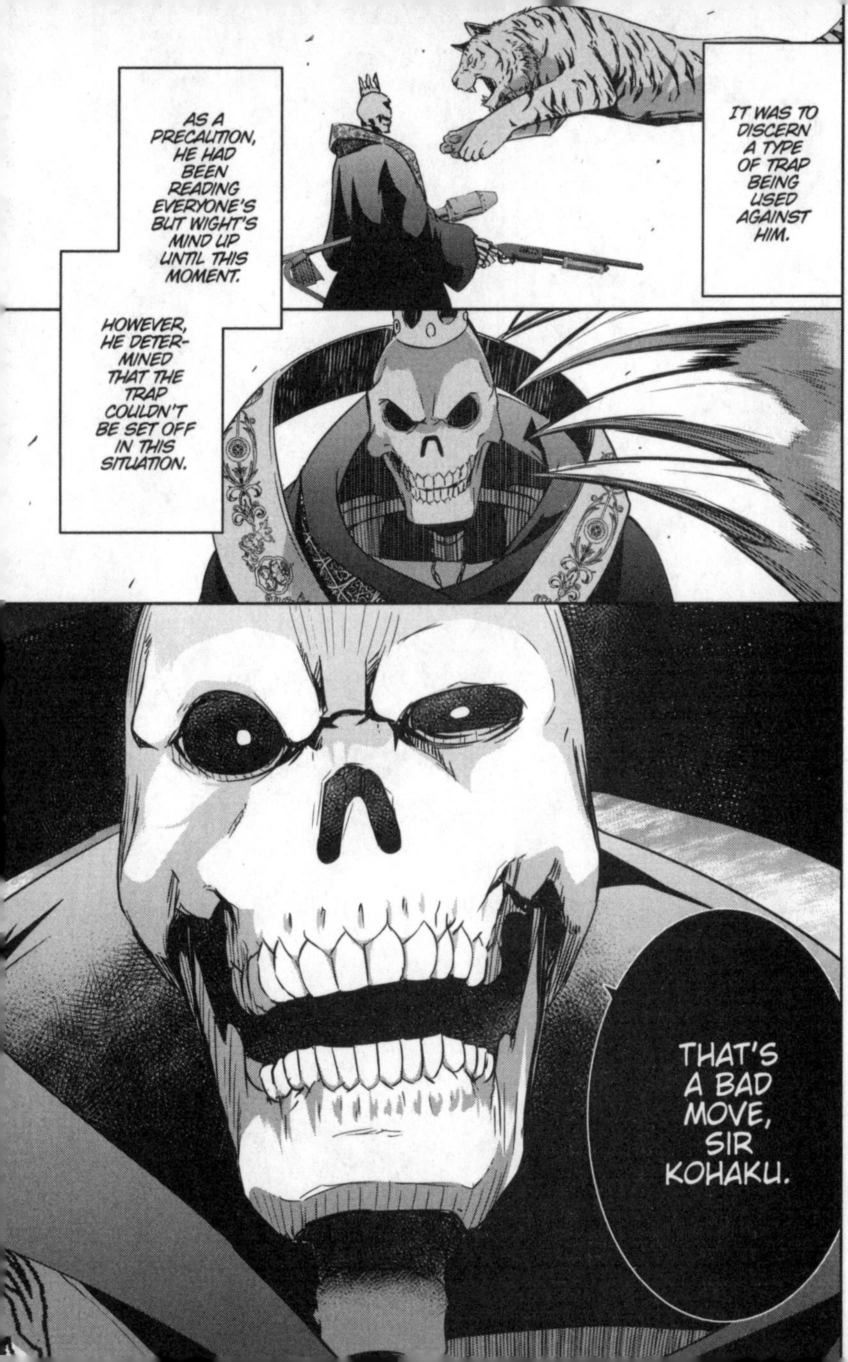

AS A PRECAUTION, HE HAD BEEN READING EVERYONE'S BUT WIGHT'S MIND UP UNTIL THIS MOMENT.
IT WAS TO DISCERN A TYPE OF TRAP BEING USED AGAINST HIM.
HOWEVER, HE DETERMINED THAT THE TRAP COULDN'T BE SET OFF IN THIS SITUATION.
THAT'S A BAD MOVE, SIR KOHAKU.

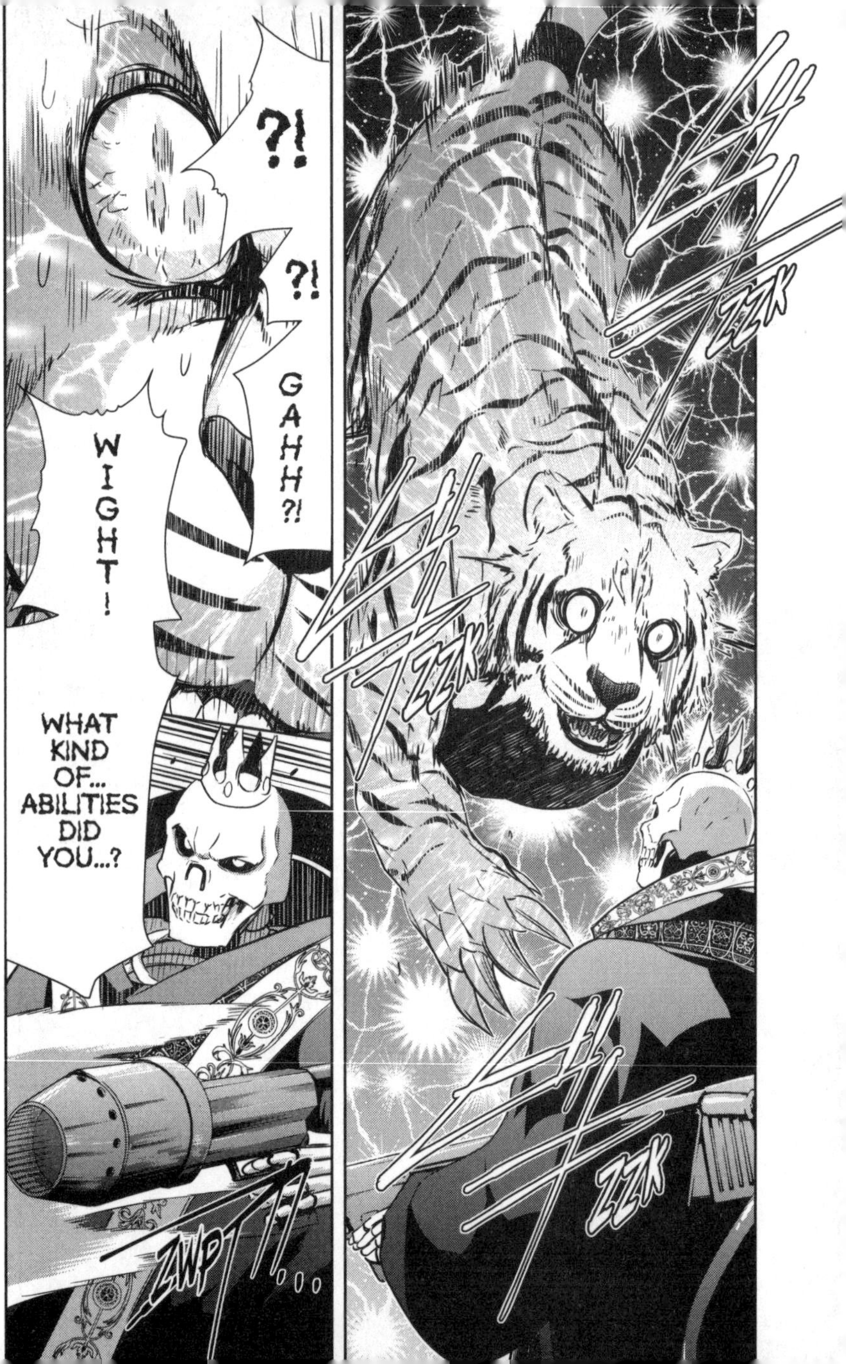
ZZZK
ZZZK
ZZZK
?!
?!
GAHHH?!
WIGHT!
WHAT KIND OF... ABILITIES DID YOU...?
ZWIP

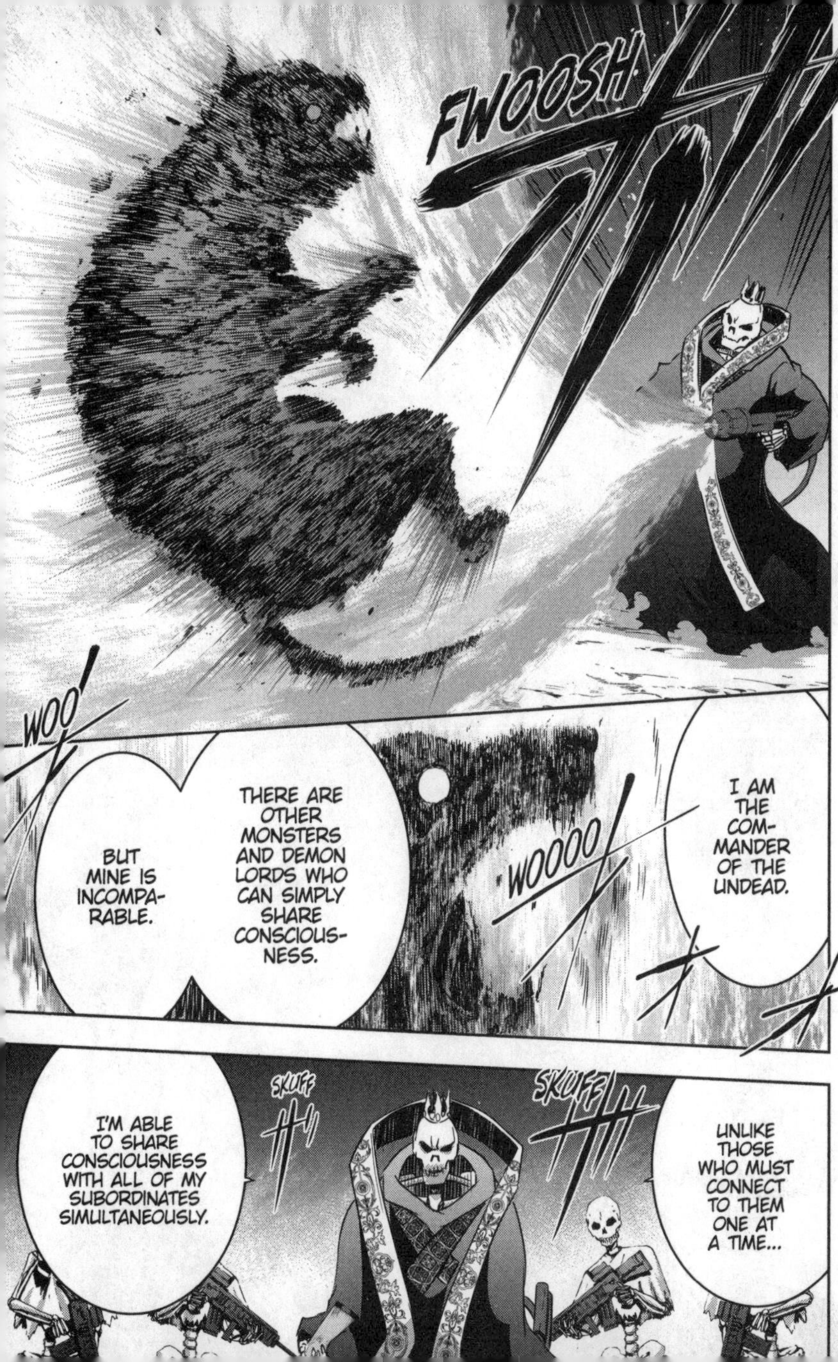
FWOOSH
I AM THE COM-MANDER OF THE UNDEAD.
WOOOO
THERE ARE OTHER MONSTERS AND DEMON LORDS WHO CAN SIMPLY SHARE CONSCIOUS-NESS.
BUT MINE IS INCOMPA-RABLE.
WOO
UNLIKE THOSE WHO MUST CONNECT TO THEM ONE AT A TIME...
SKUFF
SKUFF
I'M ABLE TO SHARE CONSCIOUSNESS WITH ALL OF MY SUBORDINATES SIMULTANEOUSLY.

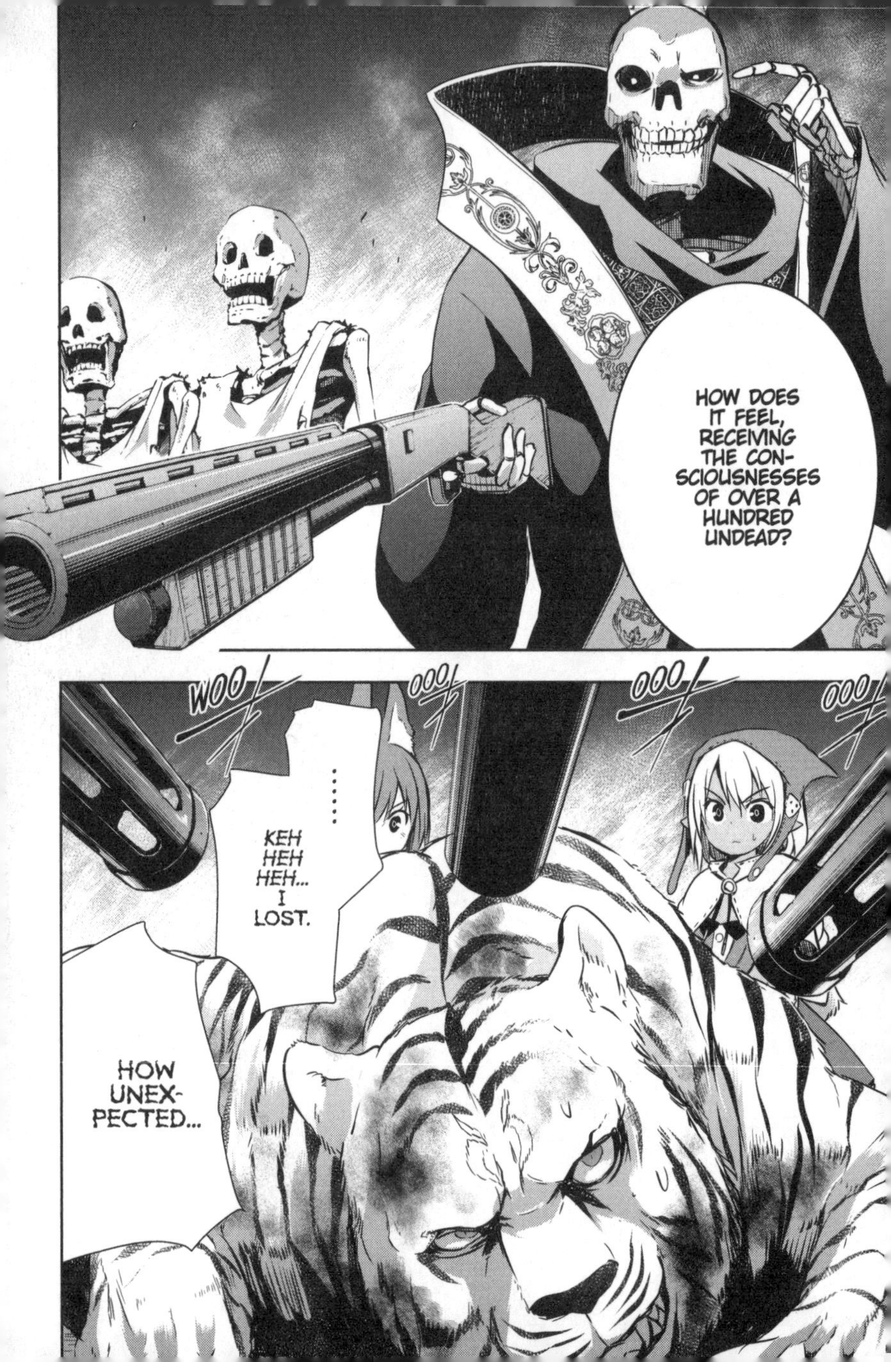
HOW DOES IT FEEL, RECEIVING THE CON-SCIOUSNESSES OF OVER A HUNDRED UNDEAD?
WOO
OOO
OOO
OOO
......
KEH HEH HEH... I LOST.
HOW UNEX-PECTED...

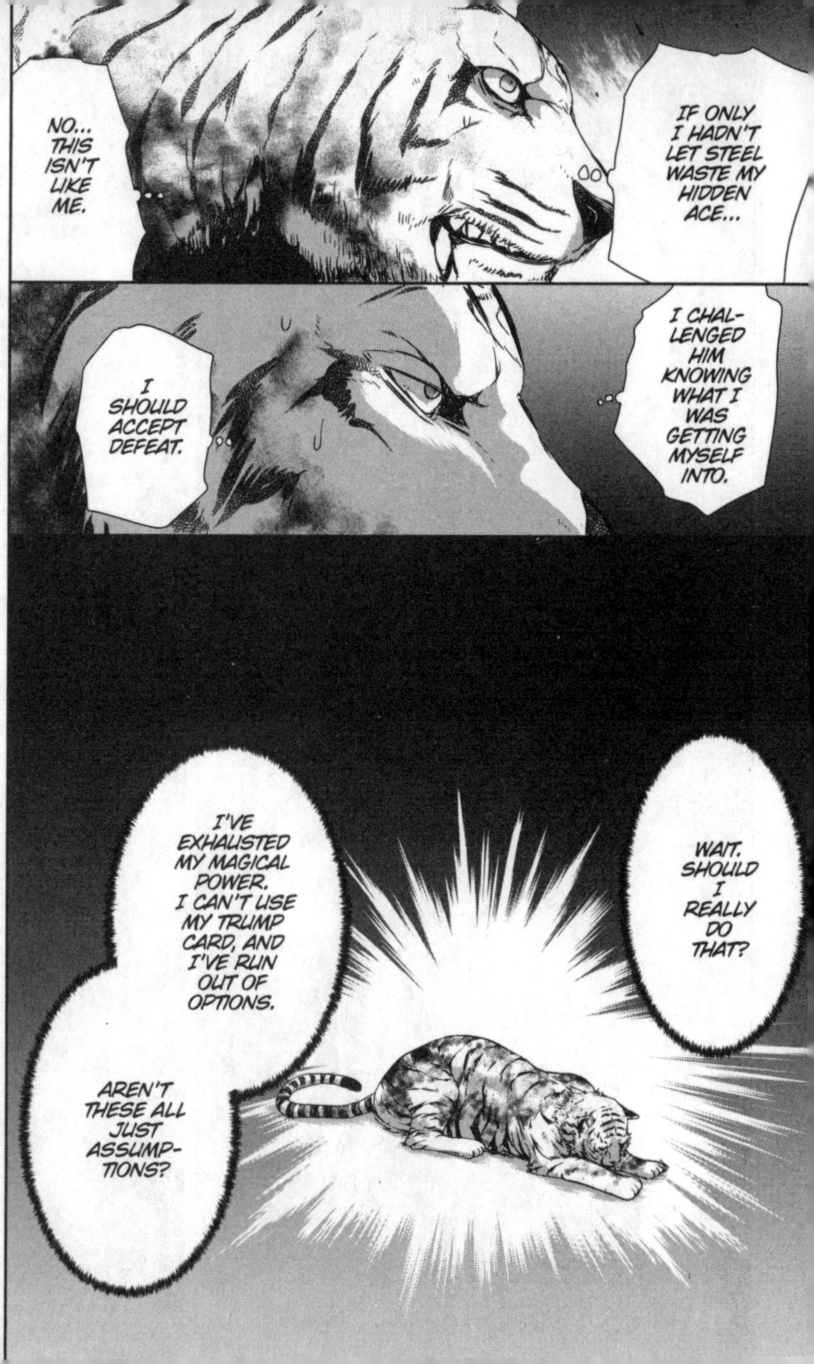
IF ONLY I HADN'T LET STEEL WASTE MY HIDDEN ACE...
NO... THIS ISN'T LIKE ME.
I CHAL-LENGED HIM KNOWING WHAT I WAS GETTING MYSELF INTO.
I SHOULD ACCEPT DEFEAT.
WAIT. SHOULD I REALLY DO THAT?
I'VE EXHAUSTED MY MAGICAL POWER. I CAN'T USE MY TRUMP CARD, AND I'VE RUN OUT OF OPTIONS.
AREN'T THESE ALL JUST ASSUMP-TIONS?

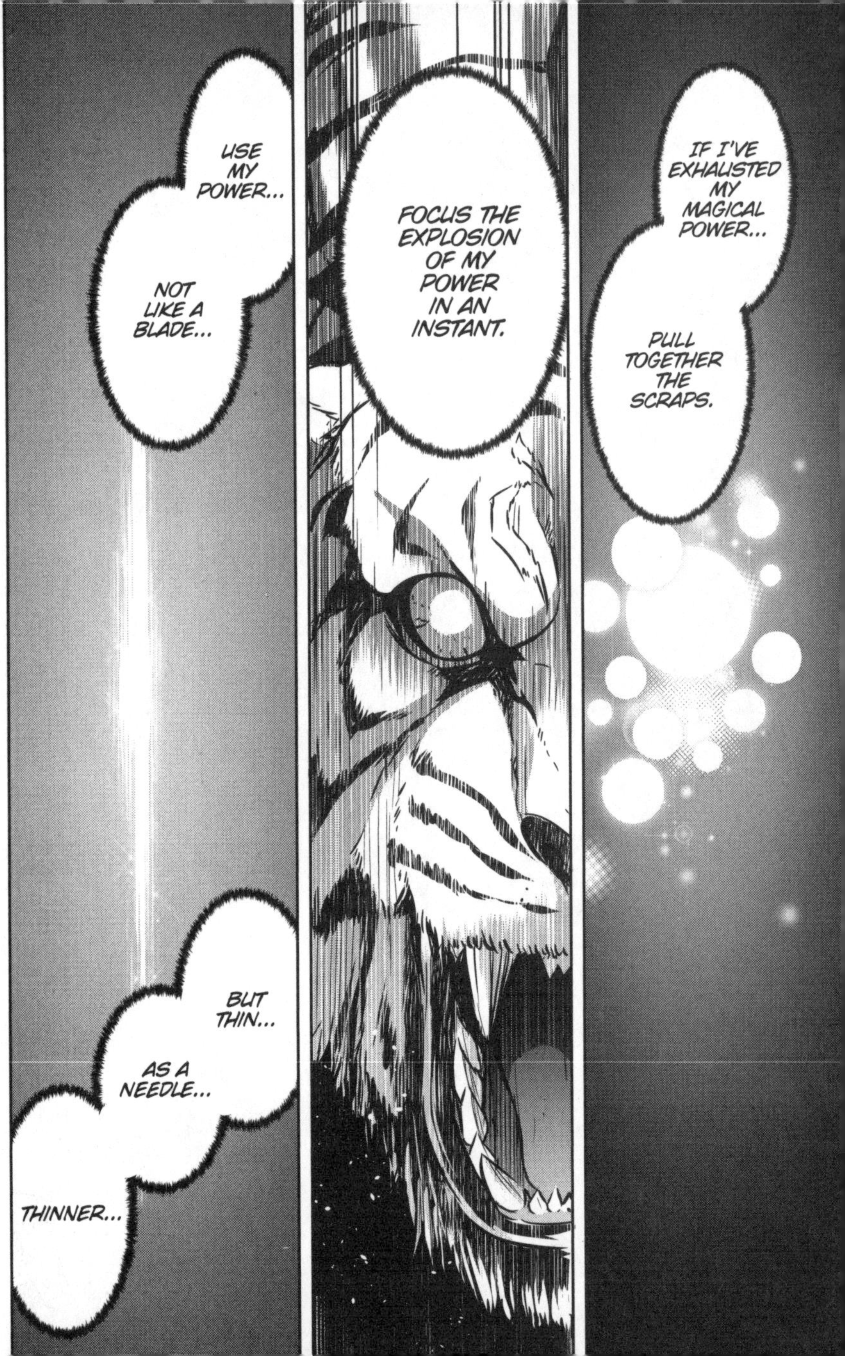
IF I'VE EXHAUSTED MY MAGICAL POWER...
PULL TOGETHER THE SCRAPS.
FOCUS THE EXPLOSION OF MY POWER IN AN INSTANT.
USE MY POWER...
NOT LIKE A BLADE...
BUT THIN...
AS A NEEDLE...
THINNER...

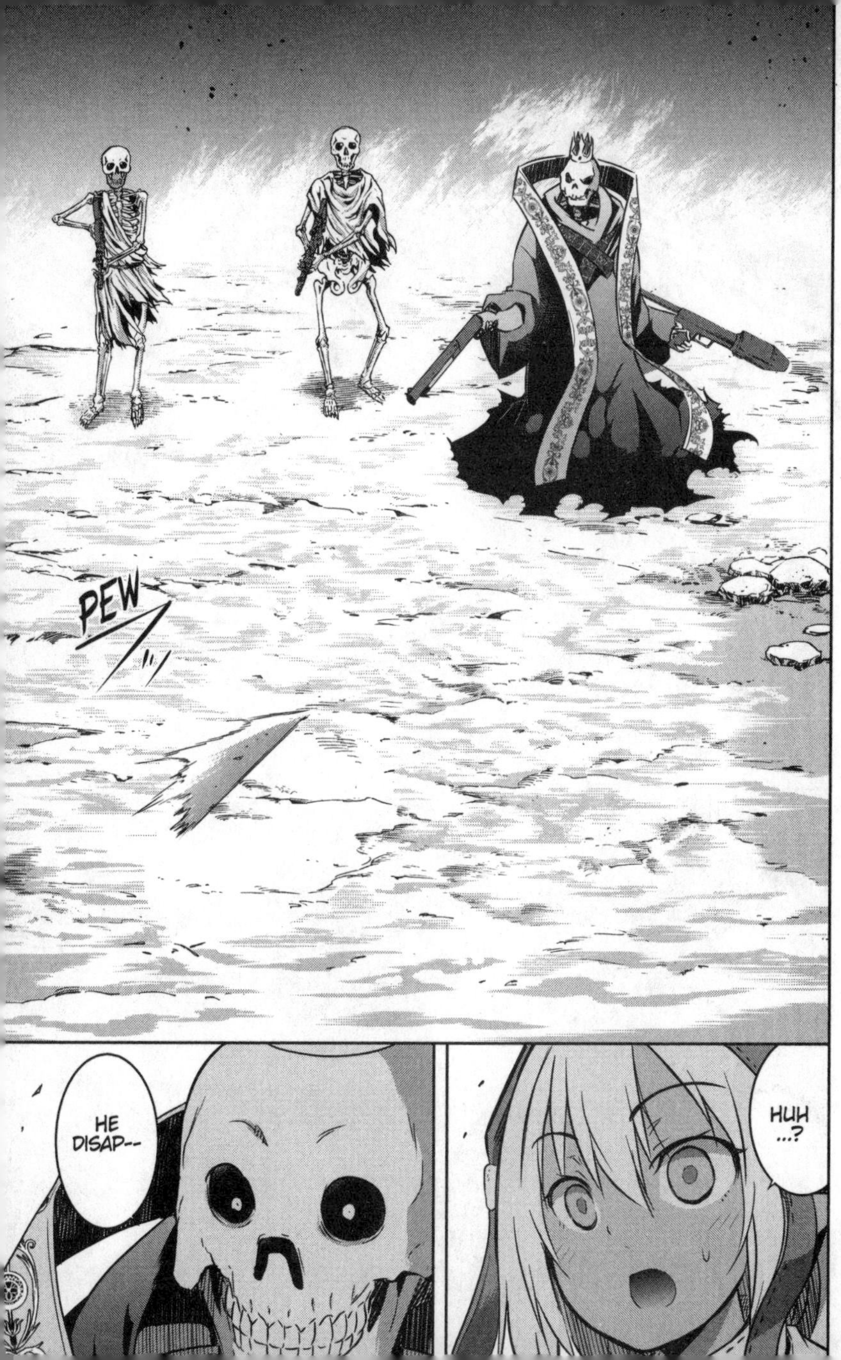
PEW
HUH ...?
HE DISAP--

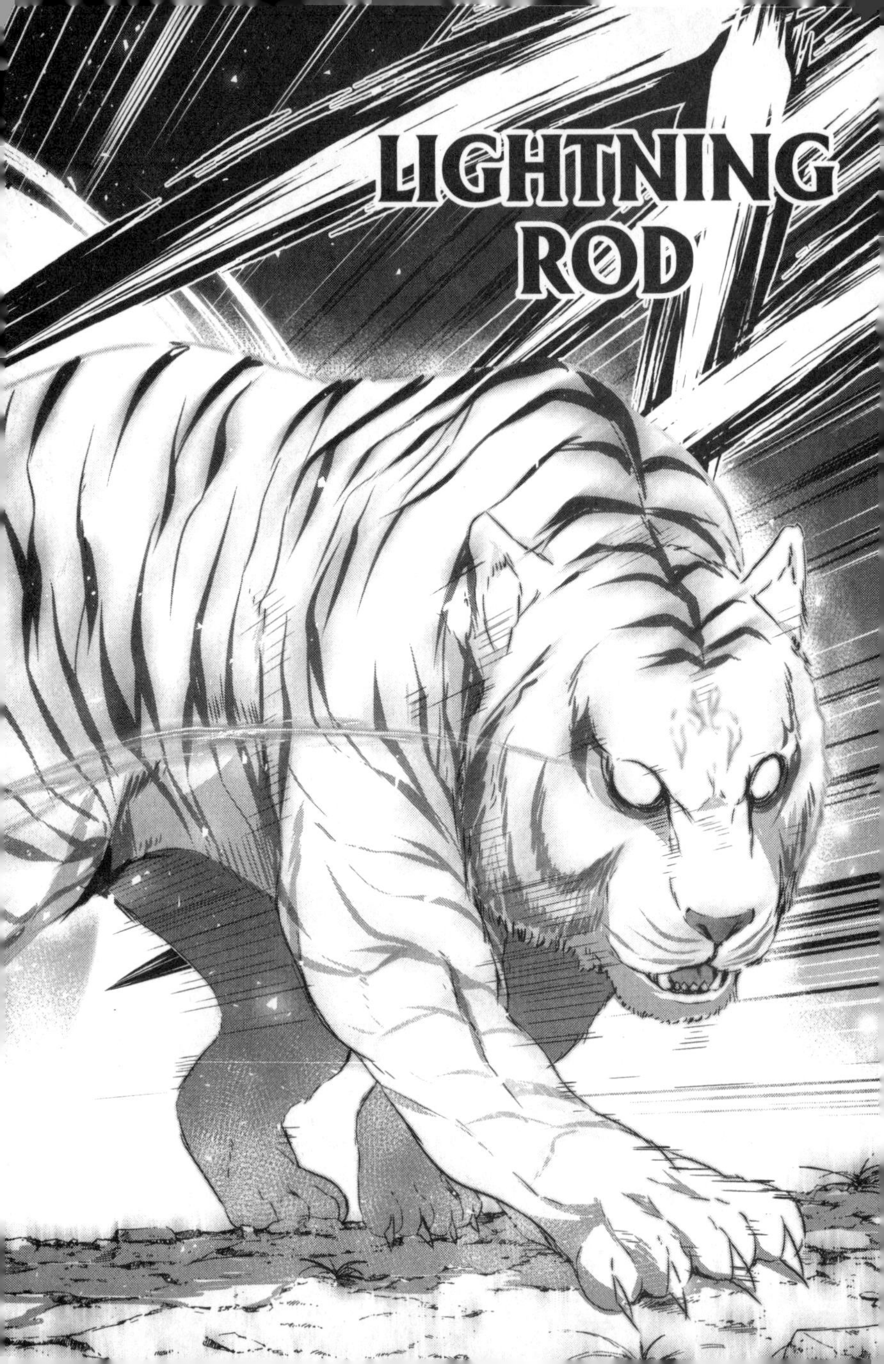
LIGHTNING
ROD

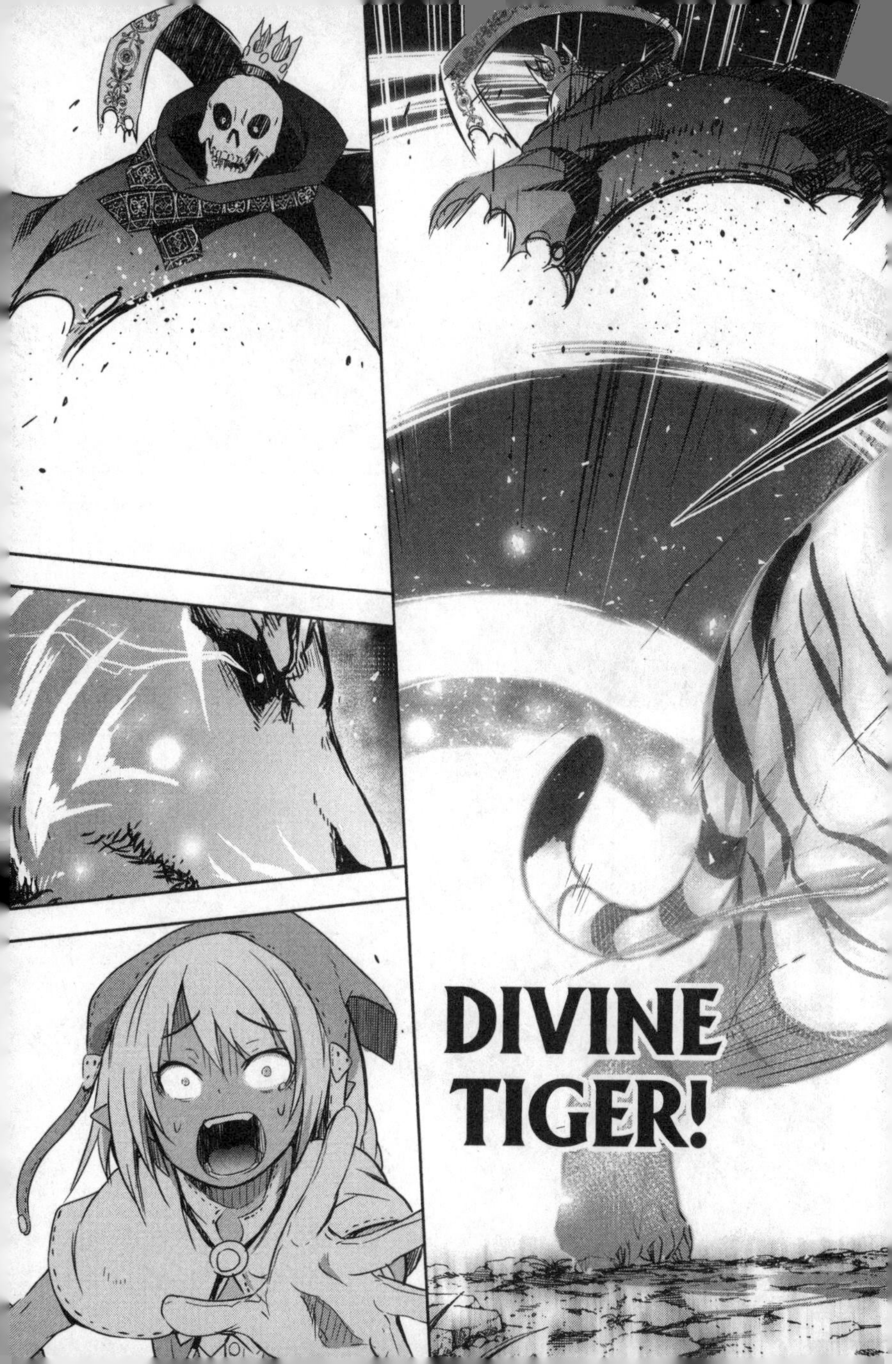
DIVINE
TIGER!

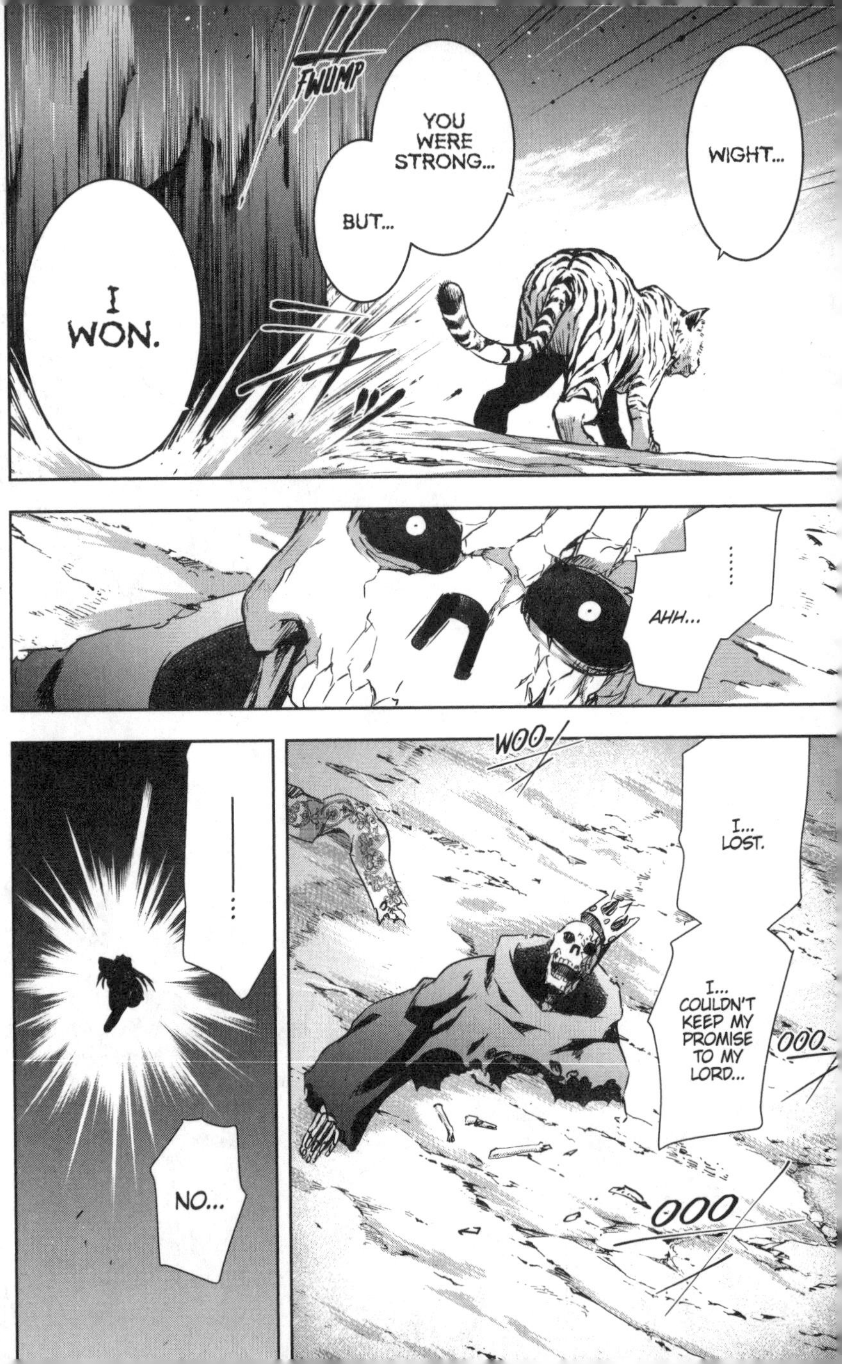
WIGHT...
YOU WERE STRONG...
BUT...
FWUMP
I WON.
......
AHH...
WOO-
I... LOST.
I... COULDN'T KEEP MY PROMISE TO MY LORD...
OOO
OOO
......
NO...

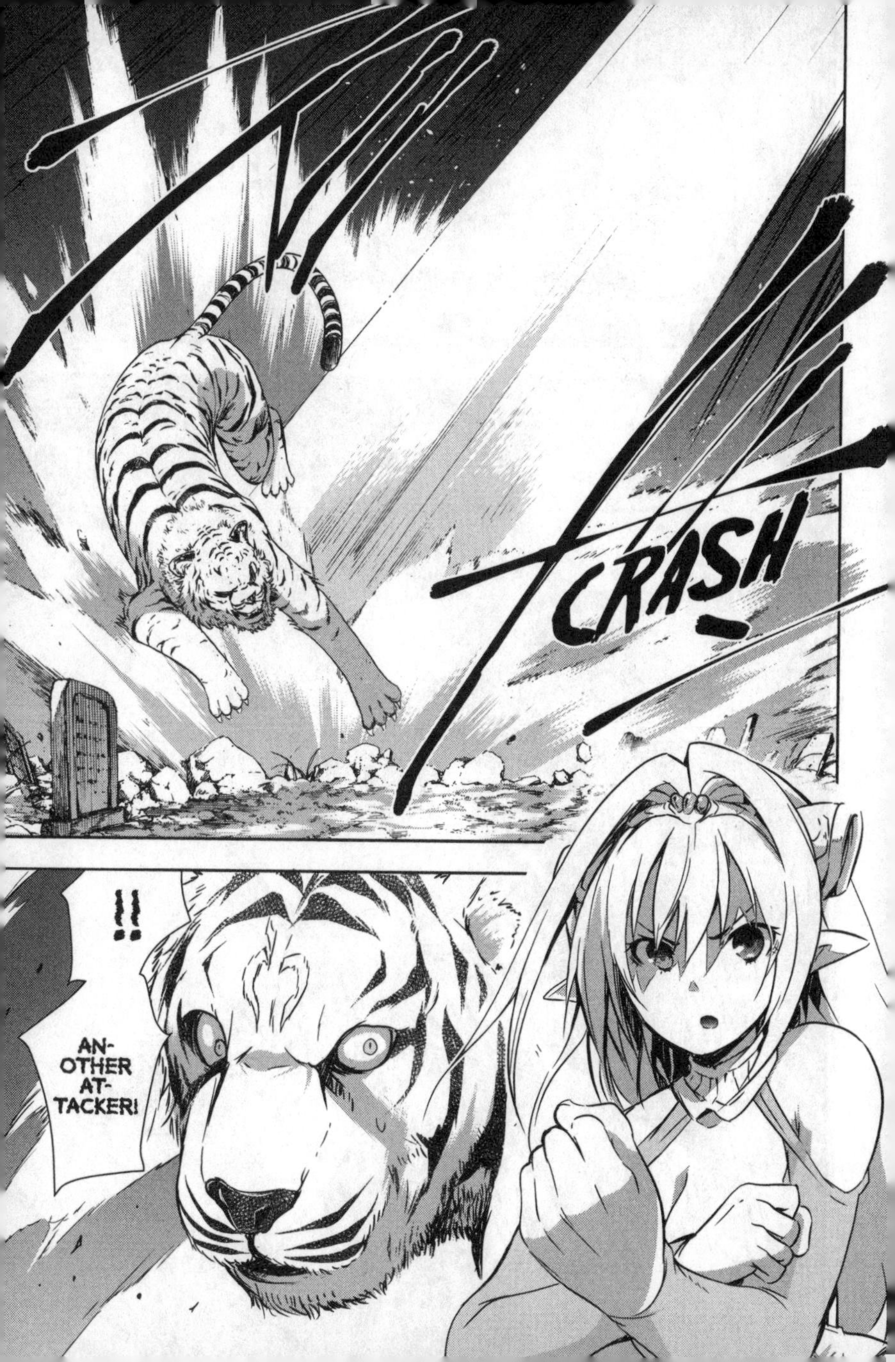
CRASH
!!
AN-OTHER AT-TACKER!

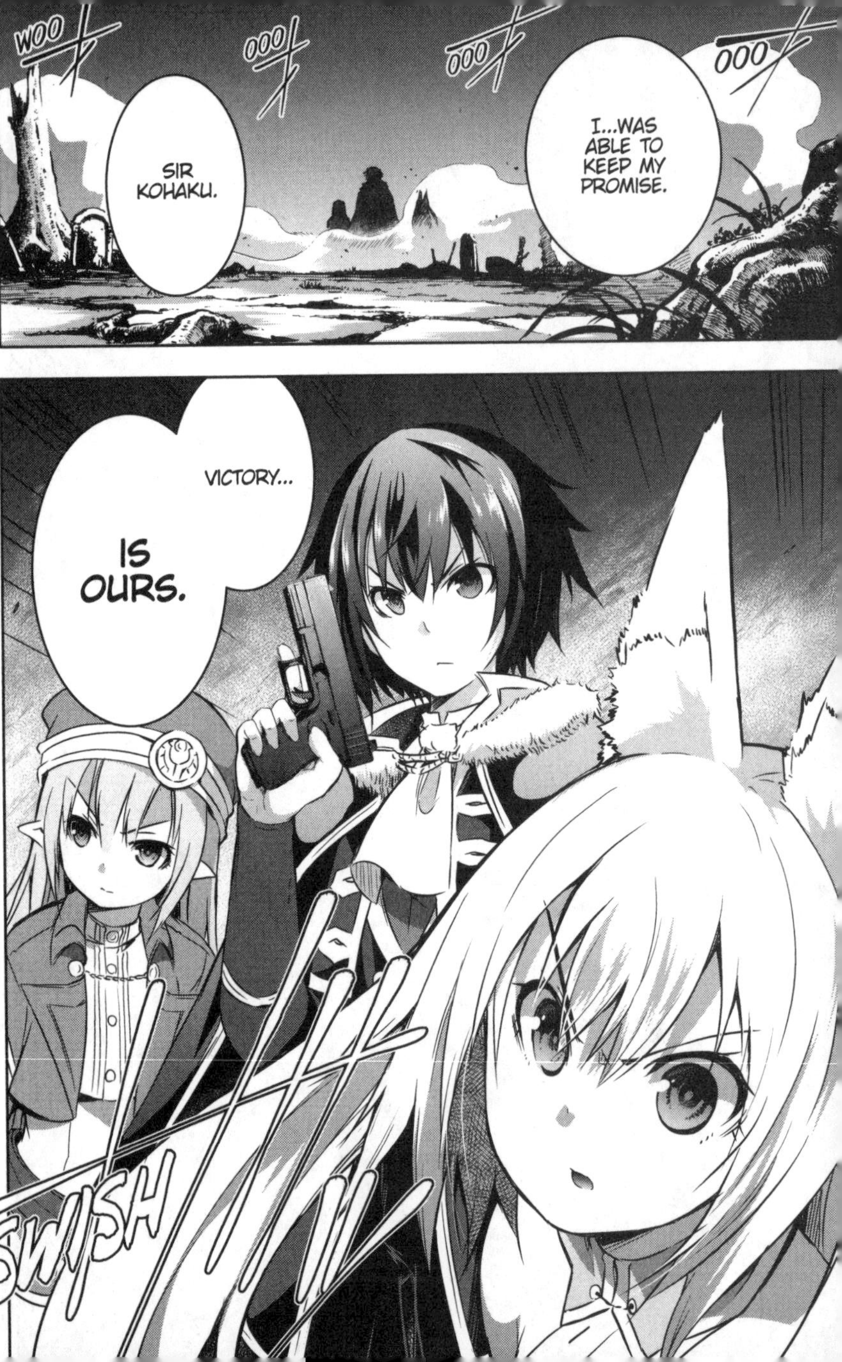
WOO
OOO
OOO
OOO
I...WAS ABLE TO KEEP MY PROMISE.
SIR KOHAKU.
VICTORY...
IS OURS.
SWISH

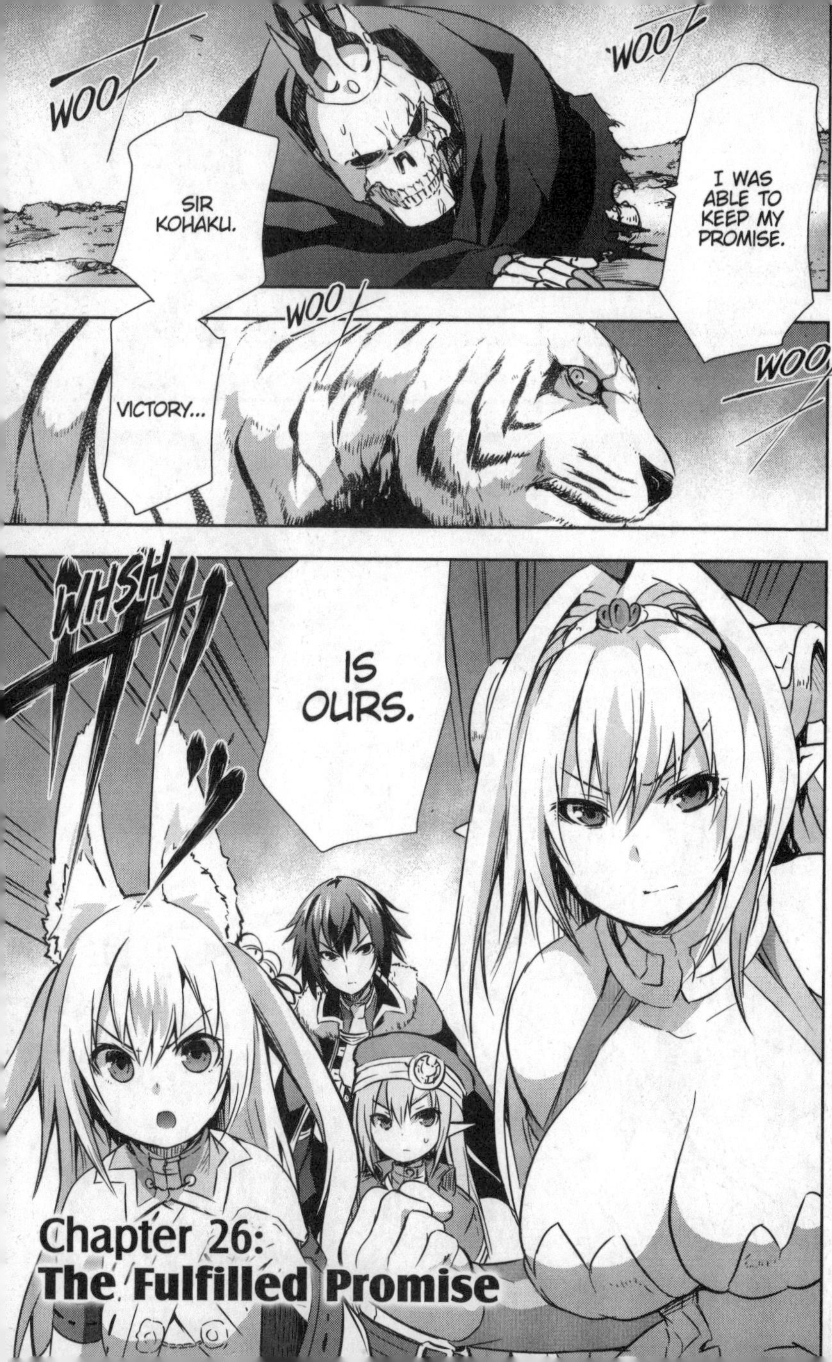
WOO
I WAS ABLE TO KEEP MY PROMISE.
WOO
SIR KOHAKU.
WOO
WOO
VICTORY...
IS OURS.
WHSH
Chapter 26:
The Fulfilled Promise

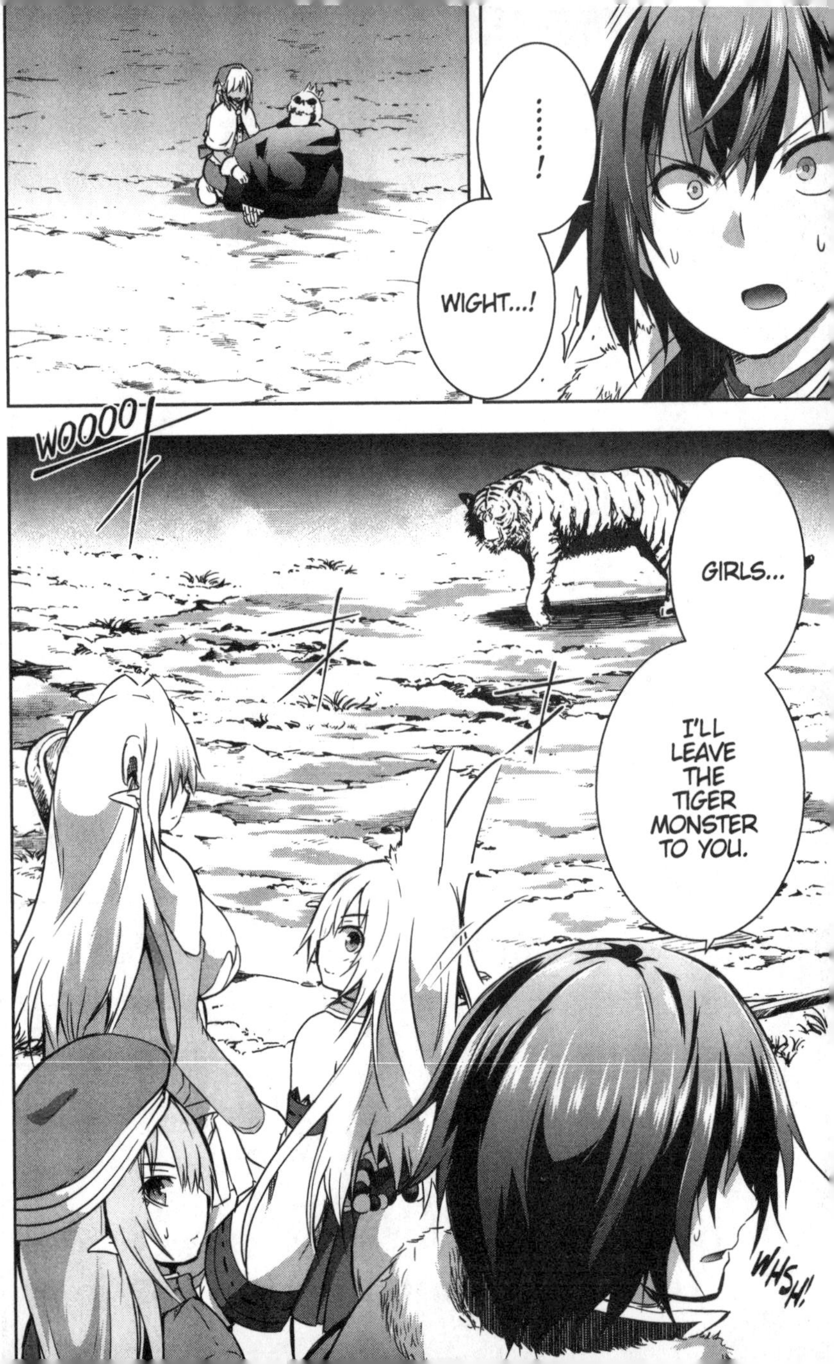
......!
WIGHT...!
WOOOO
GIRLS...
I'LL LEAVE THE TIGER MONSTER TO YOU.
WHSH!

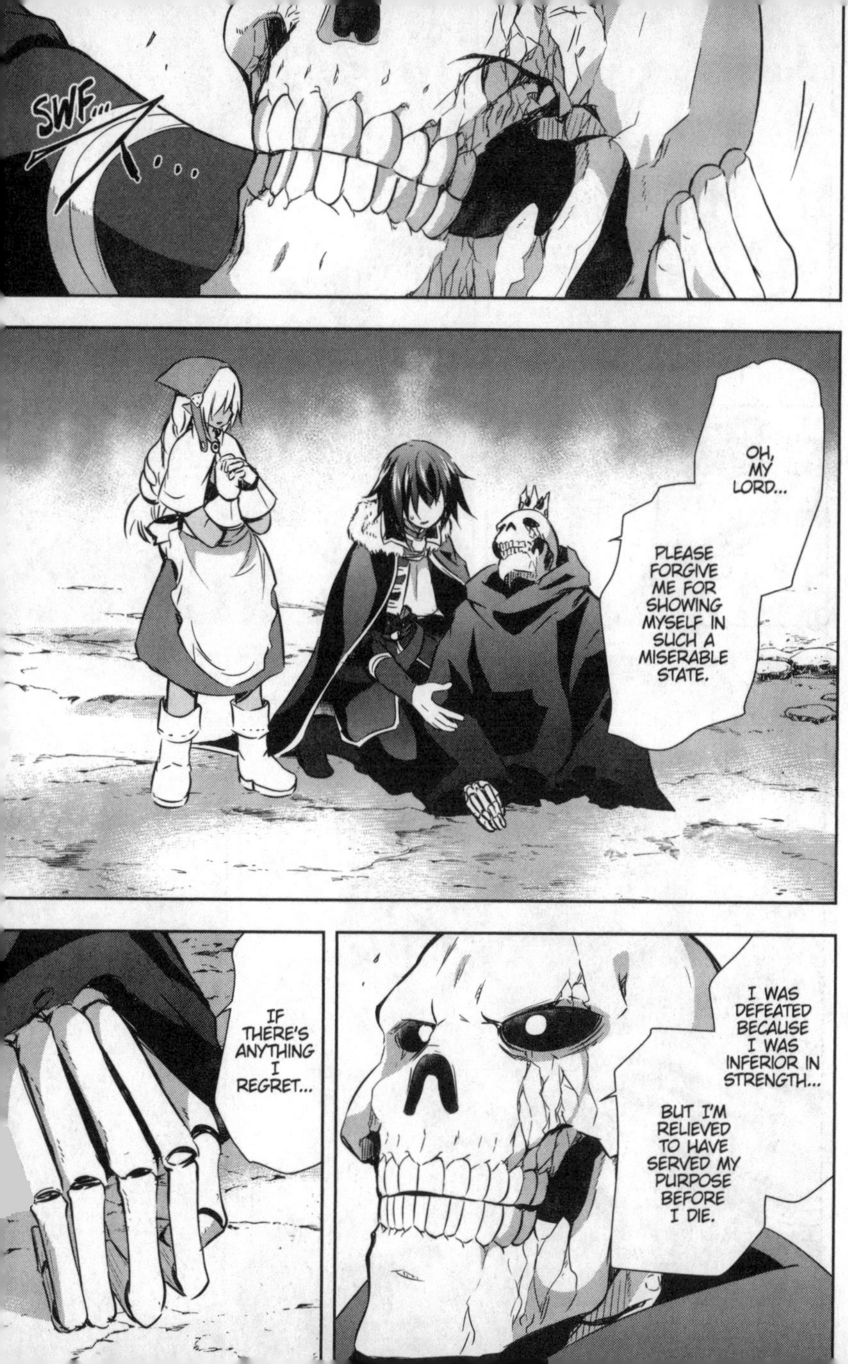
SWF...
...
OH, MY LORD...
PLEASE FORGIVE ME FOR SHOWING MYSELF IN SUCH A MISERABLE STATE.
I WAS DEFEATED BECAUSE I WAS INFERIOR IN STRENGTH...
BUT I'M RELIEVED TO HAVE SERVED MY PURPOSE BEFORE I DIE.
IF THERE'S ANYTHING I REGRET...

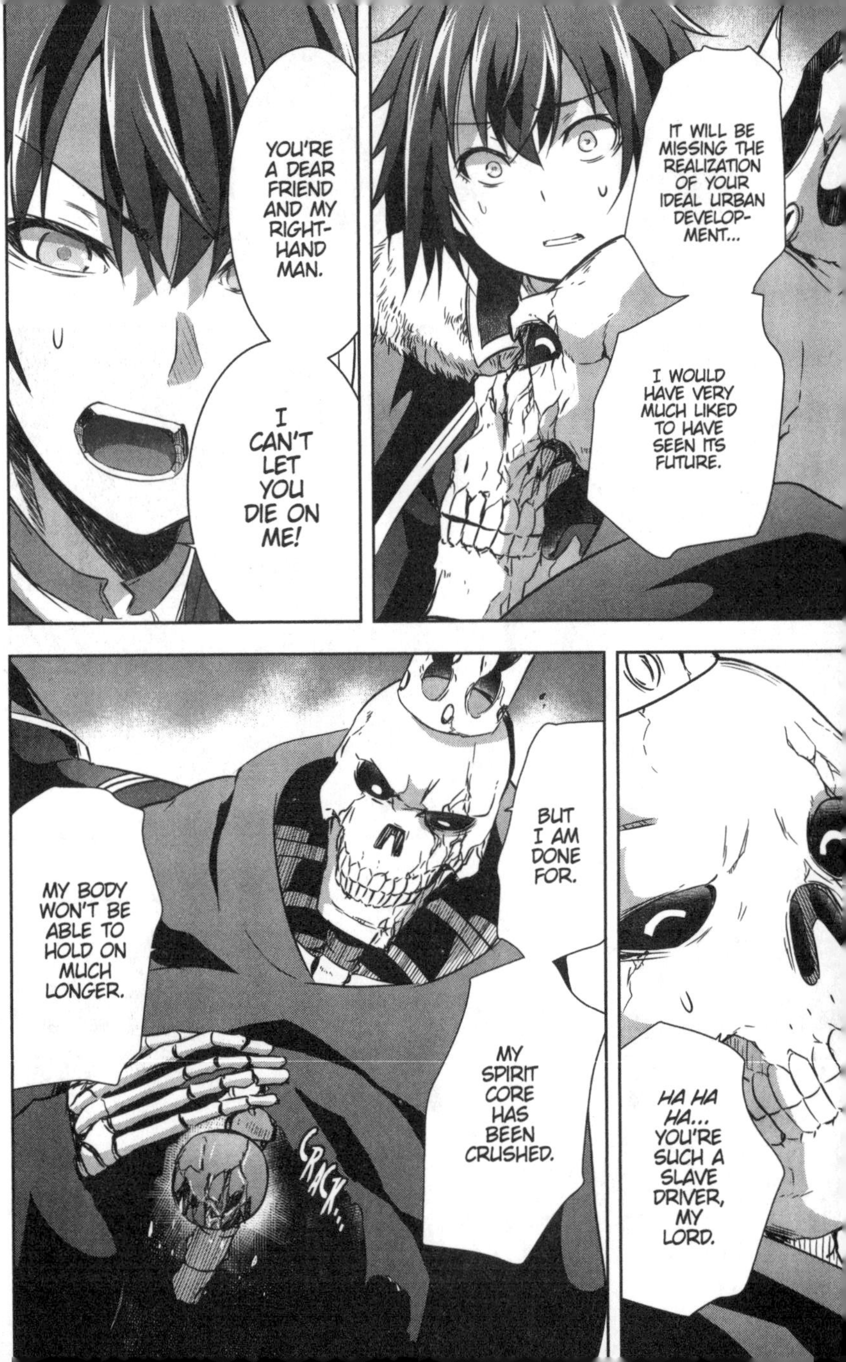
IT WILL BE MISSING THE REALIZATION OF YOUR IDEAL URBAN DEVELOP-MENT...
I WOULD HAVE VERY MUCH LIKED TO HAVE SEEN ITS FUTURE.
YOU'RE A DEAR FRIEND AND MY RIGHT-HAND MAN.
I CAN'T LET YOU DIE ON ME!
HA HA HA... YOU'RE SUCH A SLAVE DRIVER, MY LORD.
BUT I AM DONE FOR.
MY SPIRIT CORE HAS BEEN CRUSHED.
MY BODY WON'T BE ABLE TO HOLD ON MUCH LONGER.
CRACK...

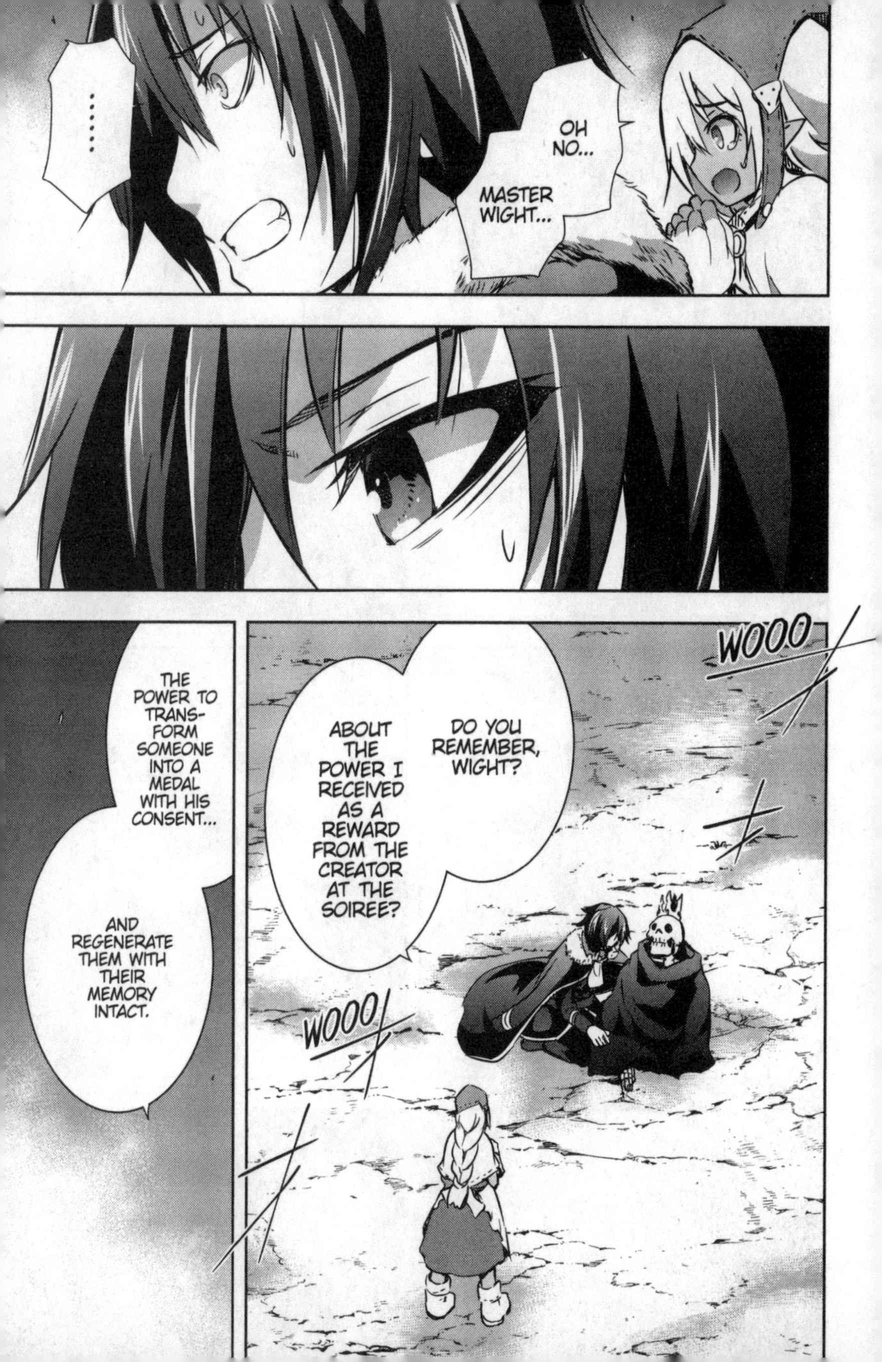
OH NO...
MASTER WIGHT...
......
WOOO
DO YOU REMEMBER, WIGHT?
ABOUT THE POWER I RECEIVED AS A REWARD FROM THE CREATOR AT THE SOIREE?
THE POWER TO TRANS-FORM SOMEONE INTO A MEDAL WITH HIS CONSENT...
AND REGENERATE THEM WITH THEIR MEMORY INTACT.
WOOO

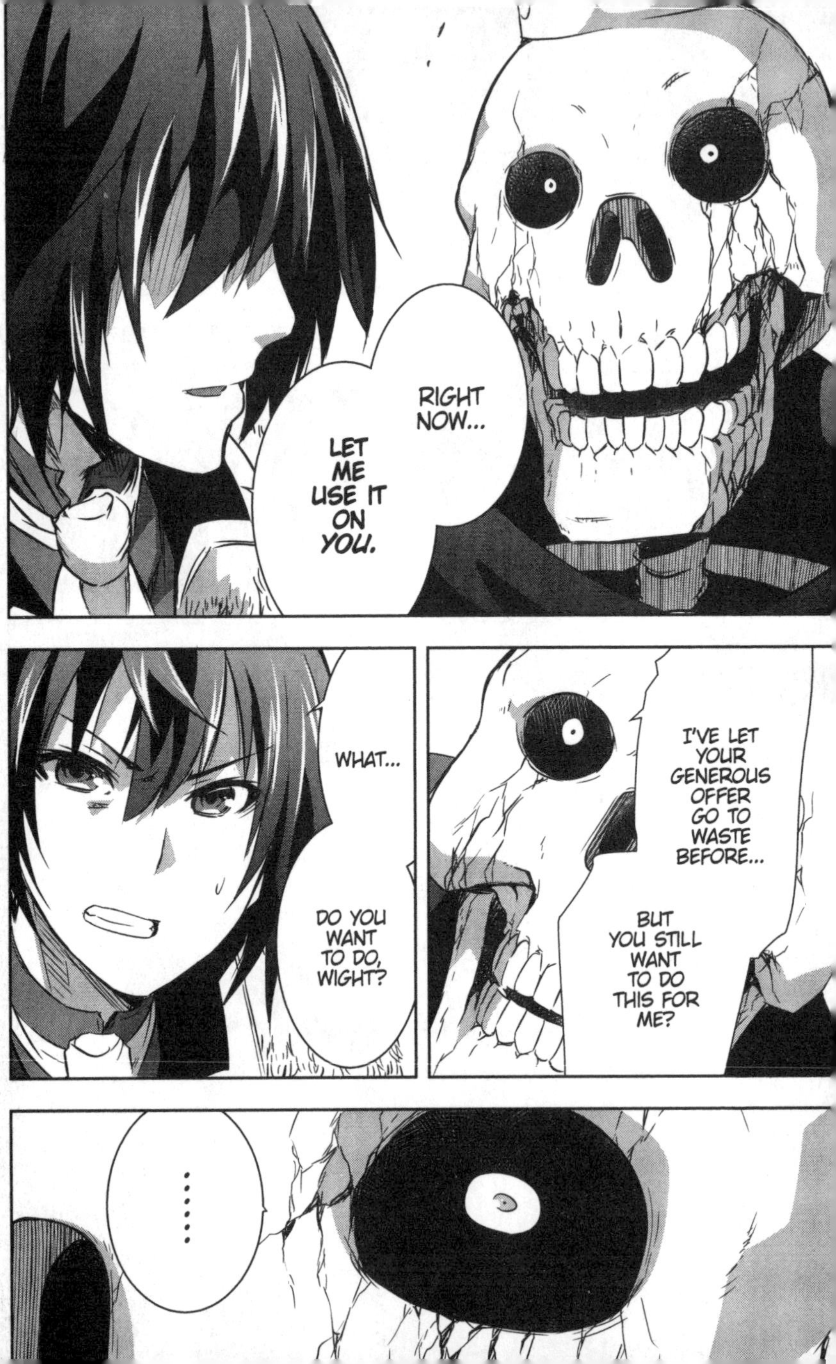
RIGHT NOW...
LET ME USE IT ON YOU.
I'VE LET YOUR GENEROUS OFFER GO TO WASTE BEFORE...
BUT YOU STILL WANT TO DO THIS FOR ME?
WHAT...
DO YOU WANT TO DO, WIGHT?
......

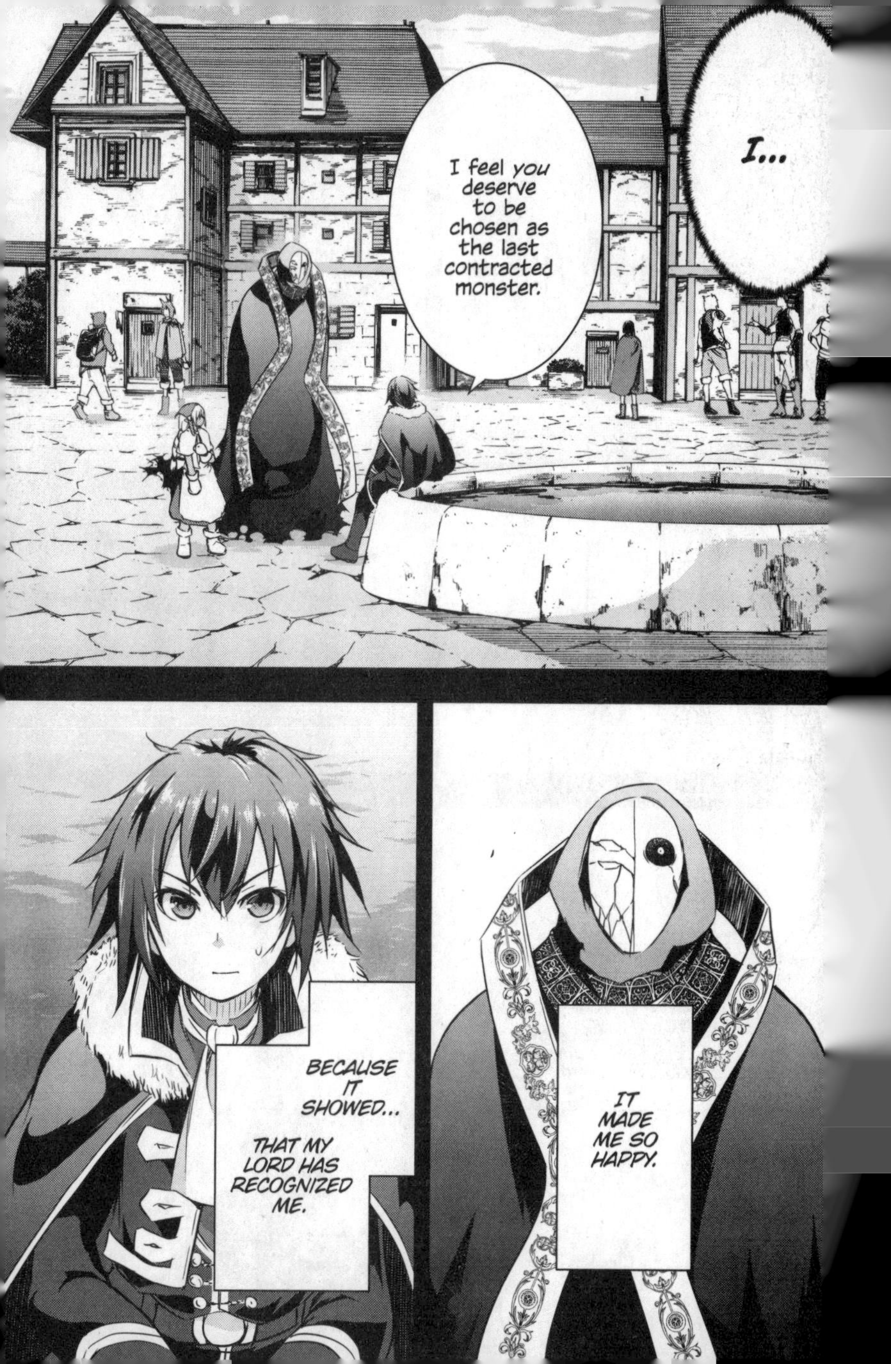
I...
I feel you deserve to be chosen as the last contracted monster.
IT MADE ME SO HAPPY.
BECAUSE IT SHOWED...
THAT MY LORD HAS RECOGNIZED ME.

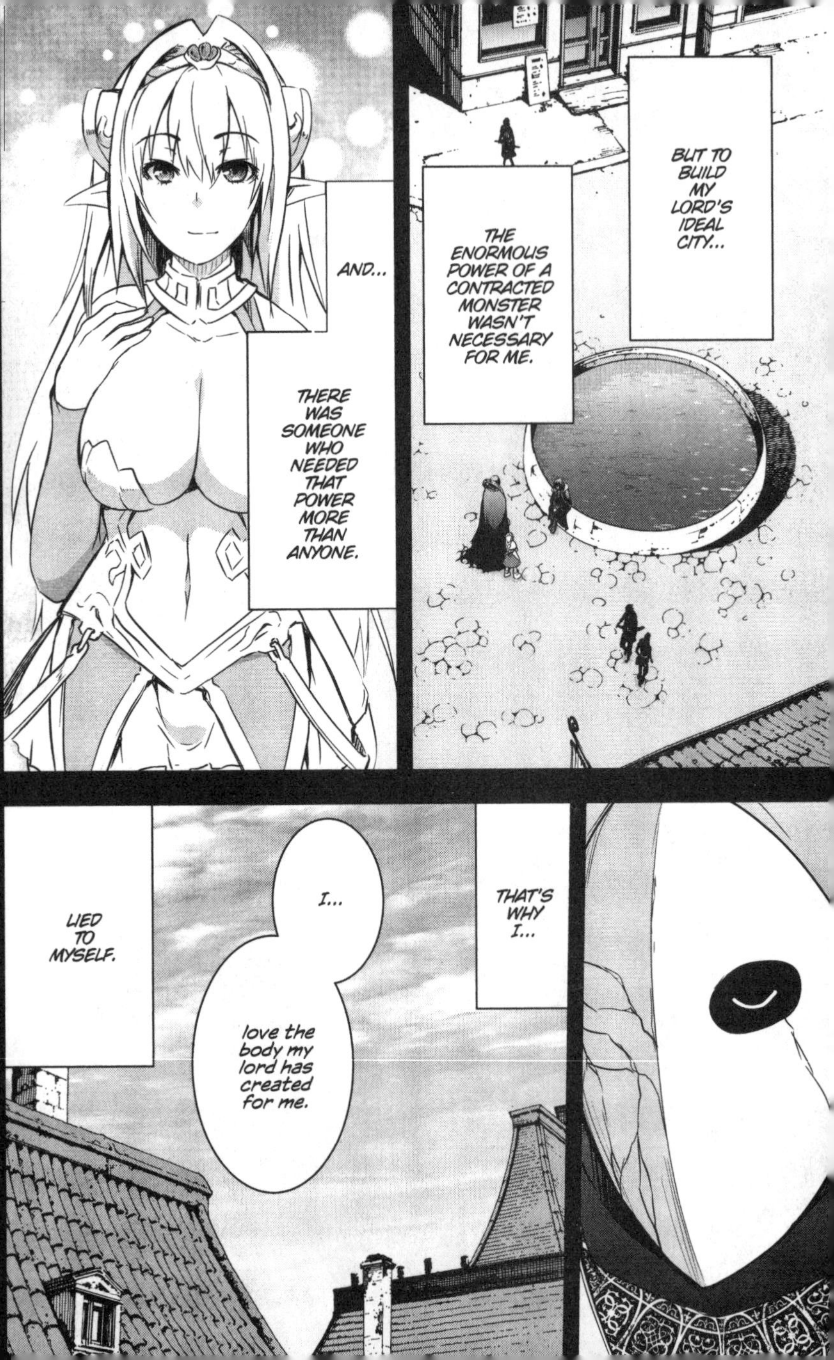
BUT TO BUILD MY LORD'S IDEAL CITY...
THE ENORMOUS POWER OF A CONTRACTED MONSTER WASN'T NECESSARY FOR ME.
AND...
THERE WAS SOMEONE WHO NEEDED THAT POWER MORE THAN ANYONE.
THAT'S WHY I...
I...
love the body my lord has created for me.
LIED TO MYSELF.

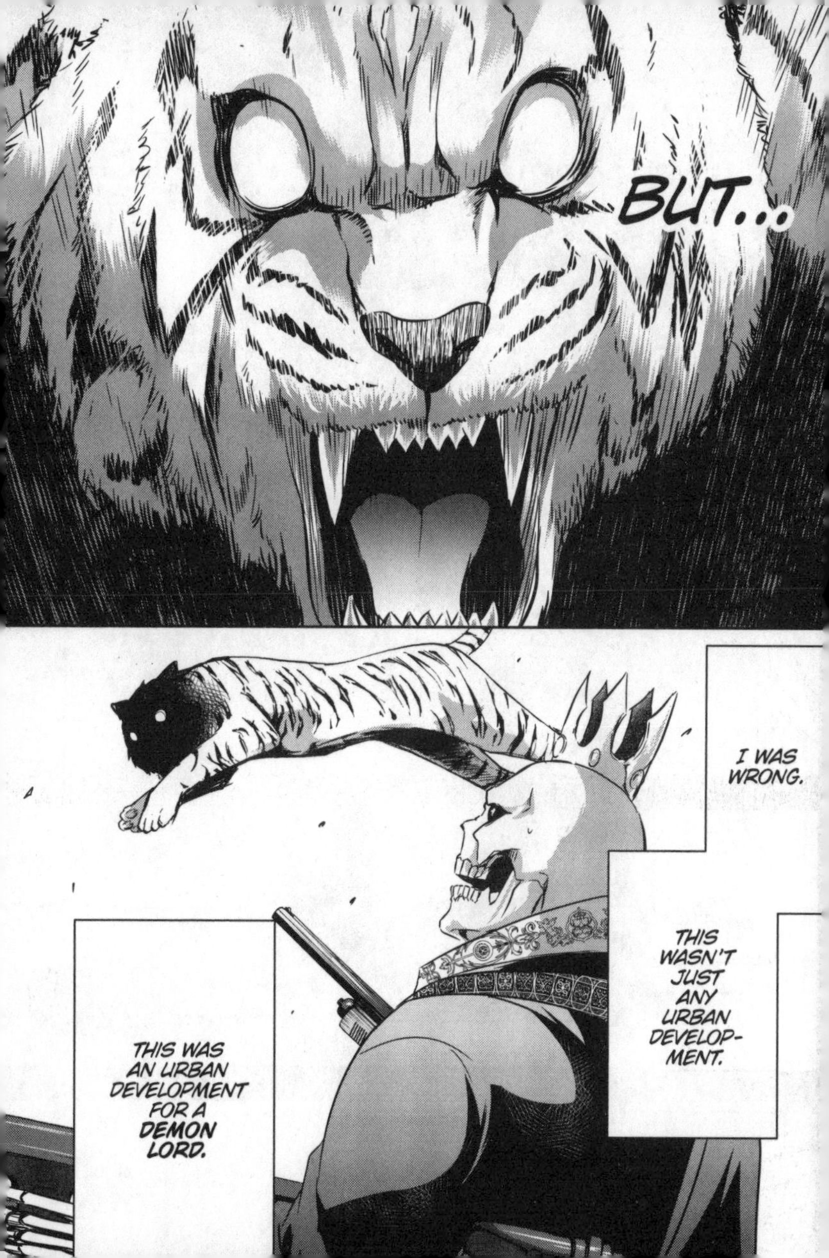
BUT...
I WAS WRONG.
THIS WASN'T JUST ANY URBAN DEVELOPMENT.
THIS WAS AN URBAN DEVELOPMENT FOR A DEMON LORD.

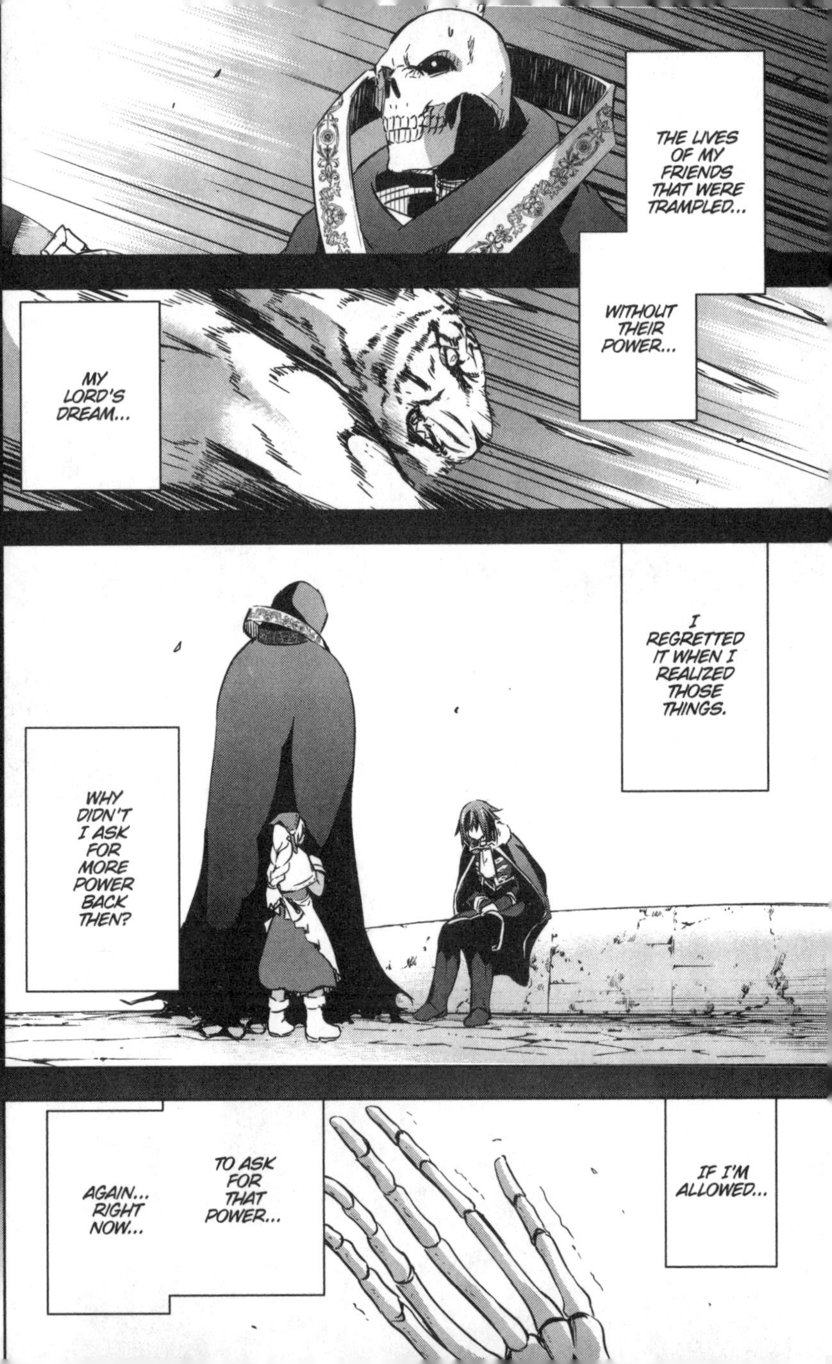
THE LIVES OF MY FRIENDS THAT WERE TRAMPLED...
WITHOUT THEIR POWER...
MY LORD'S DREAM...
I REGRETTED IT WHEN I REALIZED THOSE THINGS.
WHY DIDN'T I ASK FOR MORE POWER BACK THEN?
IF I'M ALLOWED...
TO ASK FOR THAT POWER...
AGAIN... RIGHT NOW...

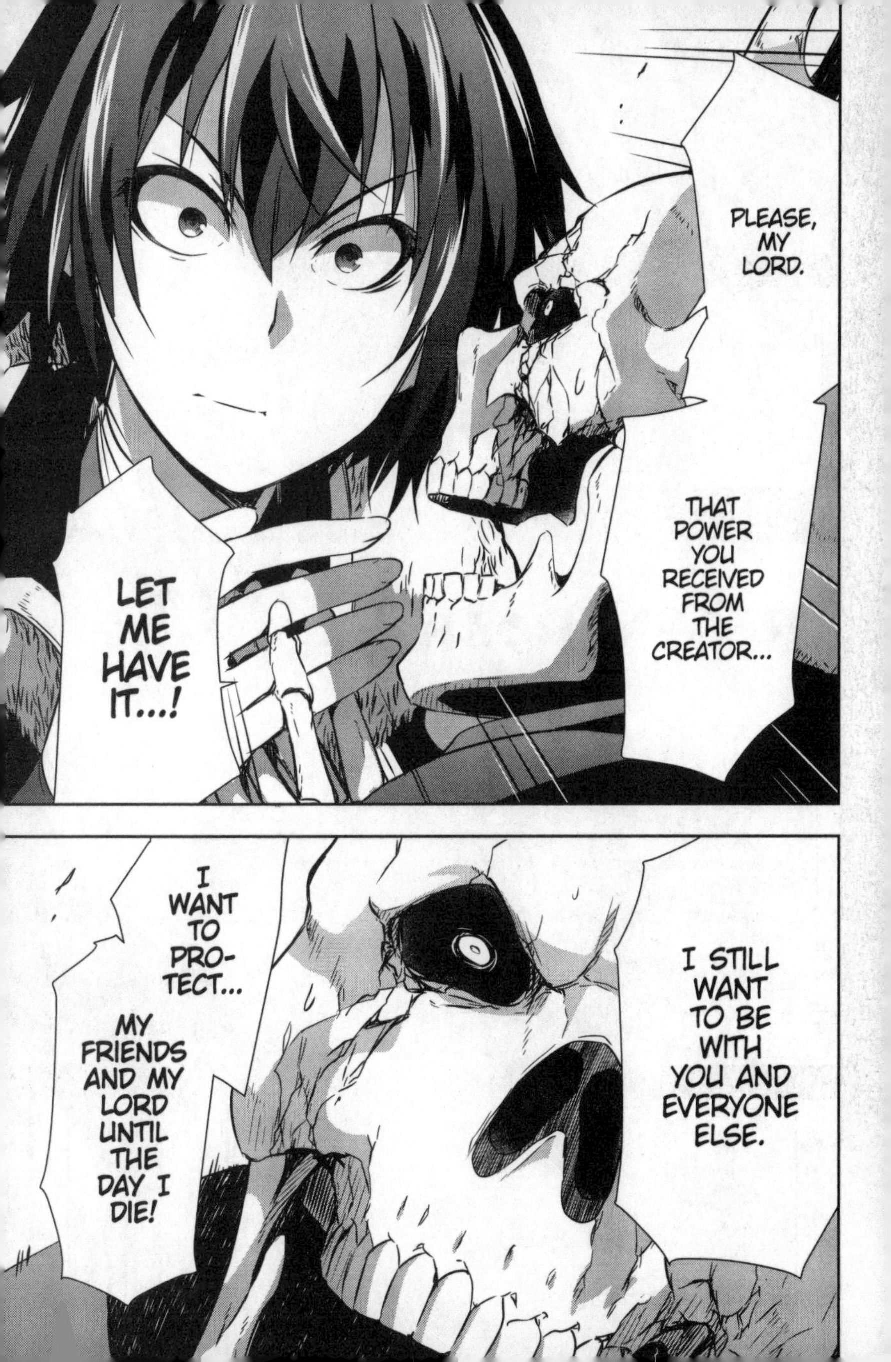
PLEASE, MY LORD.
THAT POWER YOU RECEIVED FROM THE CREATOR...
LET ME HAVE IT...!
I STILL WANT TO BE WITH YOU AND EVERYONE ELSE.
I WANT TO PROTECT...
MY FRIENDS AND MY LORD UNTIL THE DAY I DIE!

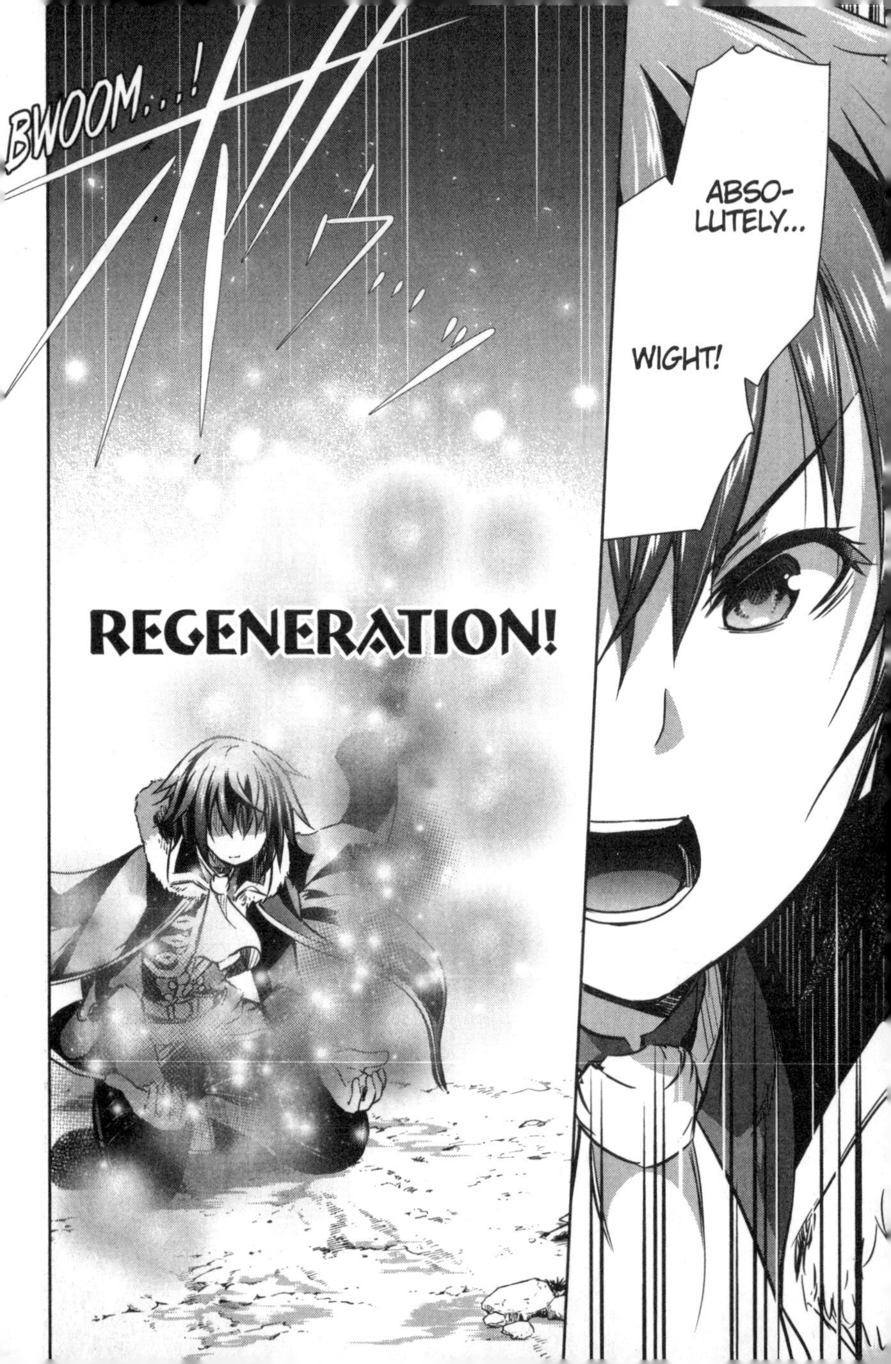
ABSO-
LUTELY...
WIGHT!
BWOOM...!
REGENERATION!

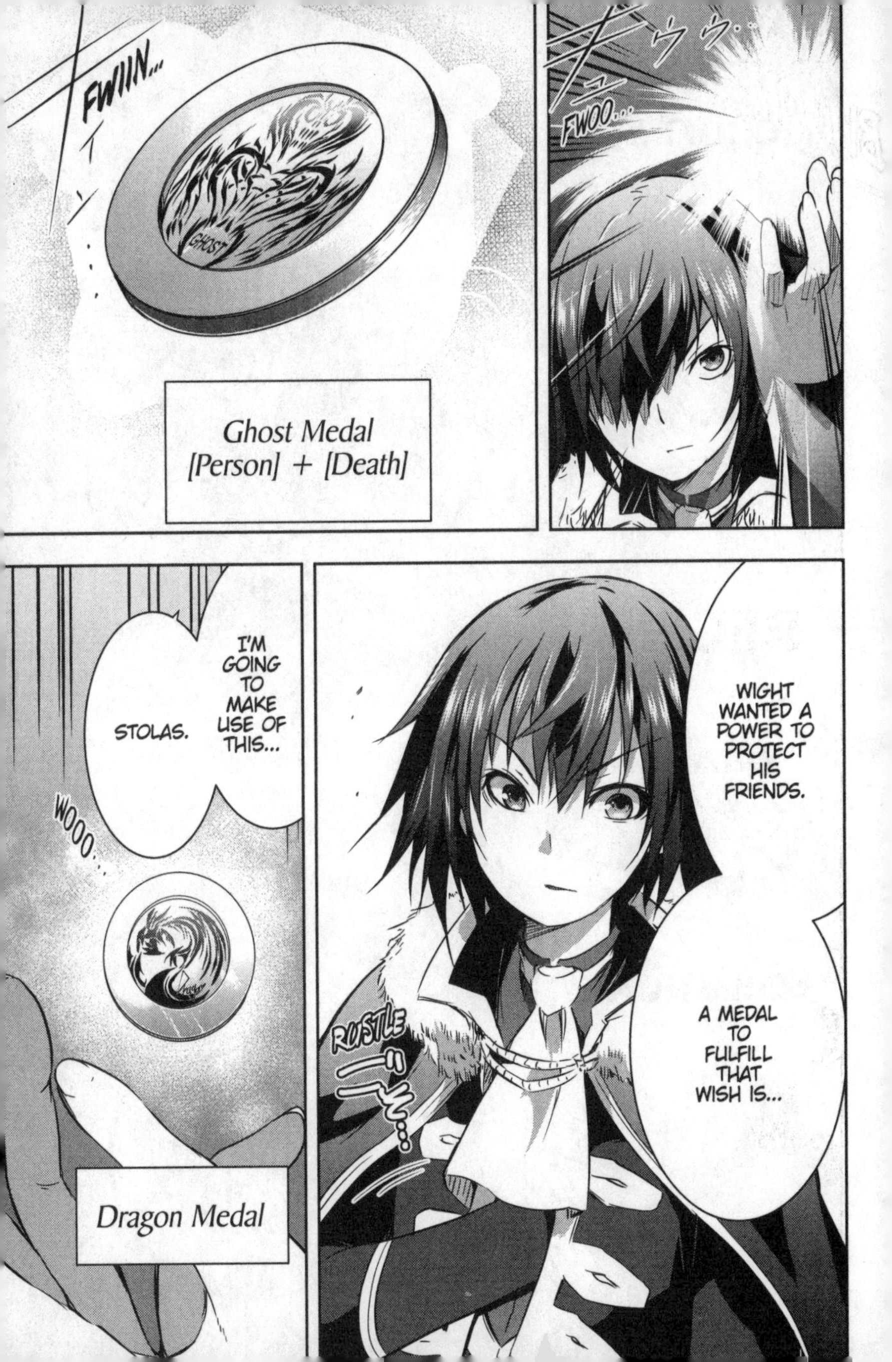
FWOO...
FWIIN...
GHOST
Ghost Medal
[Person] + [Death]
WIGHT WANTED A POWER TO PROTECT HIS FRIENDS.
A MEDAL TO FULFILL THAT WISH IS...
RUSTLE
I'M GOING TO MAKE USE OF THIS...
STOLAS.
WOOO...
Dragon Medal

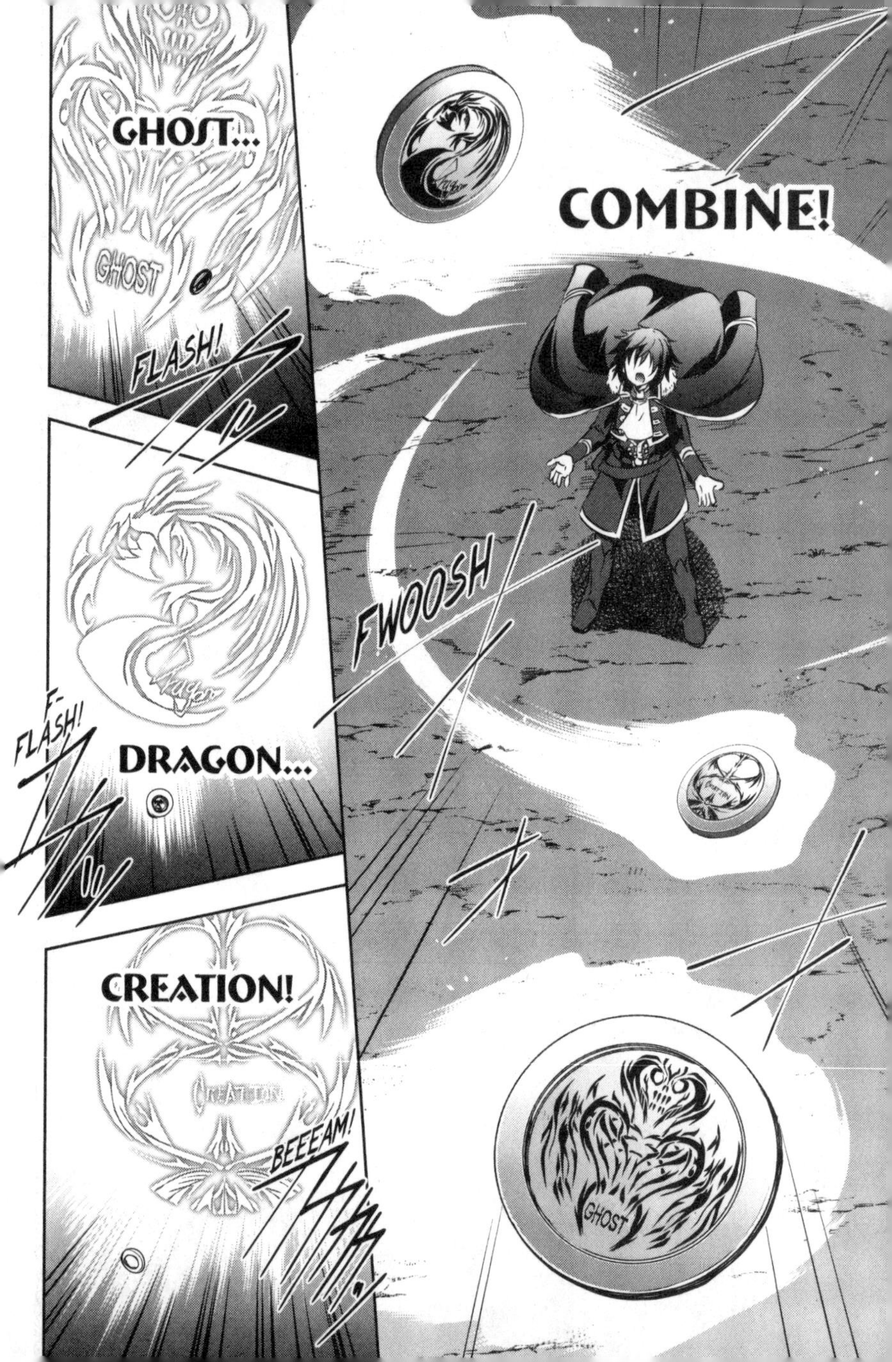
GHOST...
GHOST
FLASH!
DRAGON...
F-FLASH!
CREATION!
BEEEAM!
COMBINE!
FWOOSH
GHOST

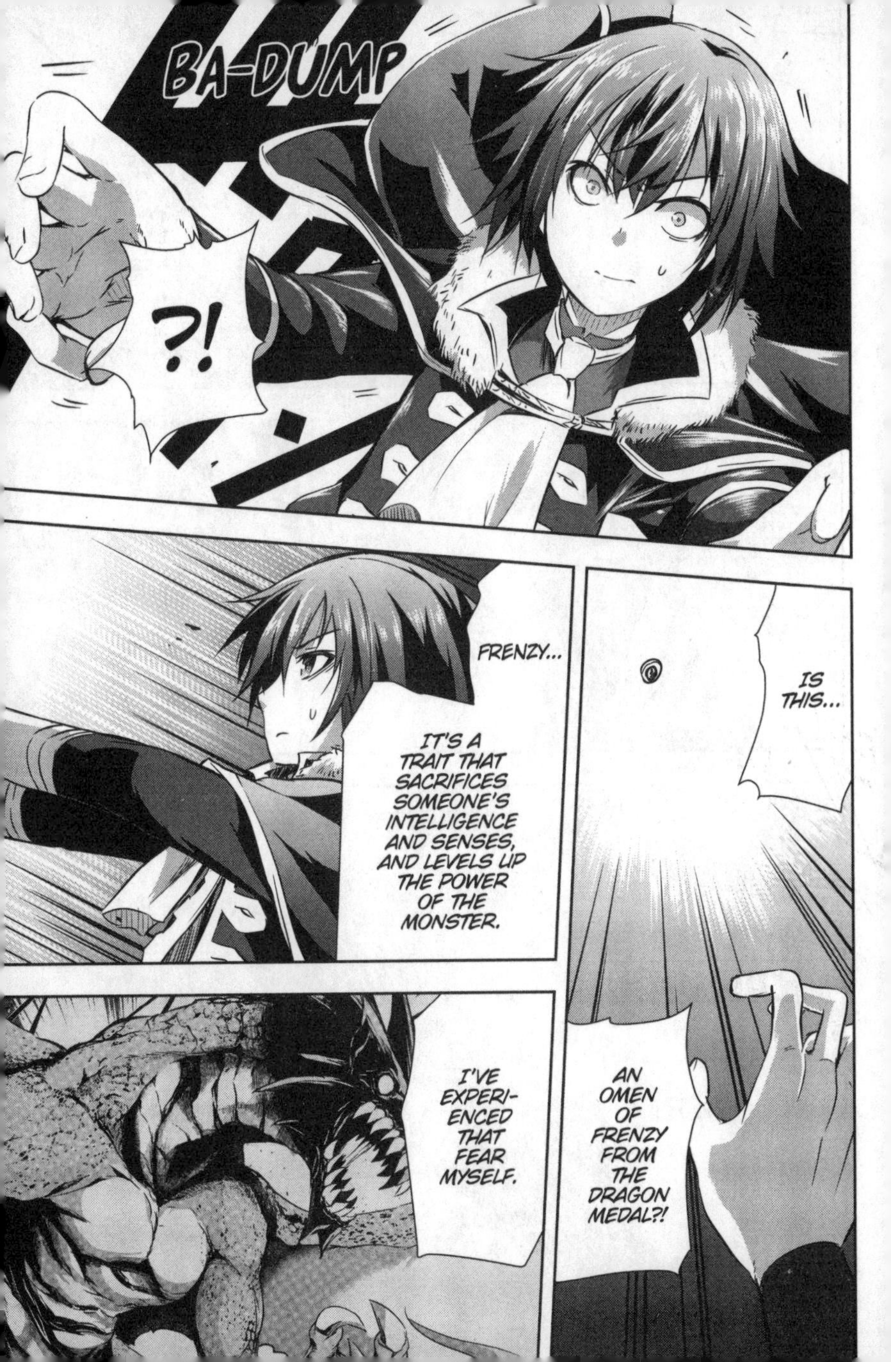
BA-DUMP
?!
IS THIS...
AN OMEN OF FRENZY FROM THE DRAGON MEDAL?!
FRENZY...
IT'S A TRAIT THAT SACRIFICES SOMEONE'S INTELLIGENCE AND SENSES, AND LEVELS UP THE POWER OF THE MONSTER.
I'VE EXPERI-ENCED THAT FEAR MYSELF.

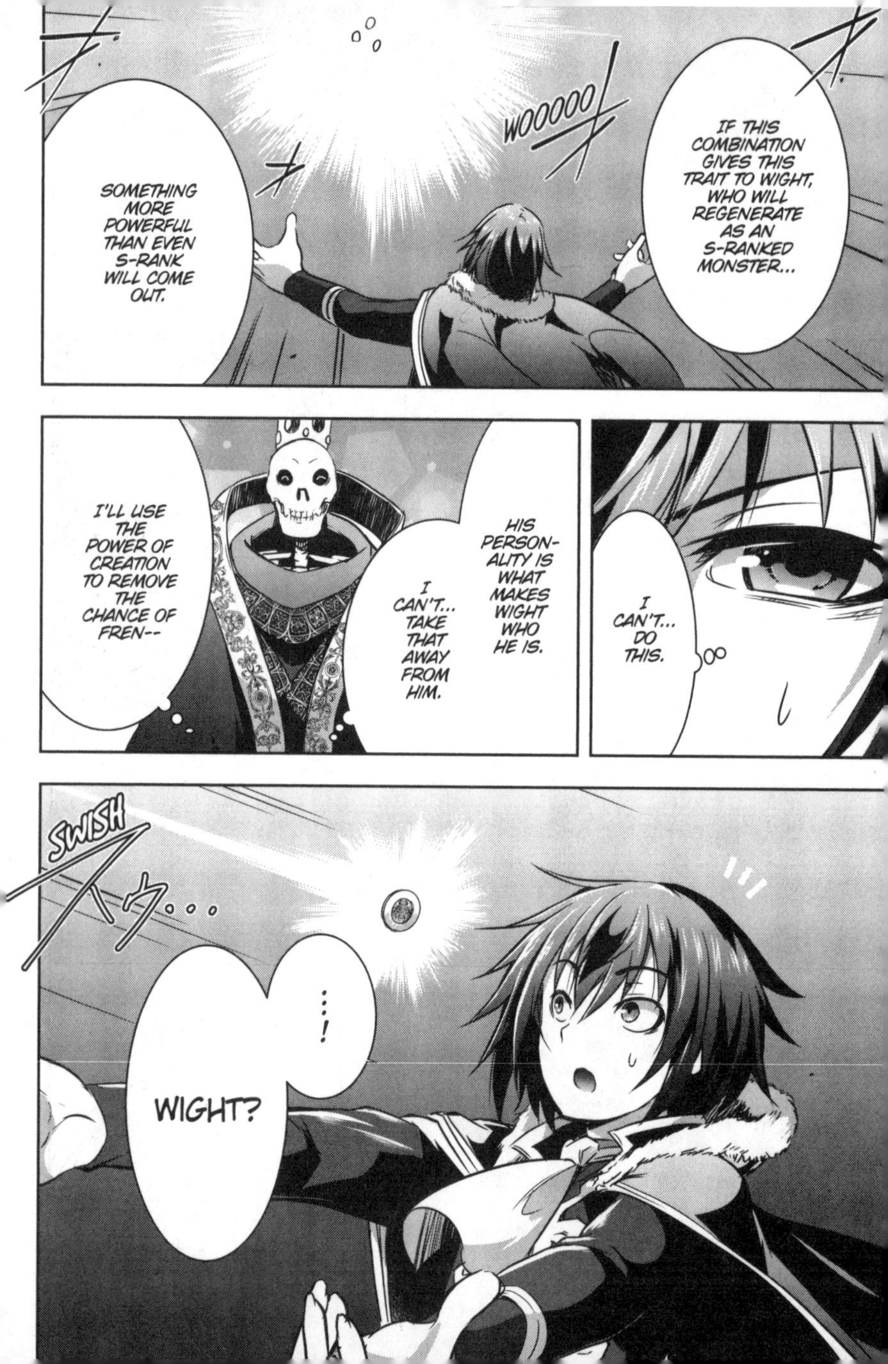
WOOOOO
IF THIS COMBINATION GIVES THIS TRAIT TO WIGHT, WHO WILL REGENERATE AS AN S-RANKED MONSTER...
SOMETHING MORE POWERFUL THAN EVEN S-RANK WILL COME OUT.
I CAN'T... DO THIS.
HIS PERSONALITY IS WHAT MAKES WIGHT WHO HE IS.
I CAN'T... TAKE THAT AWAY FROM HIM.
I'LL USE THE POWER OF CREATION TO REMOVE THE CHANCE OF FREN--
SWISH
...!
WIGHT?

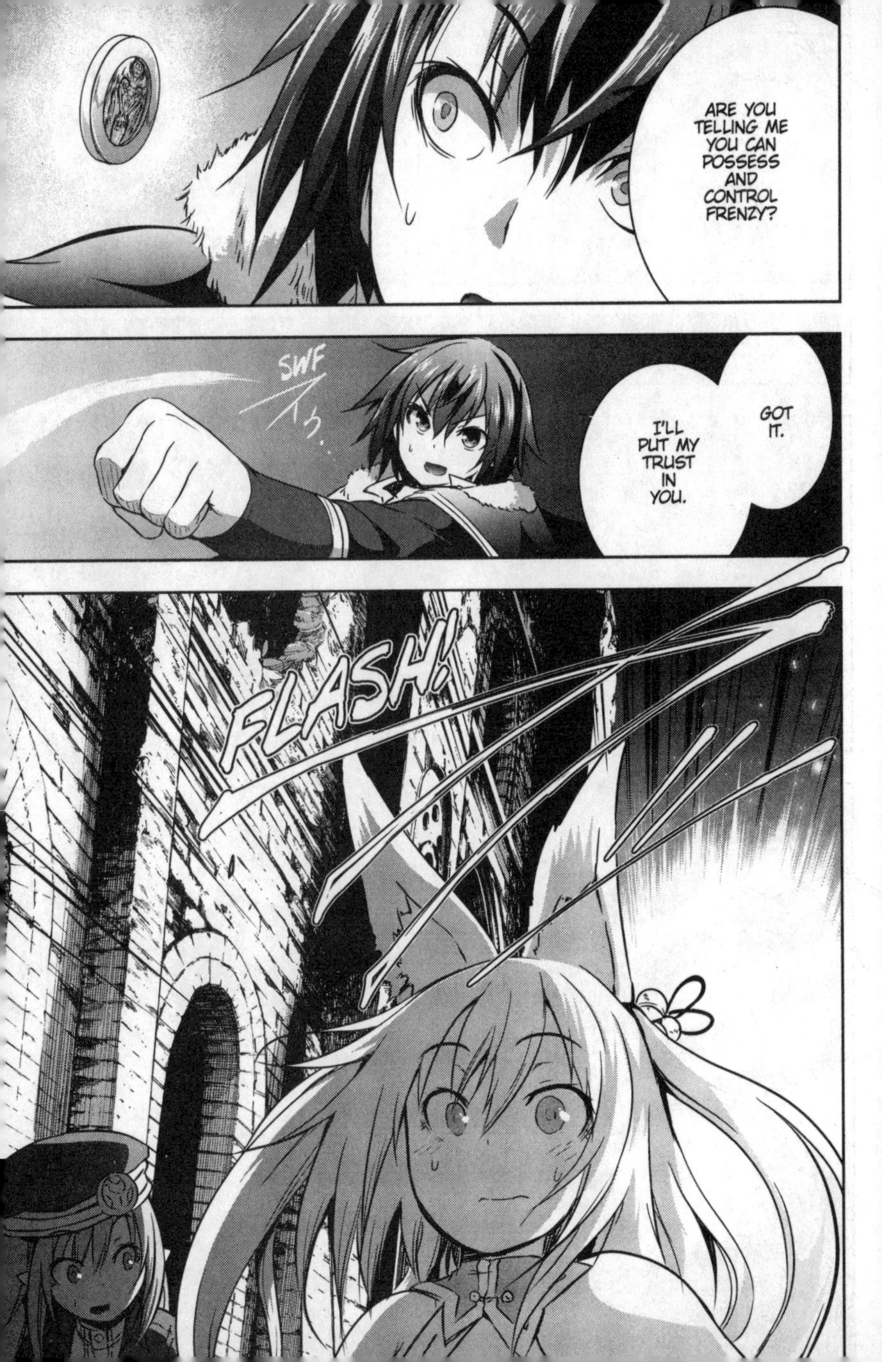
ARE YOU TELLING ME YOU CAN POSSESS AND CONTROL FRENZY?
GOT IT.
I'LL PUT MY TRUST IN YOU.
SWF
FLASH!

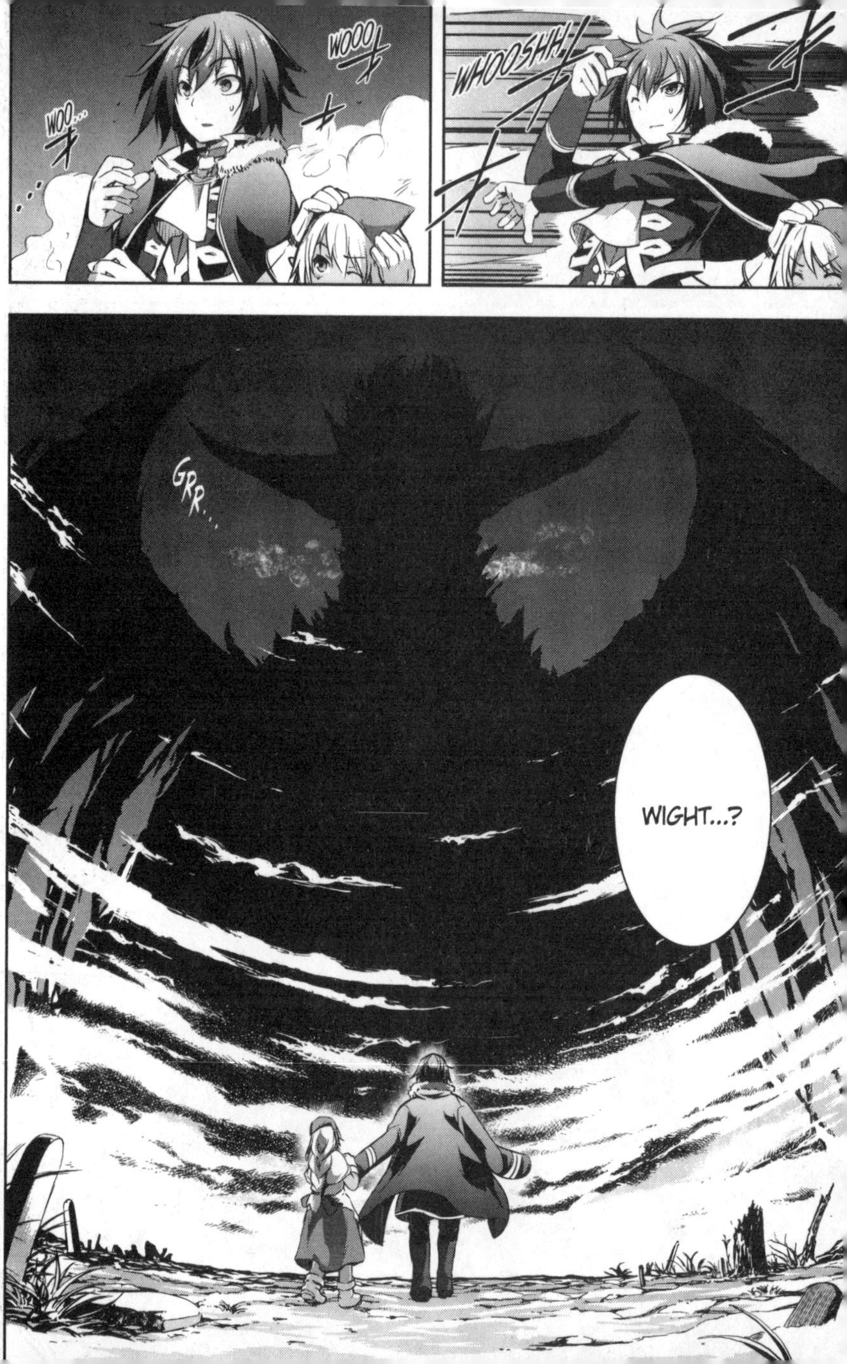
WHOOSHH
WOO...
WOOOM
GRR...
WIGHT...?

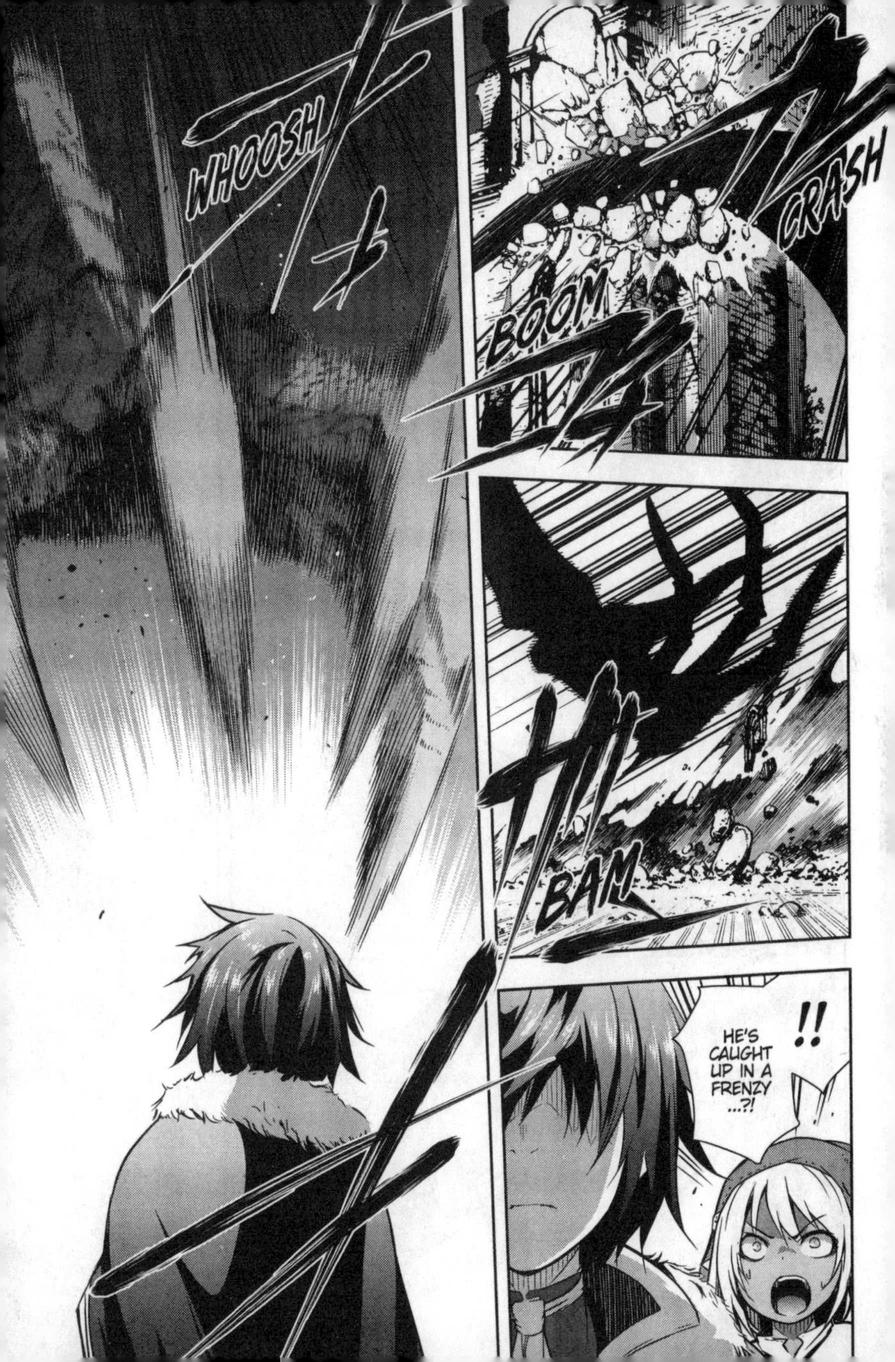
CRASH
BOOM
WHOOSH
BAM
!!
HE'S CAUGHT UP IN A FRENZY ...?!

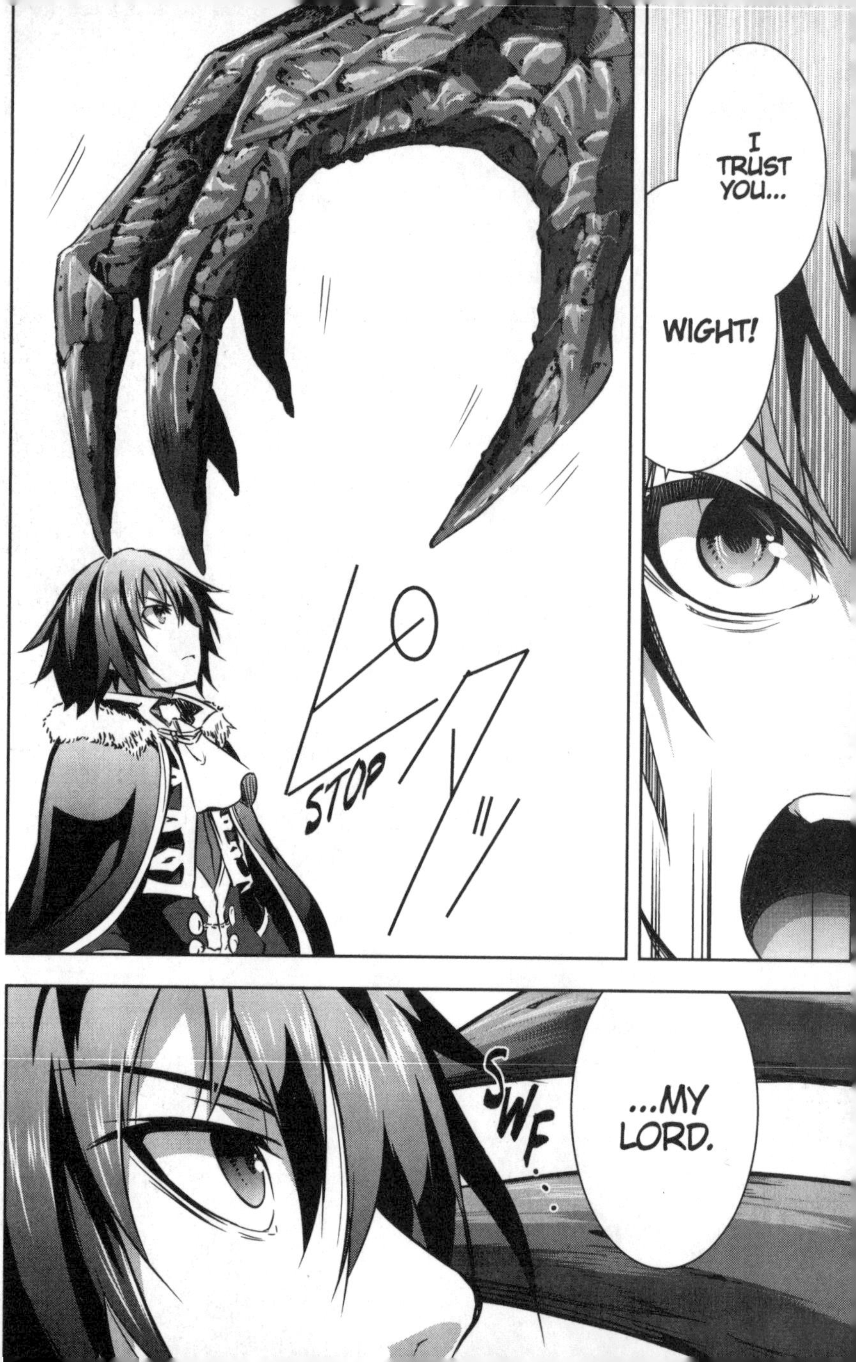
I TRUST YOU...
WIGHT!
STOP
SWF...
...MY LORD.

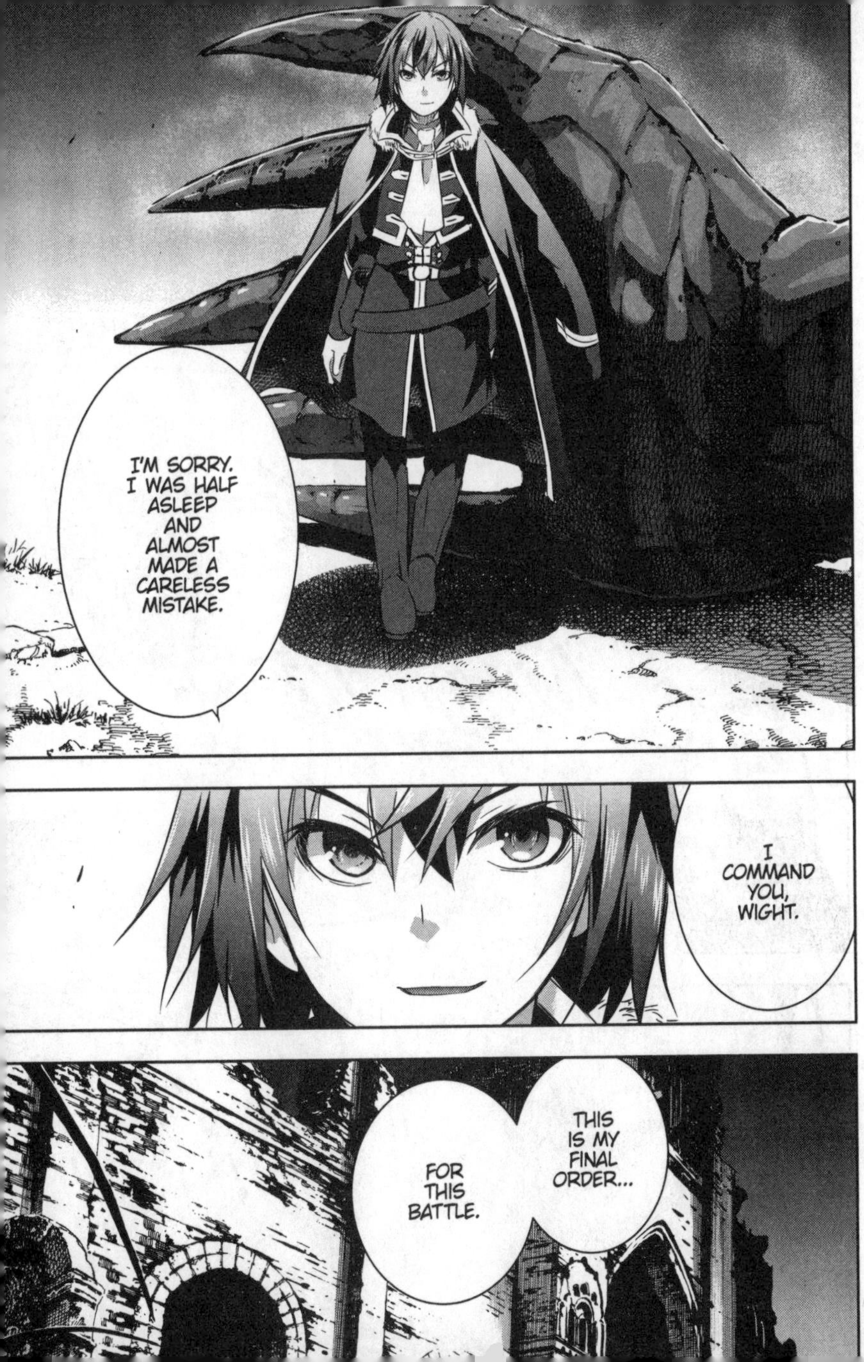
I'M SORRY. I WAS HALF ASLEEP AND ALMOST MADE A CARELESS MISTAKE.
I COMMAND YOU, WIGHT.
THIS IS MY FINAL ORDER...
FOR THIS BATTLE.

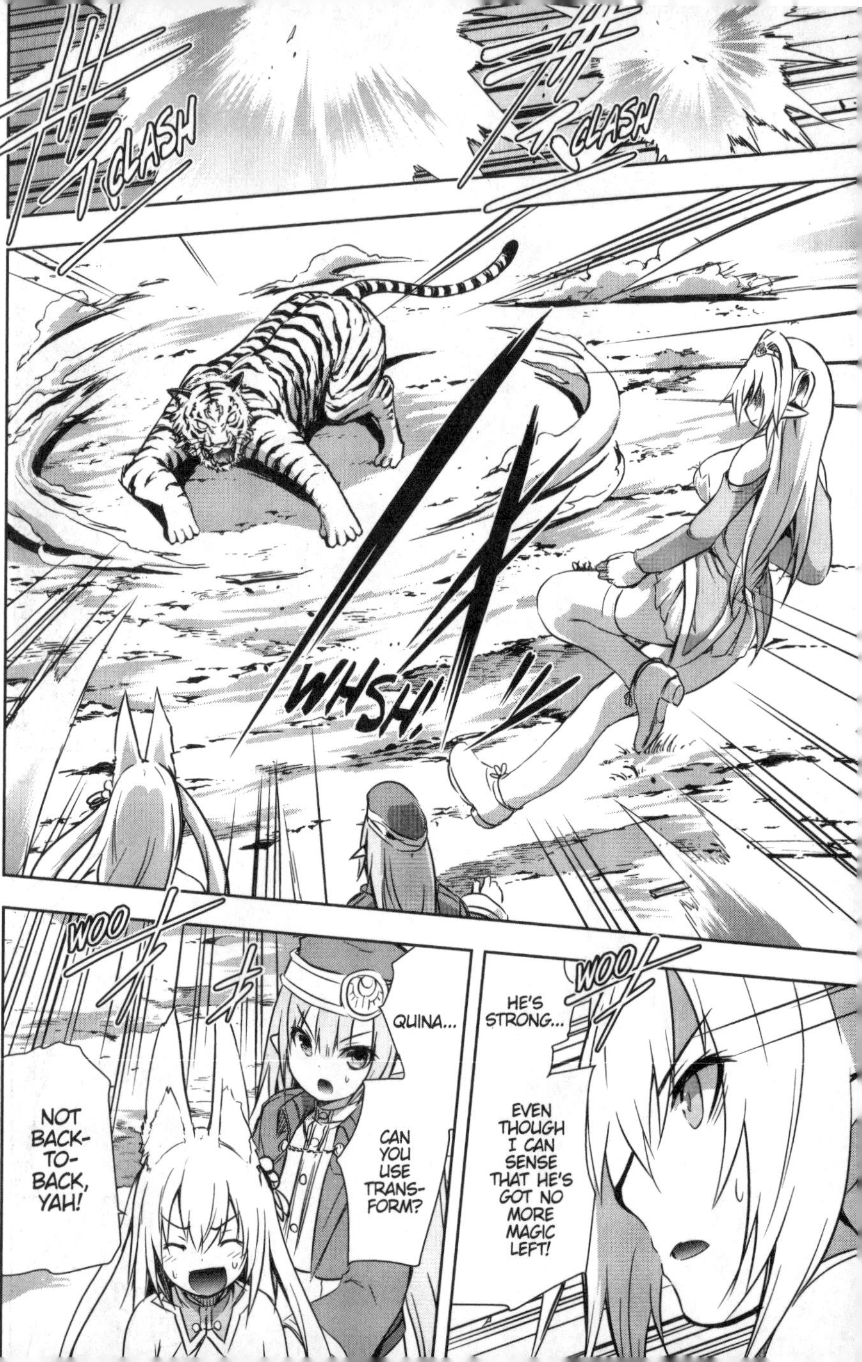
CLASH
CLASH
WHSH!
WOO
WOO
HE'S STRONG...
EVEN THOUGH I CAN SENSE THAT HE'S GOT NO MORE MAGIC LEFT!
QUINA...
CAN YOU USE TRANS-FORM?
NOT BACK-TO-BACK, YAH!

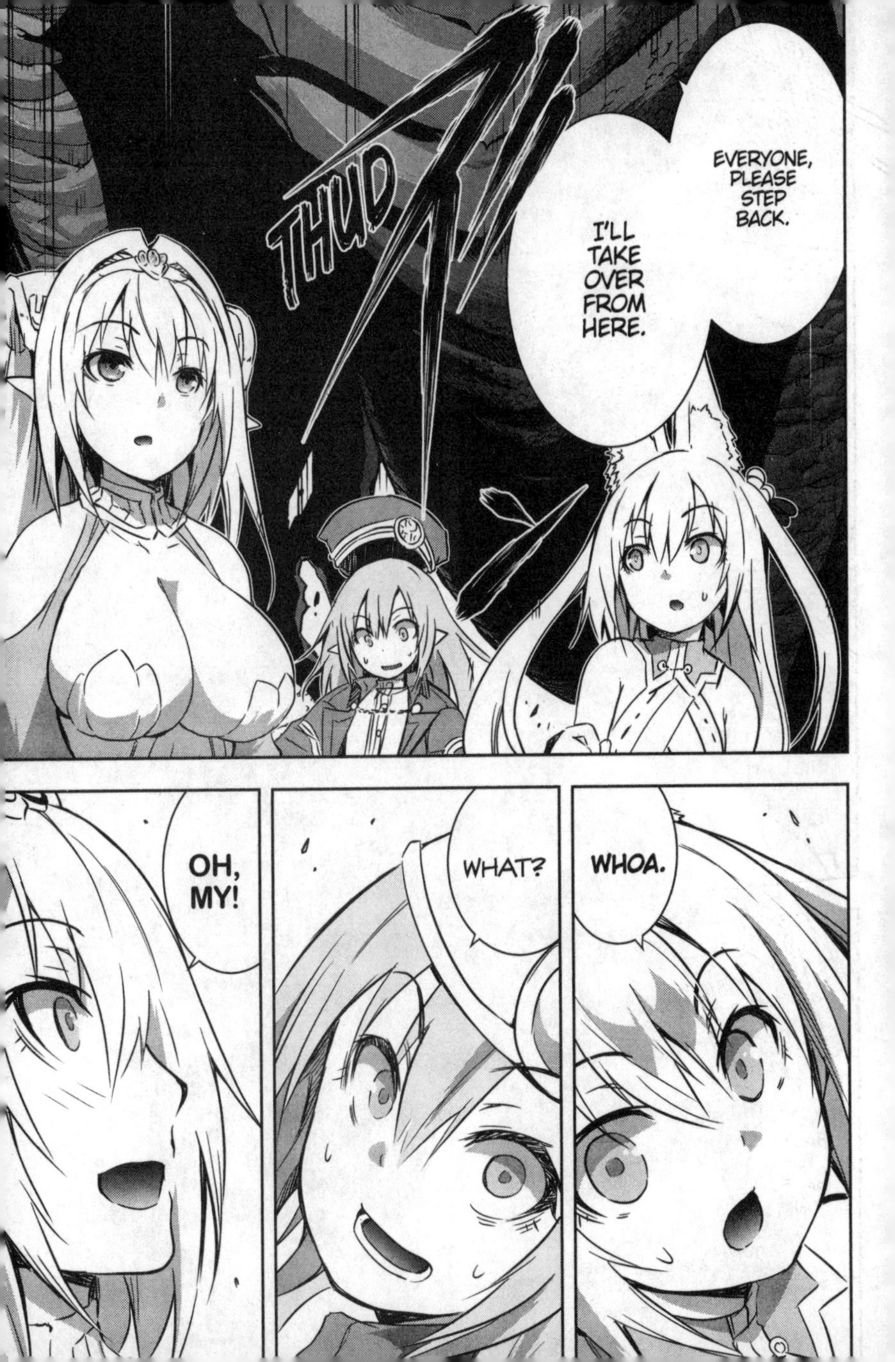
EVERYONE, PLEASE STEP BACK.
I'LL TAKE OVER FROM HERE.
THUD
WHOA.
WHAT?
OH, MY!

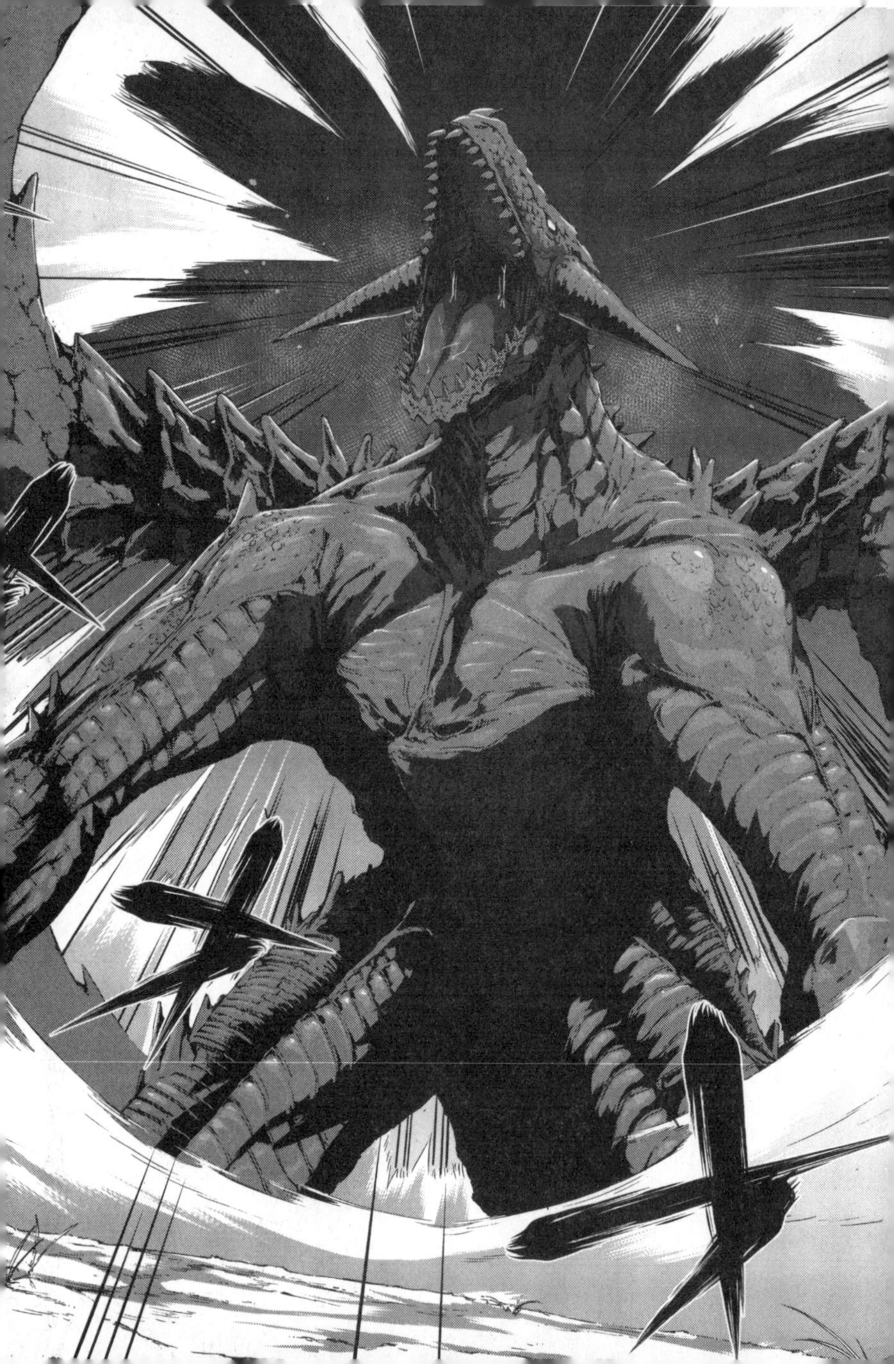

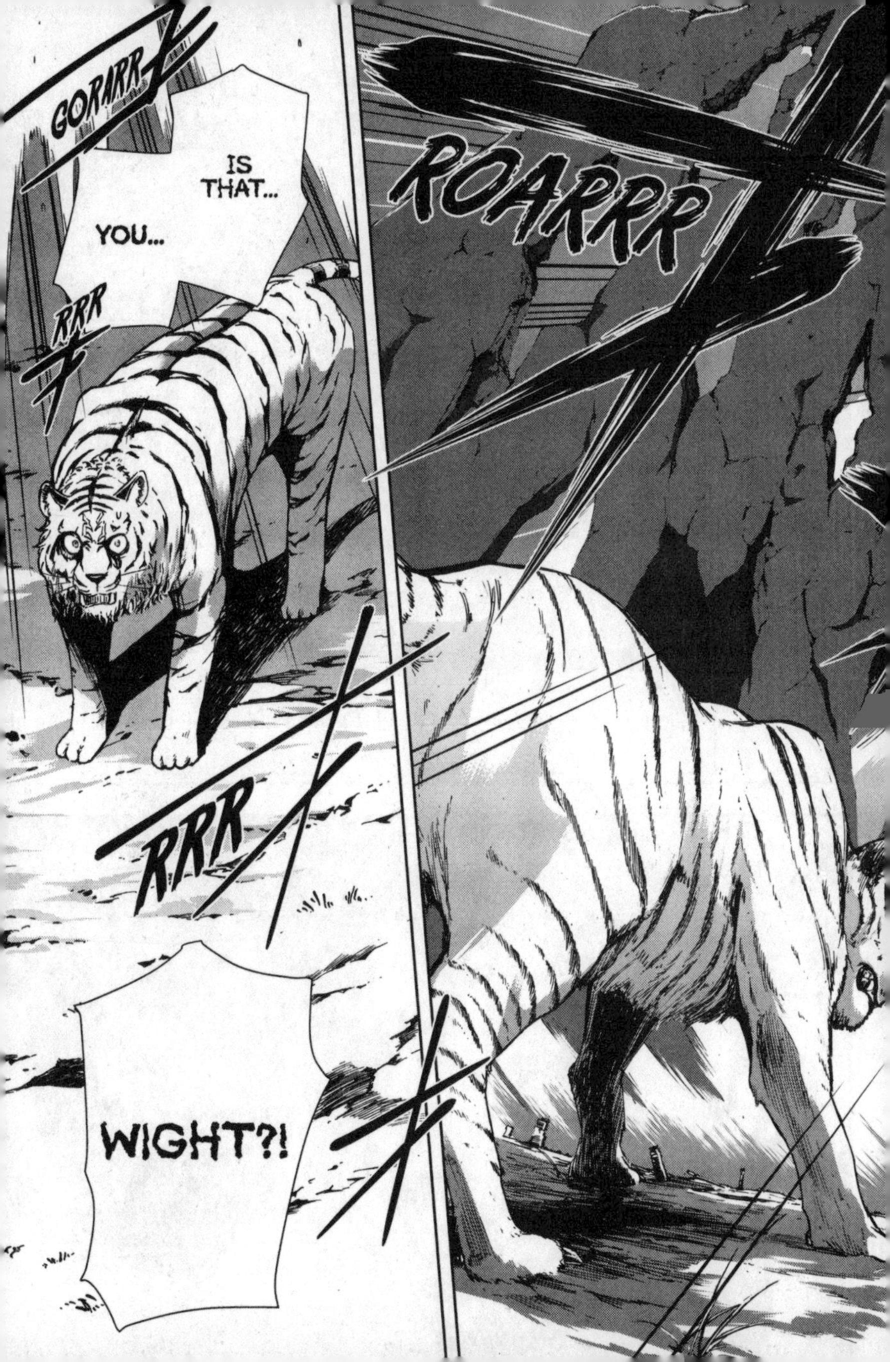
GORARR
IS THAT...
YOU...
RRR
RRR
WIGHT?!
ROARRR

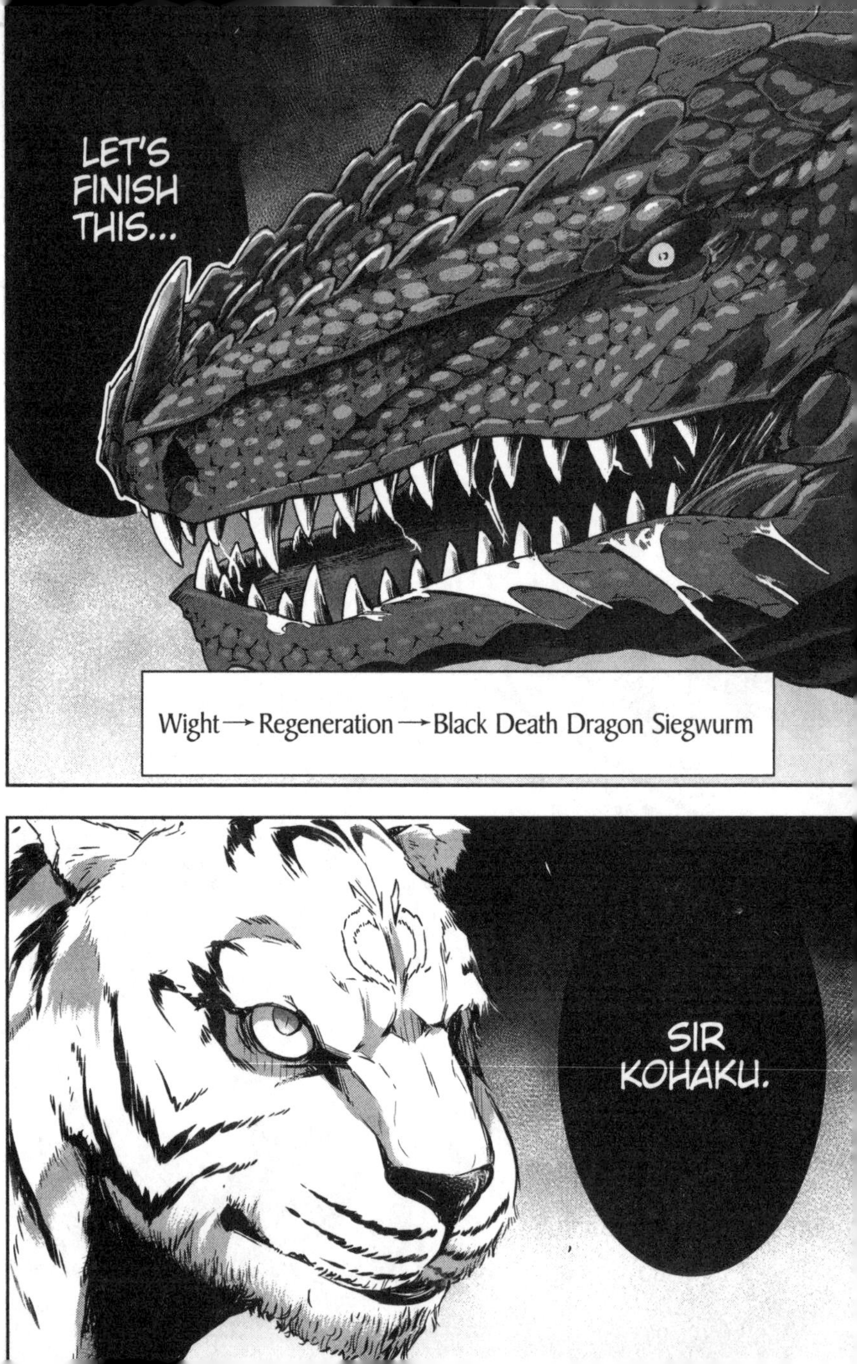
LET'S FINISH THIS...
Wight → Regeneration → Black Death Dragon Siegwurm
SIR KOHAKU.

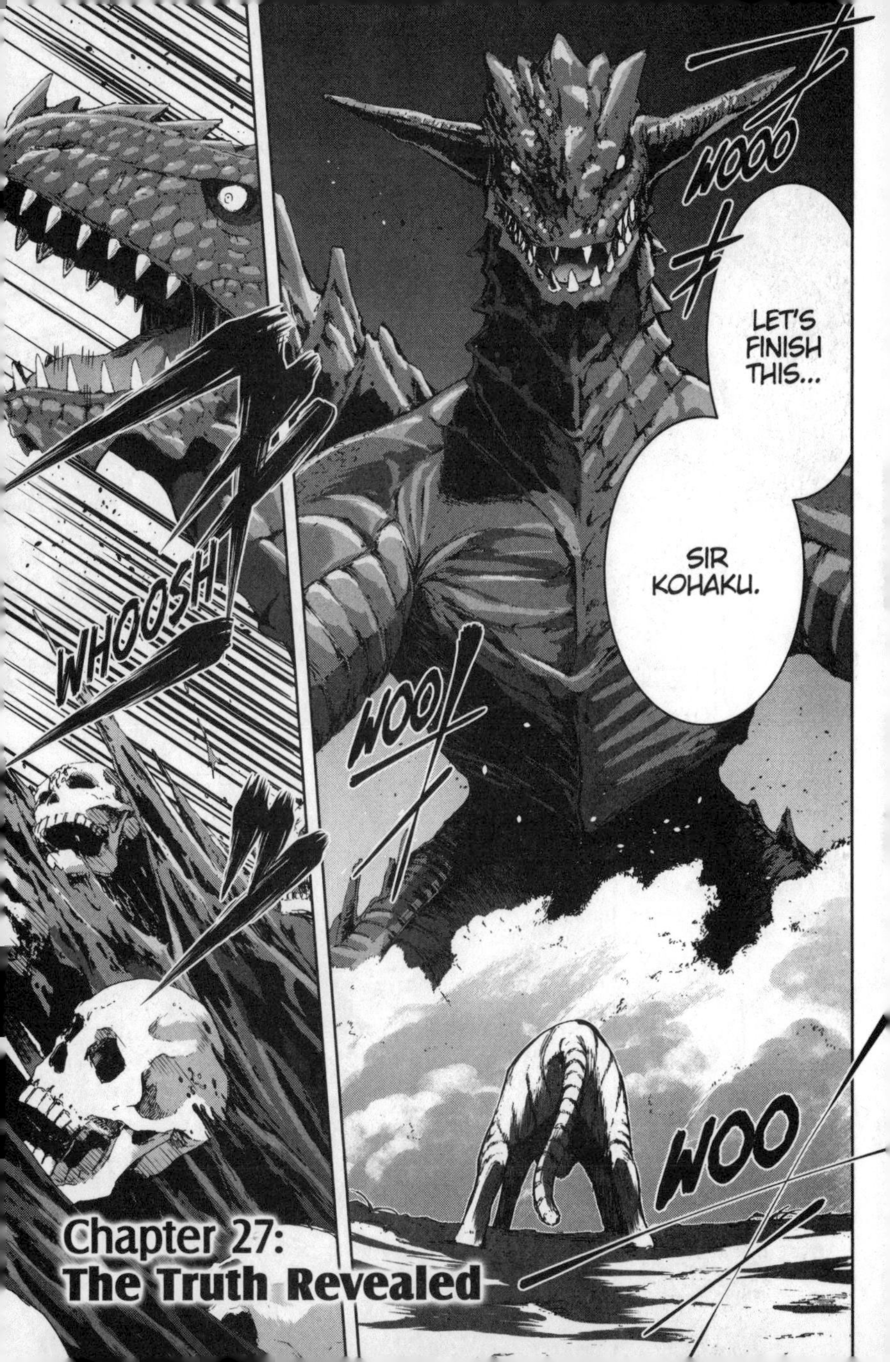
WOOO
LET'S FINISH THIS...
SIR KOHAKU.
WHOOSH
WOO
WOO
Chapter 27:
The Truth Revealed

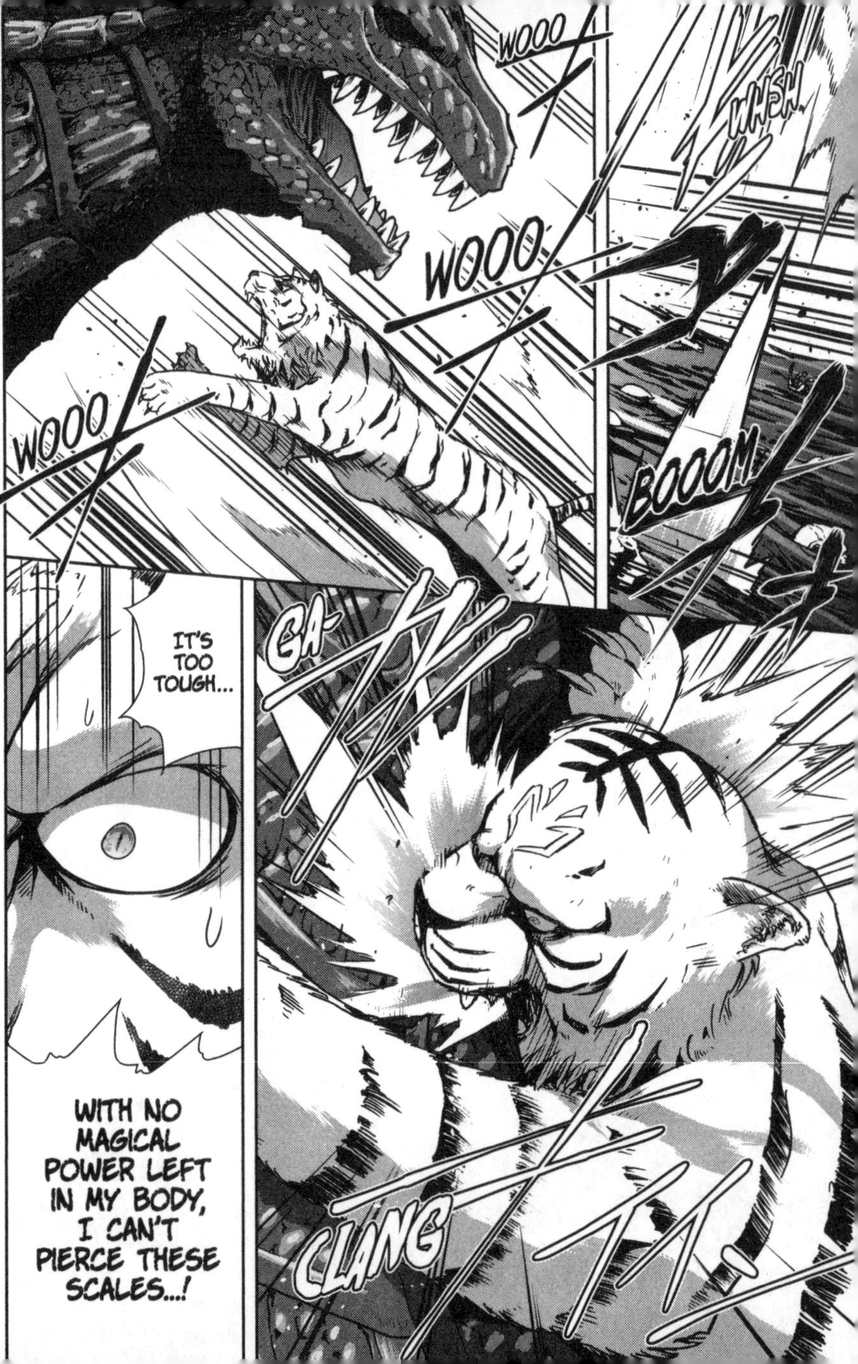

WOOO
WHSH
WOOO
WOOO
BOOOM
GA-
IT'S TOO TOUGH...
WITH NO MAGICAL POWER LEFT IN MY BODY, I CAN'T PIERCE THESE SCALES...!
CLANG

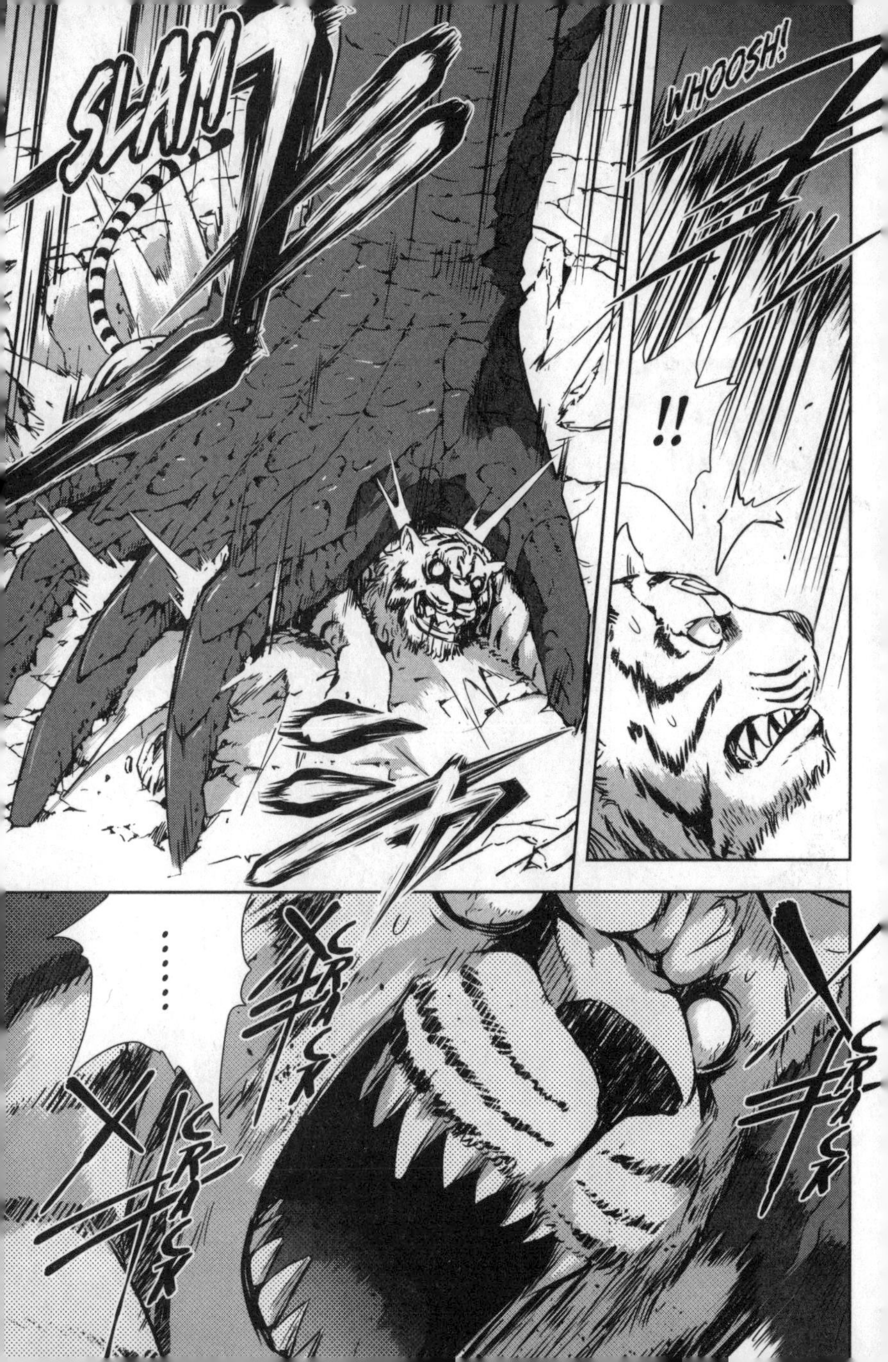
WHOOSH!
SLAM
!!
......
CRACK
CRACK
CRACK

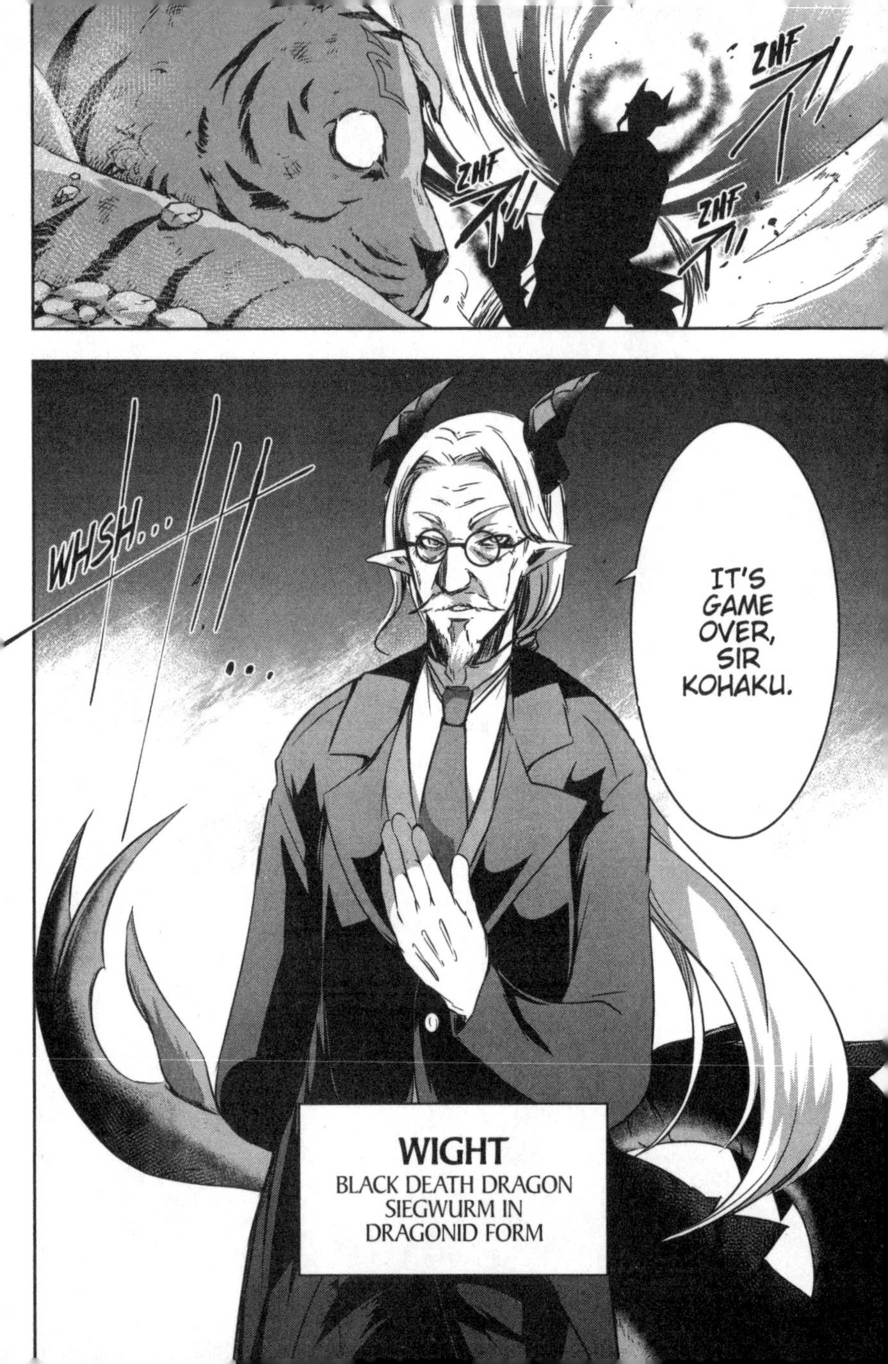
ZHF
ZHF
ZHF
WHSH...
...
IT'S GAME OVER, SIR KOHAKU.
WIGHT
BLACK DEATH DRAGON SIEGWURM IN DRAGONID FORM

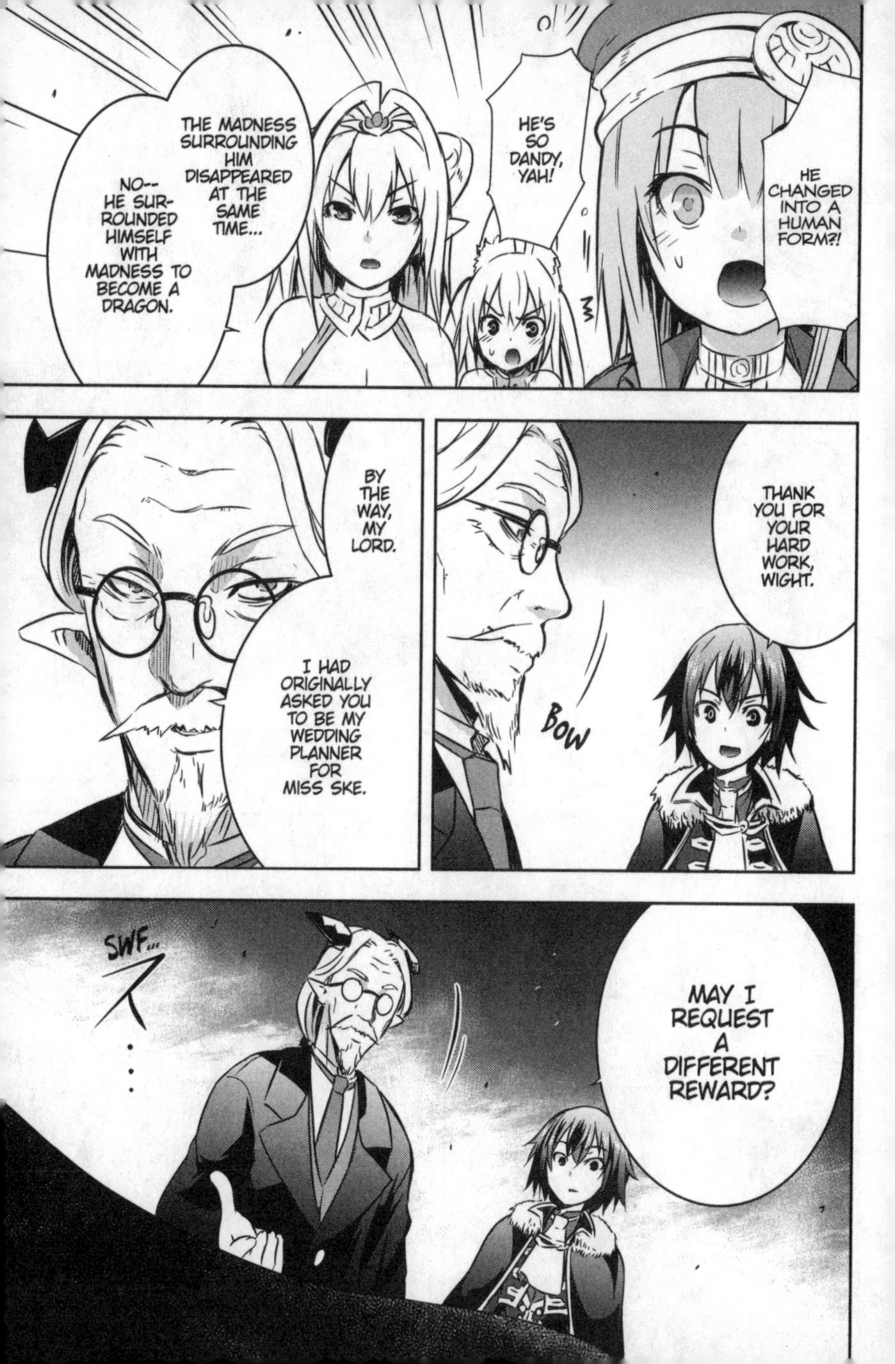
HE CHANGED INTO A HUMAN FORM?!
HE'S SO DANDY, YAH!
THE MADNESS SURROUNDING HIM DISAPPEARED AT THE SAME TIME...
NO-- HE SURROUNDED HIMSELF WITH MADNESS TO BECOME A DRAGON.
THANK YOU FOR YOUR HARD WORK, WIGHT.
BOW
BY THE WAY, MY LORD.
I HAD ORIGINALLY ASKED YOU TO BE MY WEDDING PLANNER FOR MISS SKE.
MAY I REQUEST A DIFFERENT REWARD?
SWF...

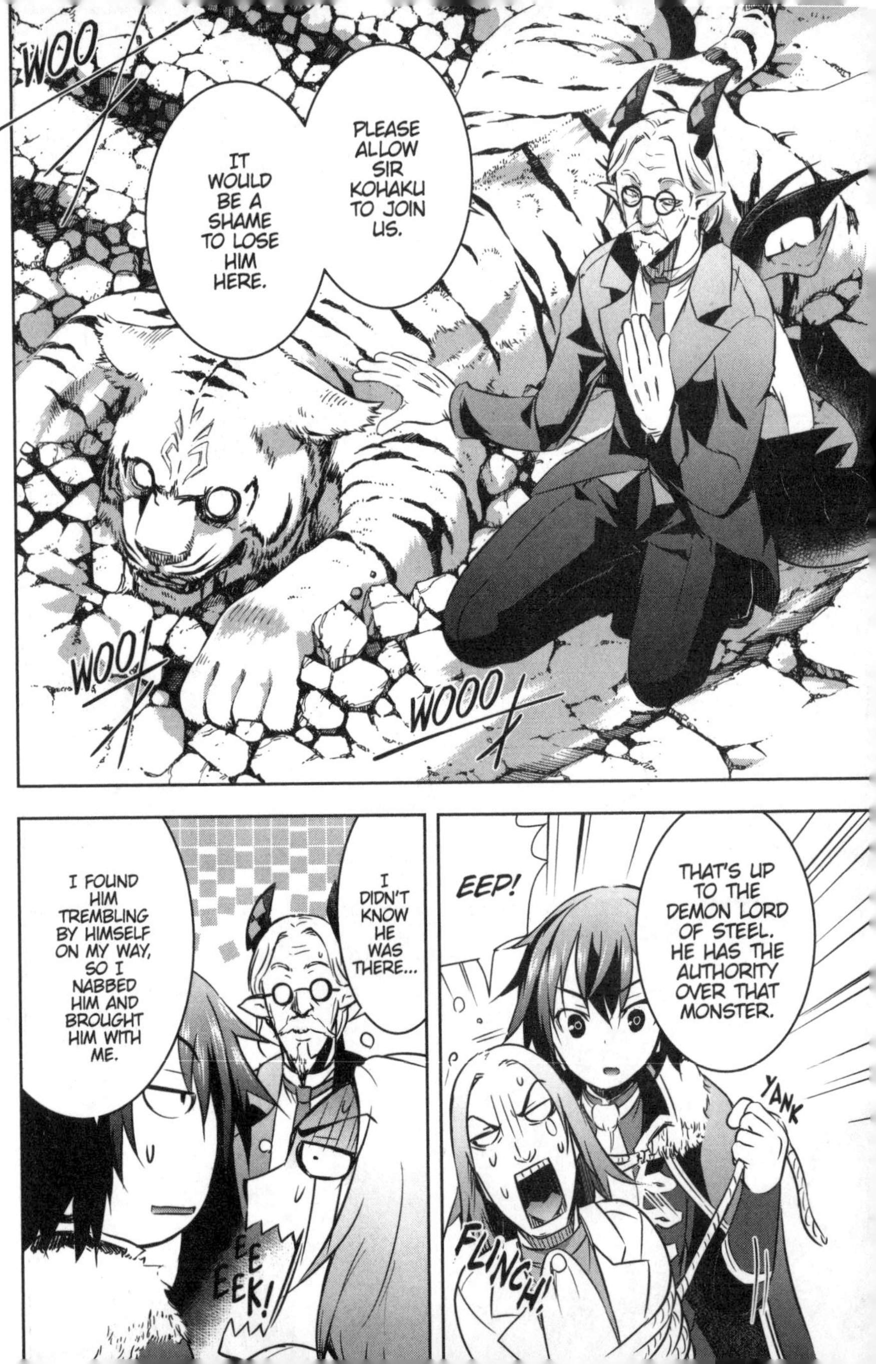
WOO
PLEASE ALLOW SIR KOHAKU TO JOIN US.
IT WOULD BE A SHAME TO LOSE HIM HERE.
WOO
WOOO
THAT'S UP TO THE DEMON LORD OF STEEL. HE HAS THE AUTHORITY OVER THAT MONSTER.
EEP!
YANK
FLINCH!
I DIDN'T KNOW HE WAS THERE...
I FOUND HIM TREMBLING BY HIMSELF ON MY WAY, SO I NABBED HIM AND BROUGHT HIM WITH ME.
EEEK!

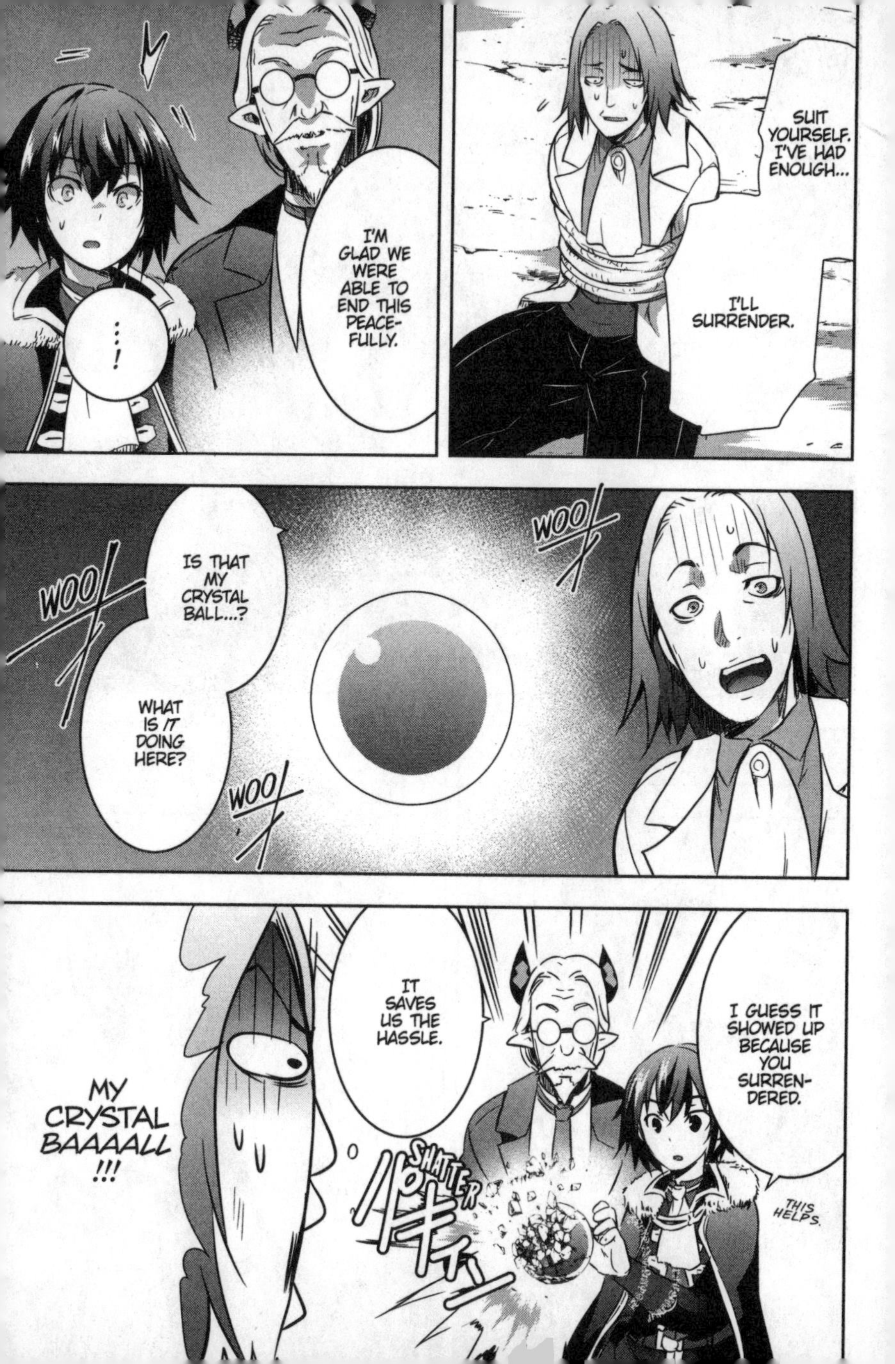
SUIT YOURSELF. I'VE HAD ENOUGH...
I'LL SURRENDER.
I'M GLAD WE WERE ABLE TO END THIS PEACEFULLY.
...!
WOO
IS THAT MY CRYSTAL BALL...?
WHAT IS IT DOING HERE?
WOO
WOO
I GUESS IT SHOWED UP BECAUSE YOU SURRENDERED.
THIS HELPS.
IT SAVES US THE HASSLE.
SHATTER
MY CRYSTAL BAAAALL!!!

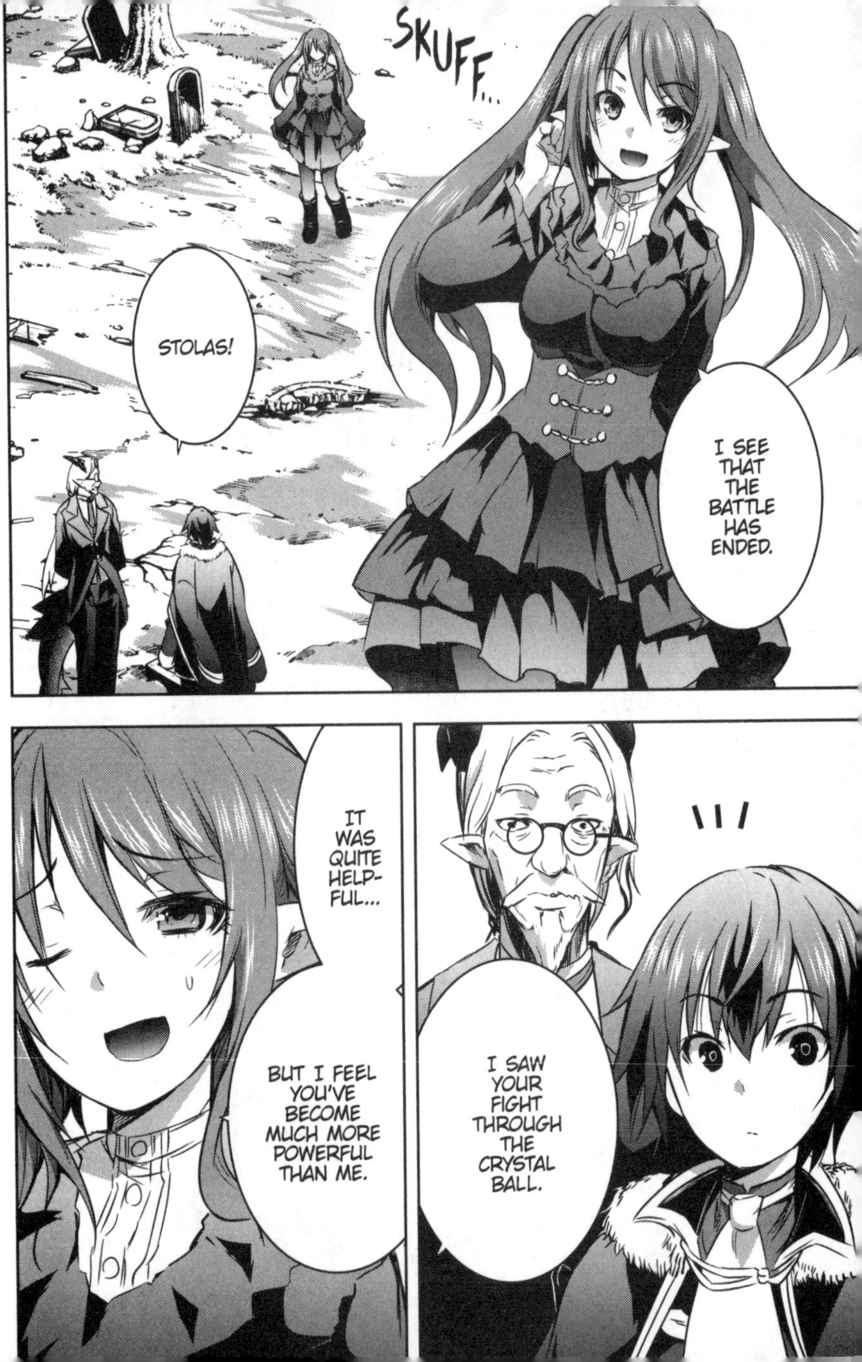

SKUFF...
I SEE THAT THE BATTLE HAS ENDED.
STOLAS!
I SAW YOUR FIGHT THROUGH THE CRYSTAL BALL.
IT WAS QUITE HELPFUL...
BUT I FEEL YOU'VE BECOME MUCH MORE POWERFUL THAN ME.

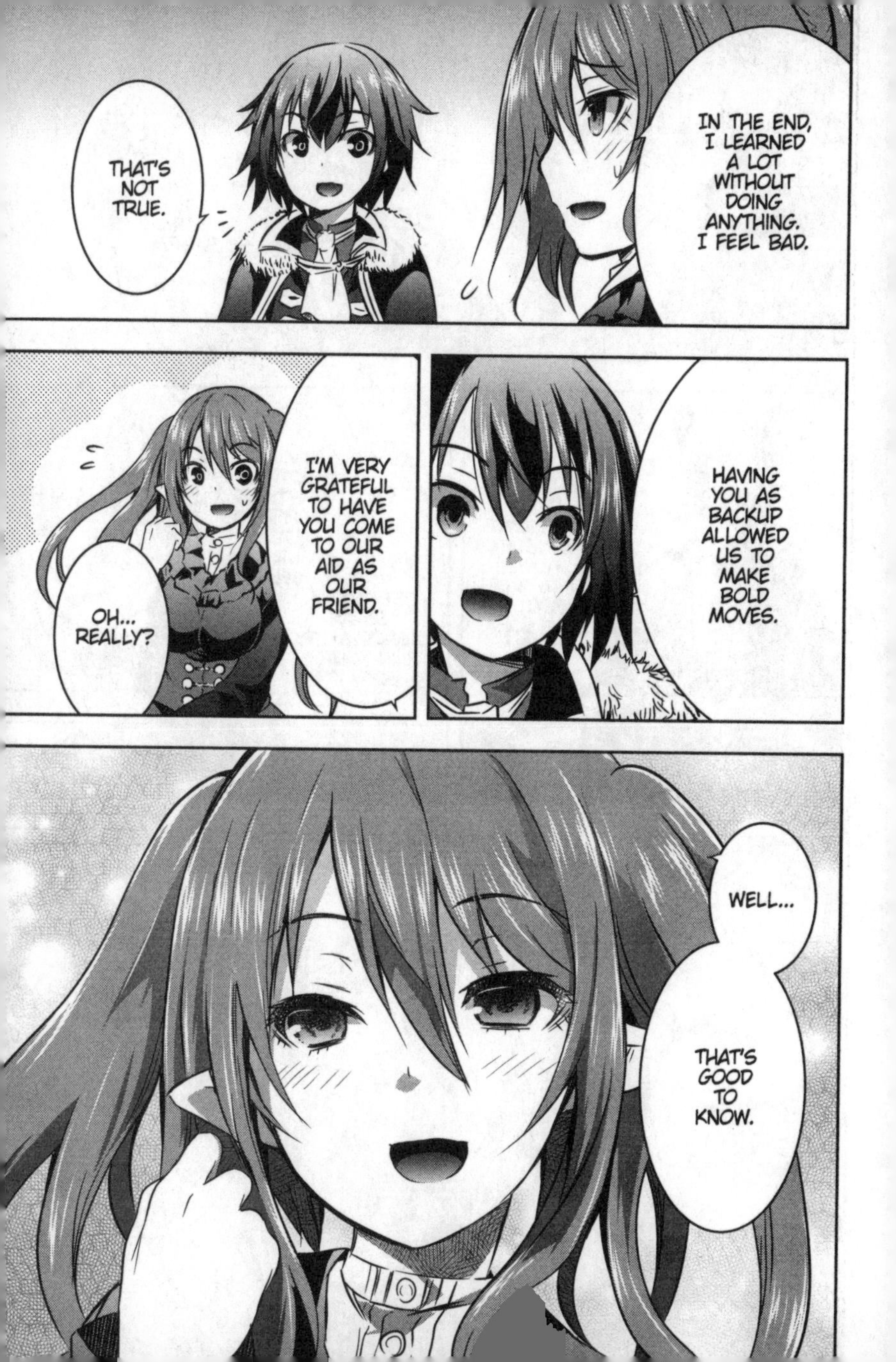
IN THE END, I LEARNED A LOT WITHOUT DOING ANYTHING. I FEEL BAD.
THAT'S NOT TRUE.
HAVING YOU AS BACKUP ALLOWED US TO MAKE BOLD MOVES.
I'M VERY GRATEFUL TO HAVE YOU COME TO OUR AID AS OUR FRIEND.
OH... REALLY?
WELL...
THAT'S GOOD TO KNOW.

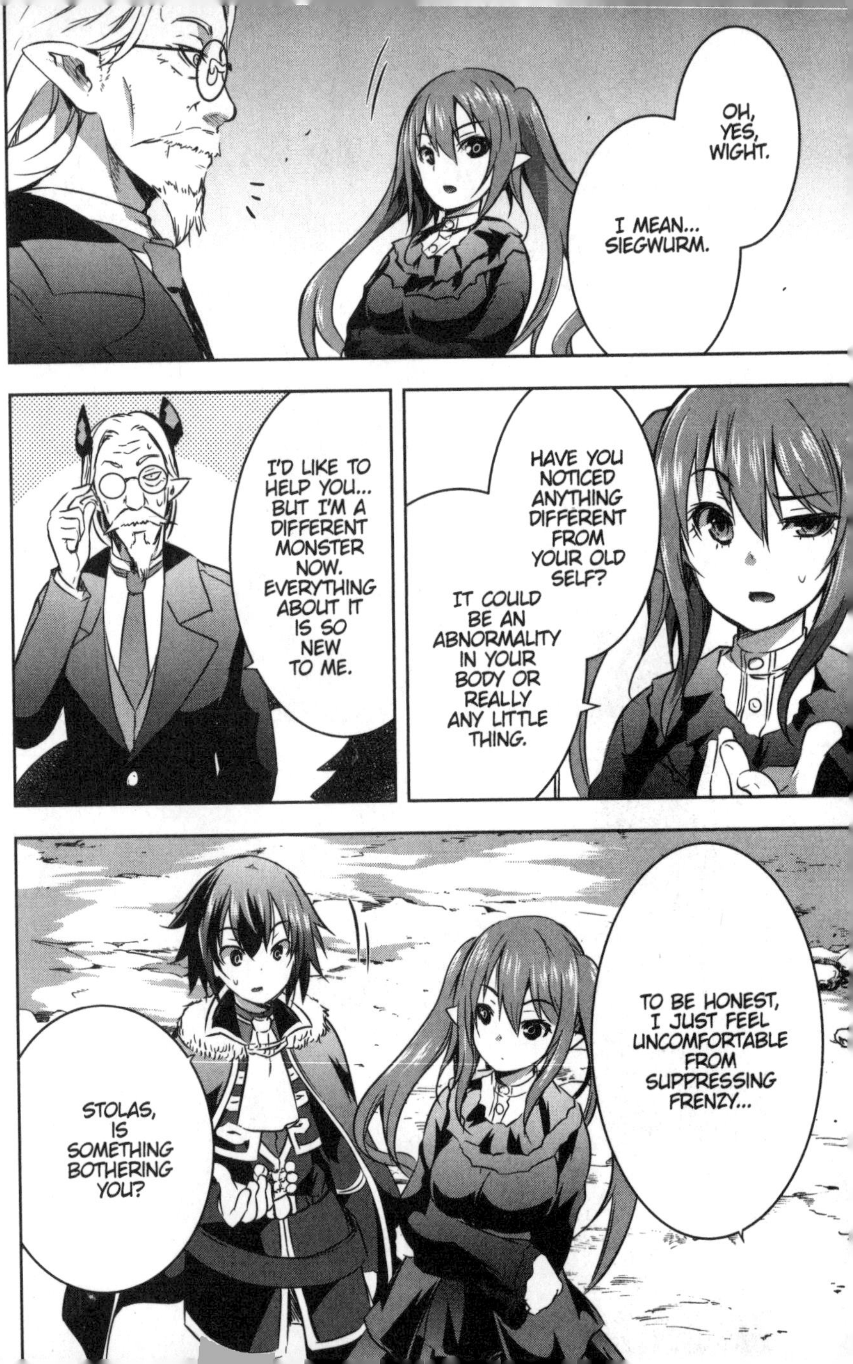
OH, YES, WIGHT.
I MEAN... SIEGWURM.
HAVE YOU NOTICED ANYTHING DIFFERENT FROM YOUR OLD SELF?
IT COULD BE AN ABNORMALITY IN YOUR BODY OR REALLY ANY LITTLE THING.
I'D LIKE TO HELP YOU... BUT I'M A DIFFERENT MONSTER NOW. EVERYTHING ABOUT IT IS SO NEW TO ME.
TO BE HONEST, I JUST FEEL UNCOMFORTABLE FROM SUPPRESSING FRENZY...
STOLAS, IS SOMETHING BOTHERING YOU?

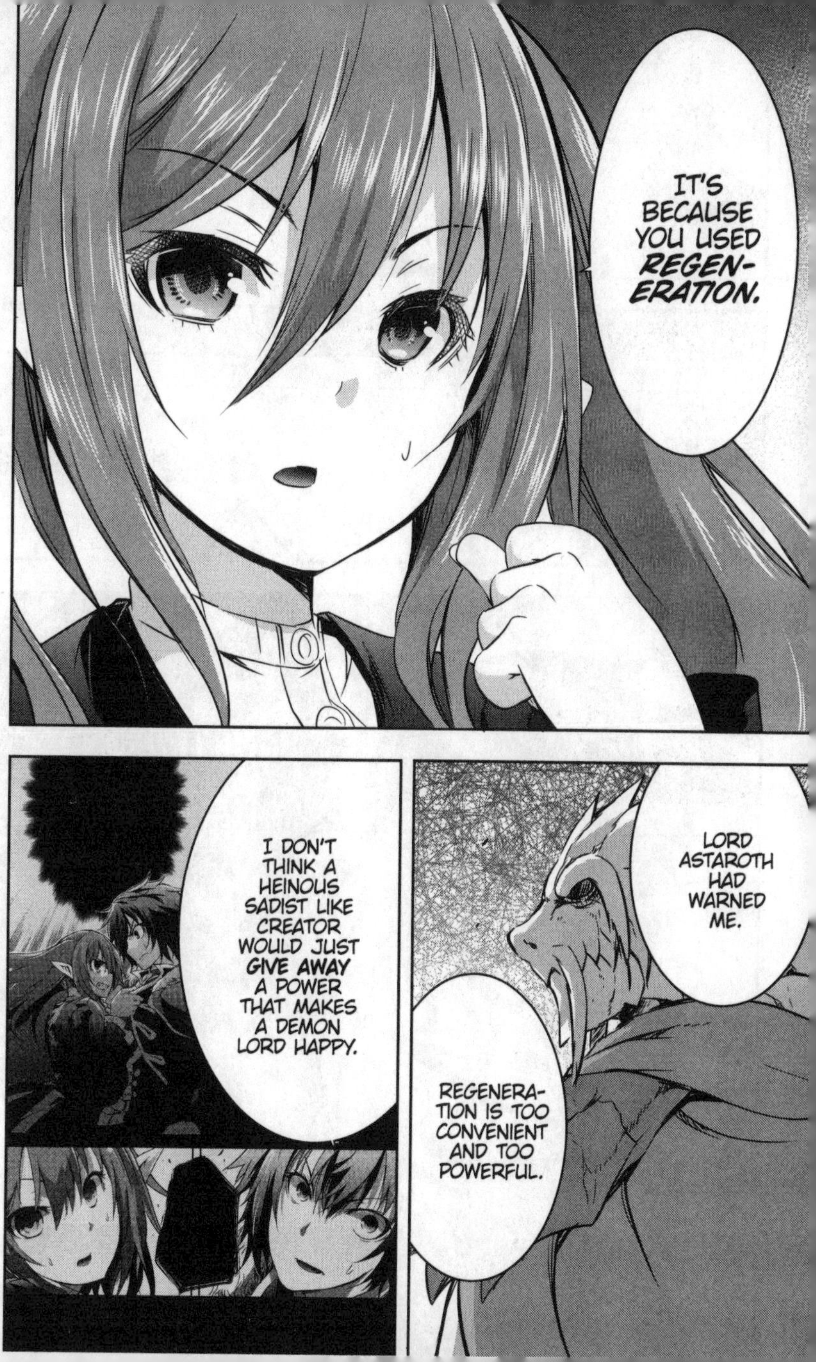
IT'S BECAUSE YOU USED *REGEN-ERATION.*
LORD ASTAROTH HAD WARNED ME.
REGENERA-TION IS TOO CONVENIENT AND TOO POWERFUL.
I DON'T THINK A HEINOUS SADIST LIKE CREATOR WOULD JUST **GIVE AWAY** A POWER THAT MAKES A DEMON LORD HAPPY.

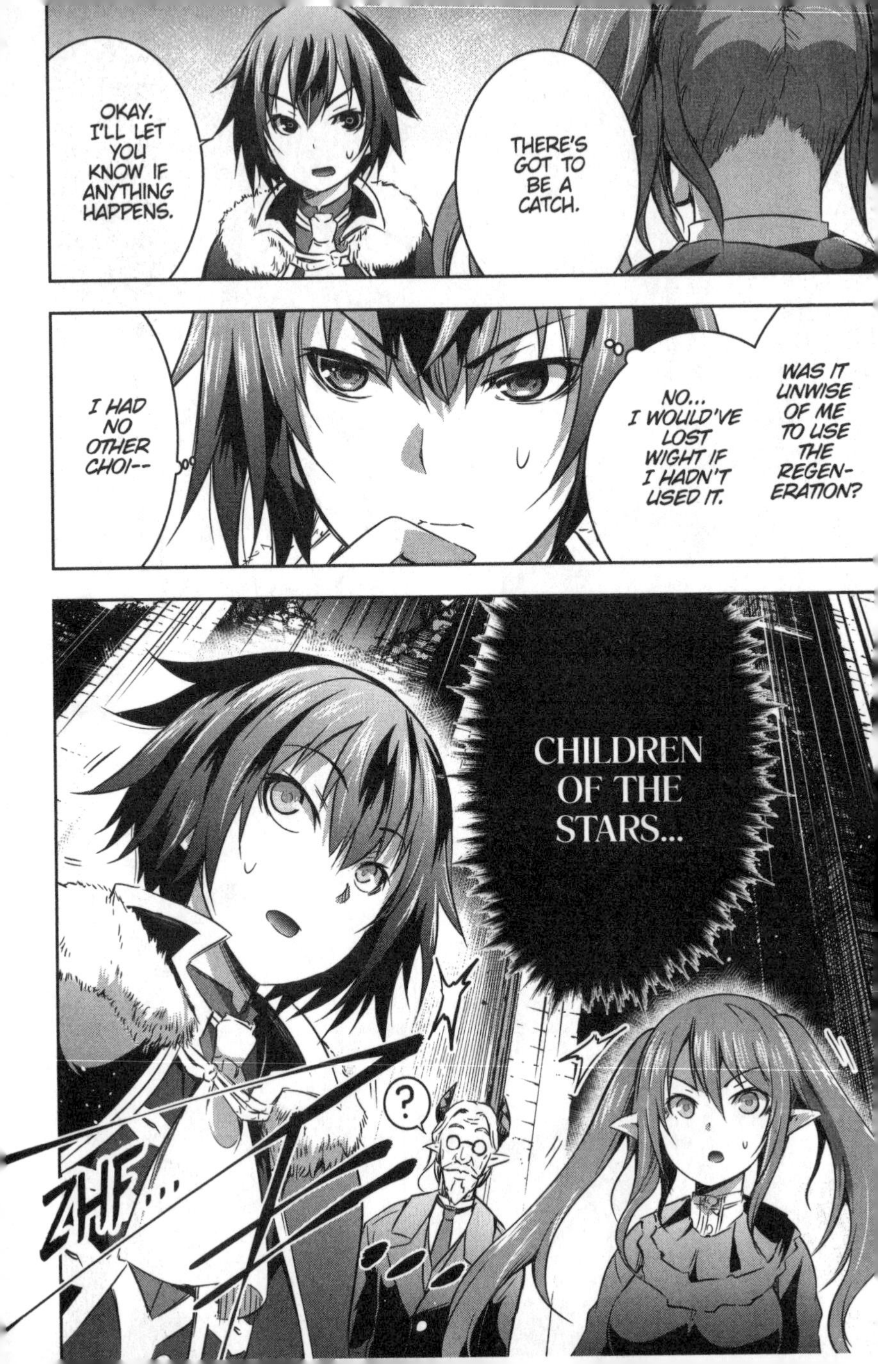
THERE'S GOT TO BE A CATCH.
OKAY. I'LL LET YOU KNOW IF ANYTHING HAPPENS.
WAS IT UNWISE OF ME TO USE THE REGEN-ERATION?
NO... I WOULD'VE LOST WIGHT IF I HADN'T USED IT.
I HAD NO OTHER CHOI--
CHILDREN OF THE STARS...
?
ZHF...

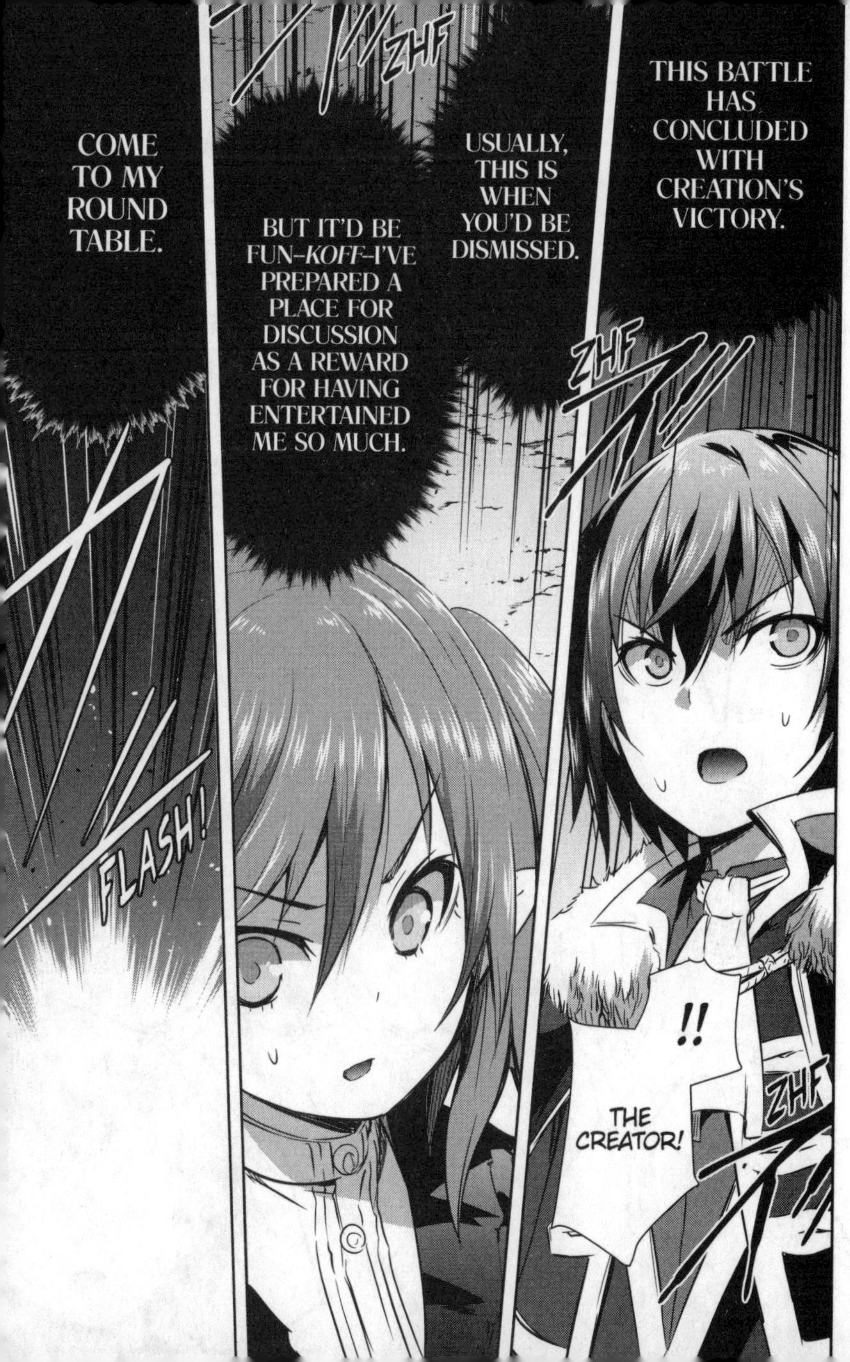
THIS BATTLE HAS CONCLUDED WITH CREATION'S VICTORY.
USUALLY, THIS IS WHEN YOU'D BE DISMISSED.
ZHF
!!
THE CREATOR!
ZHF
ZHF
BUT IT'D BE FUN--*KOFF*--I'VE PREPARED A PLACE FOR DISCUSSION AS A REWARD FOR HAVING ENTERTAINED ME SO MUCH.
COME TO MY ROUND TABLE.
FLASH!

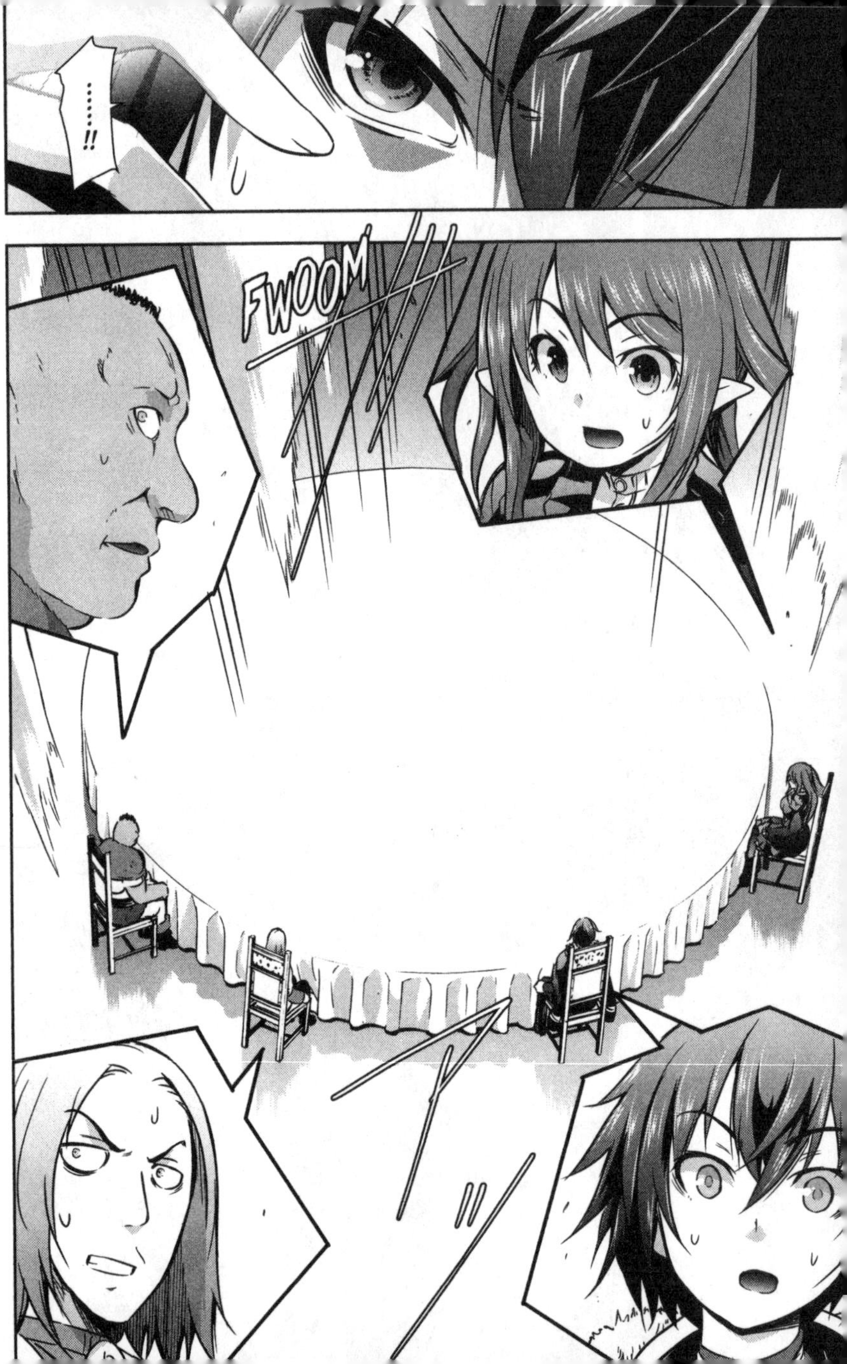
......!!
FWOOM

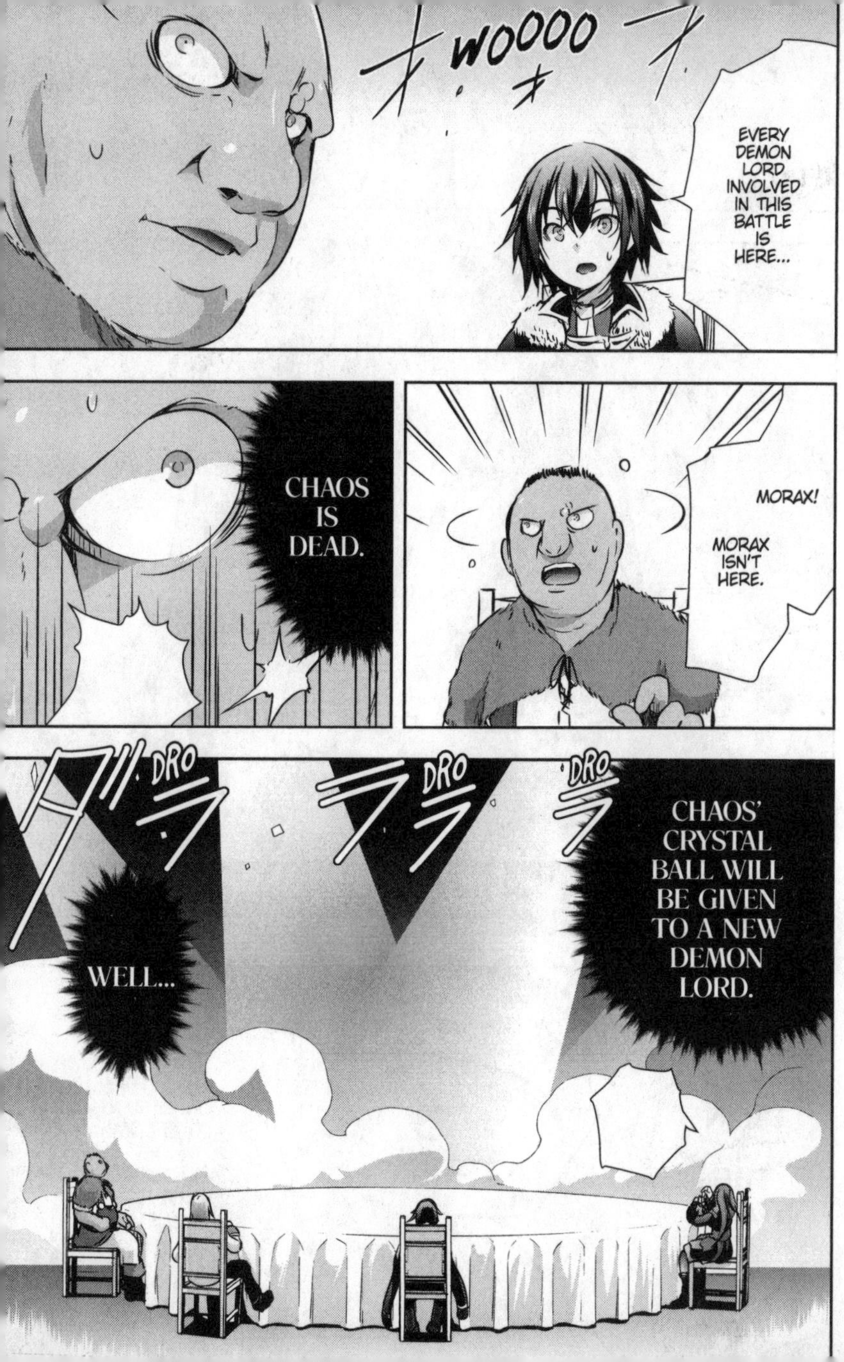
WOOOO
EVERY DEMON LORD INVOLVED IN THIS BATTLE IS HERE...
MORAX!
MORAX ISN'T HERE.
CHAOS IS DEAD.
DRO
DRO
DRO
CHAOS' CRYSTAL BALL WILL BE GIVEN TO A NEW DEMON LORD.
WELL...

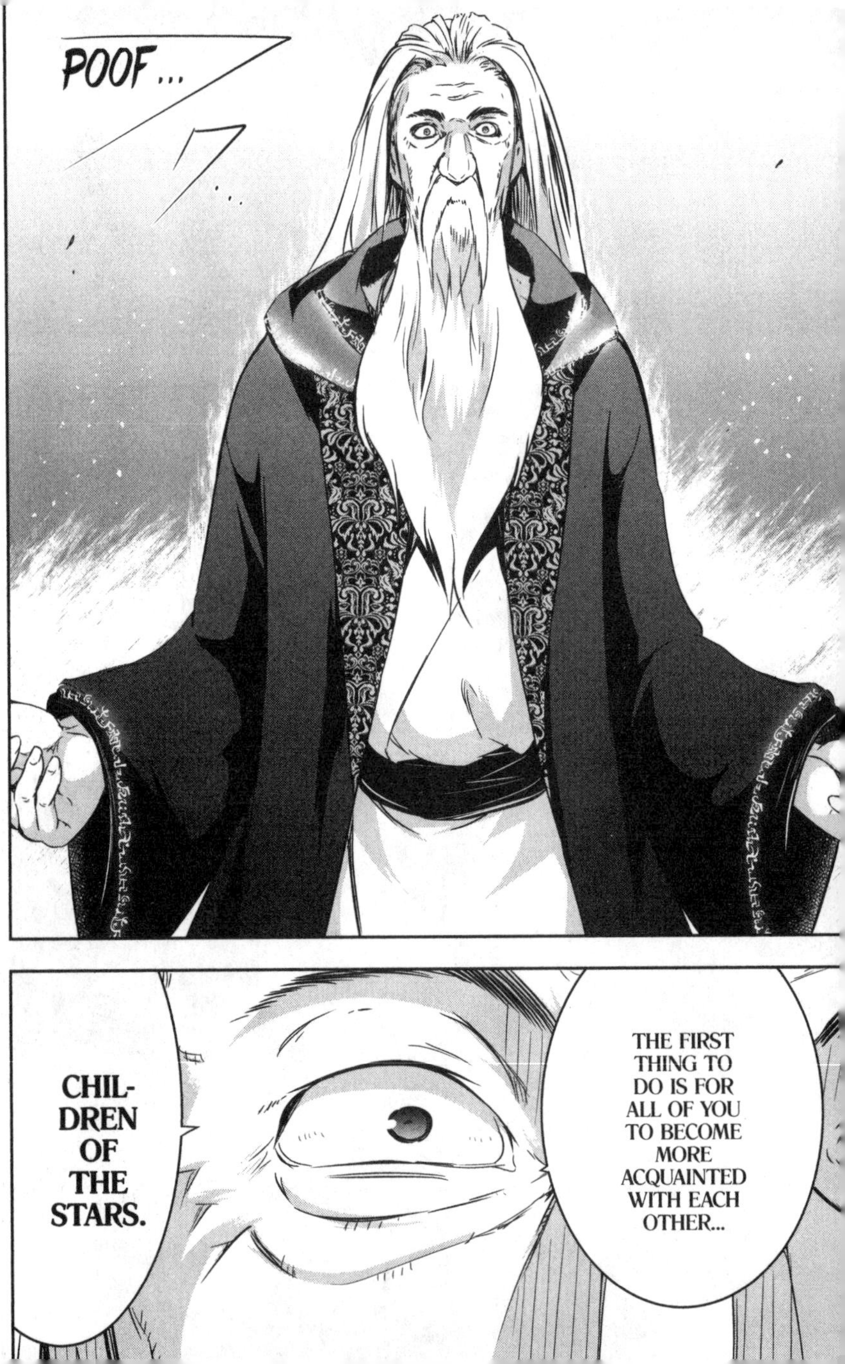
POOF...
THE FIRST THING TO DO IS FOR ALL OF YOU TO BECOME MORE ACQUAINTED WITH EACH OTHER...
CHIL-DREN OF THE STARS.

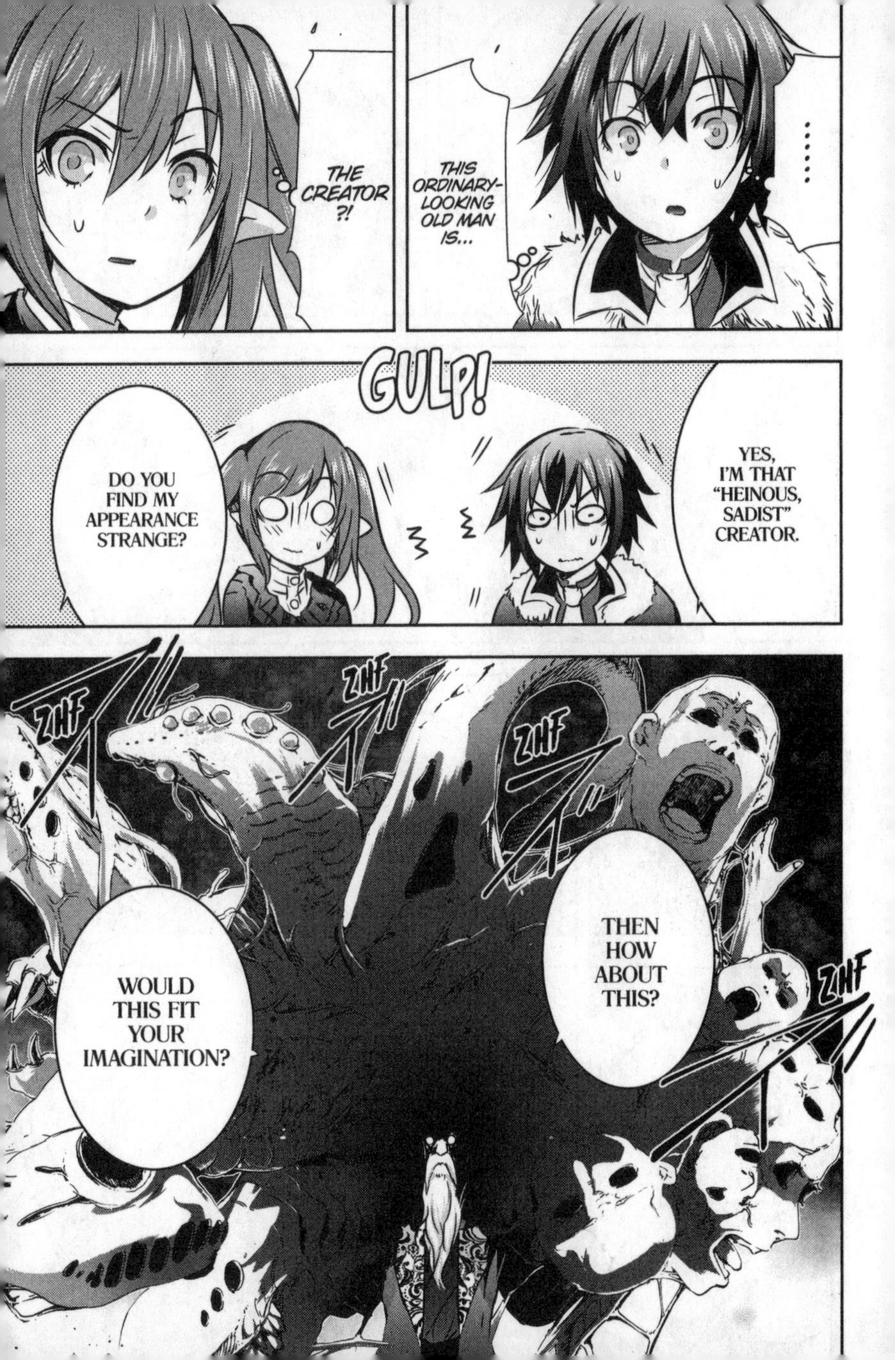
......
THIS ORDINARY-LOOKING OLD MAN IS...
THE CREATOR ?!
GULP!
YES, I'M THAT "HEINOUS, SADIST" CREATOR.
DO YOU FIND MY APPEARANCE STRANGE?
ZHF
ZHF
ZHF
ZHF
THEN HOW ABOUT THIS?
WOULD THIS FIT YOUR IMAGINATION?

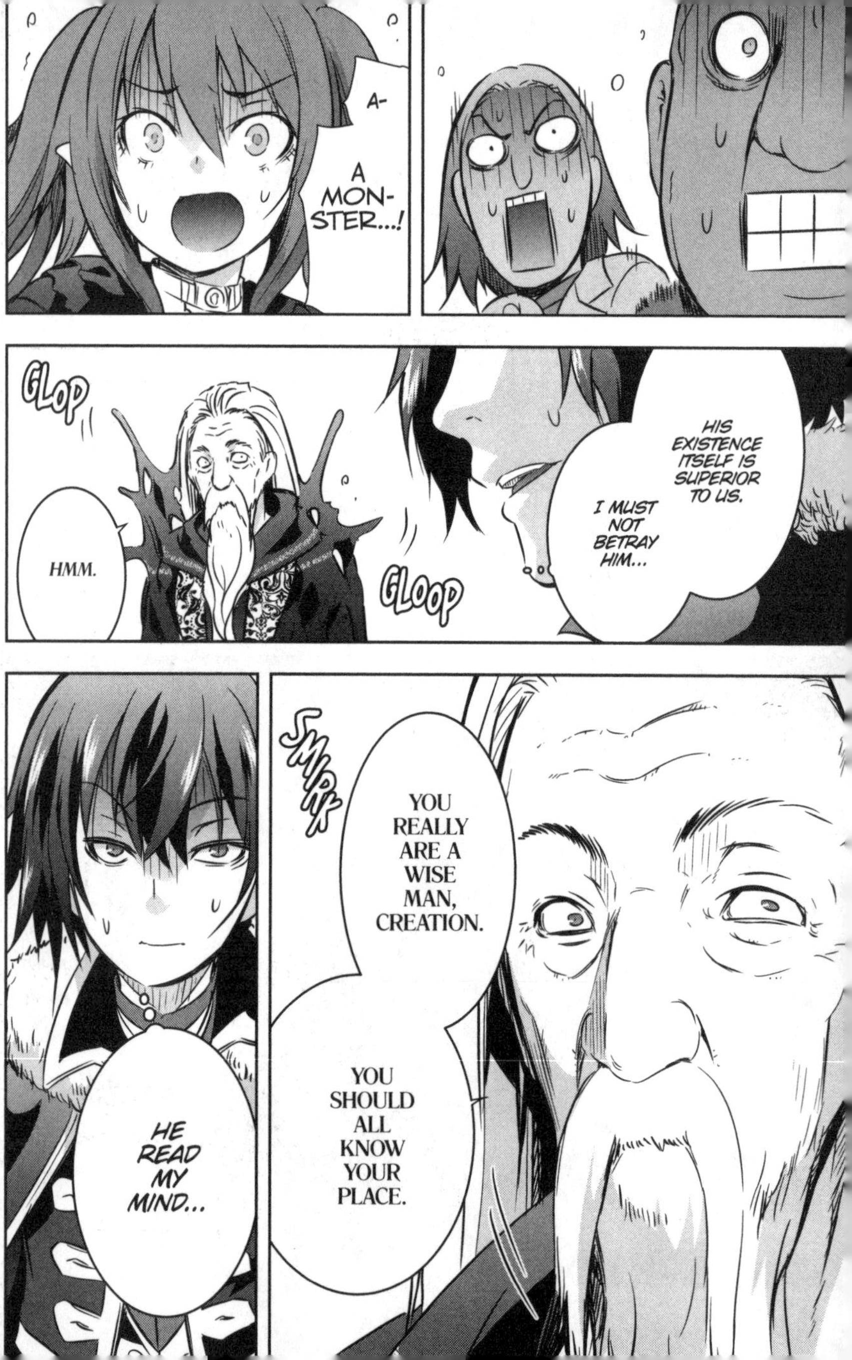
A-
A MONSTER...!
HIS EXISTENCE ITSELF IS SUPERIOR TO US.
I MUST NOT BETRAY HIM...
GLOOP
GLOP
HMM.
SMIRK
YOU REALLY ARE A WISE MAN, CREATION.
YOU SHOULD ALL KNOW YOUR PLACE.
HE READ MY MIND...

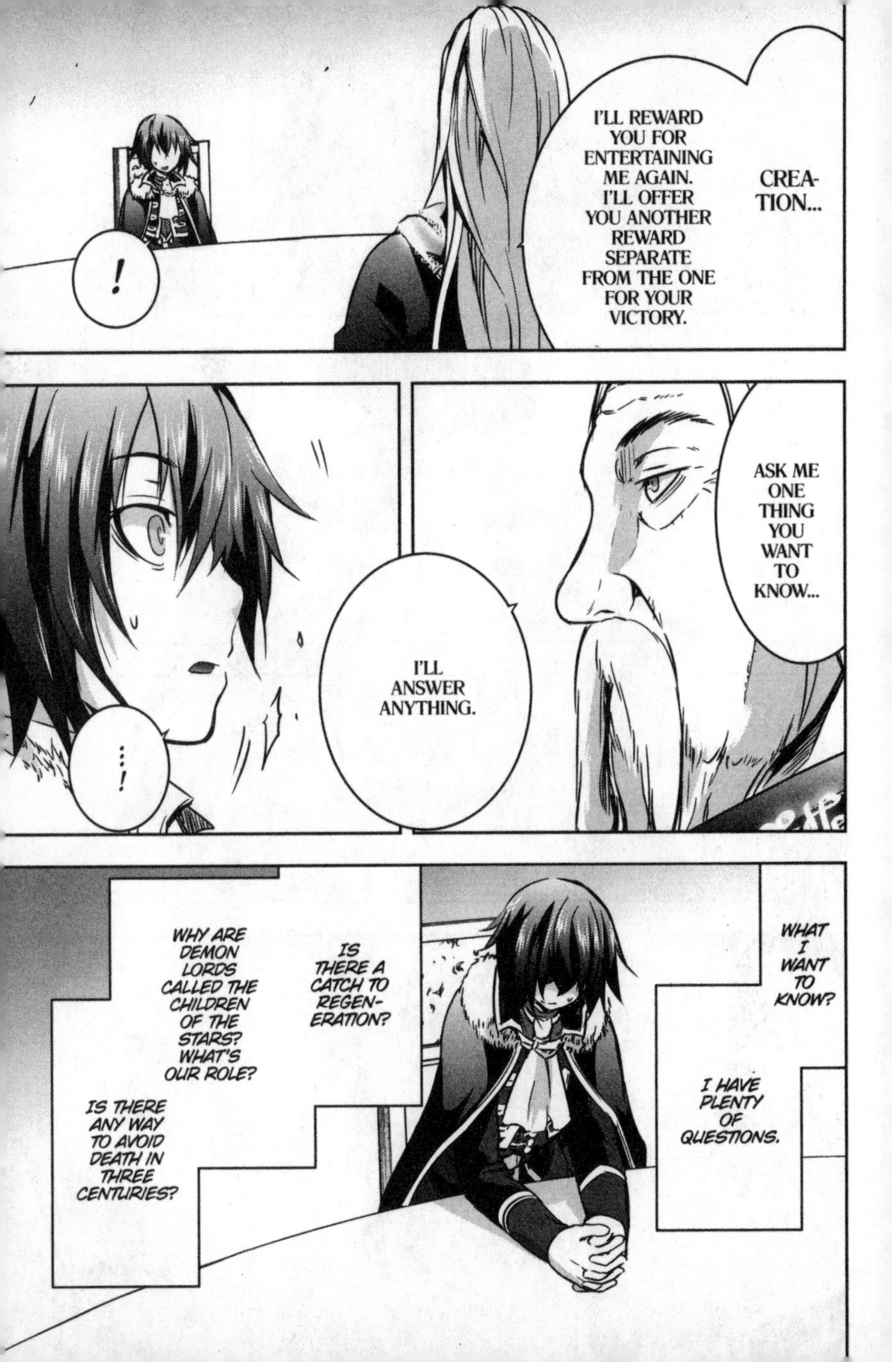
CREATION...
I'LL REWARD YOU FOR ENTERTAINING ME AGAIN. I'LL OFFER YOU ANOTHER REWARD SEPARATE FROM THE ONE FOR YOUR VICTORY.
!
ASK ME ONE THING YOU WANT TO KNOW...
I'LL ANSWER ANYTHING.
...!
WHAT I WANT TO KNOW?
I HAVE PLENTY OF QUESTIONS.
IS THERE A CATCH TO REGEN-ERATION?
WHY ARE DEMON LORDS CALLED THE CHILDREN OF THE STARS? WHAT'S OUR ROLE?
IS THERE ANY WAY TO AVOID DEATH IN THREE CENTURIES?

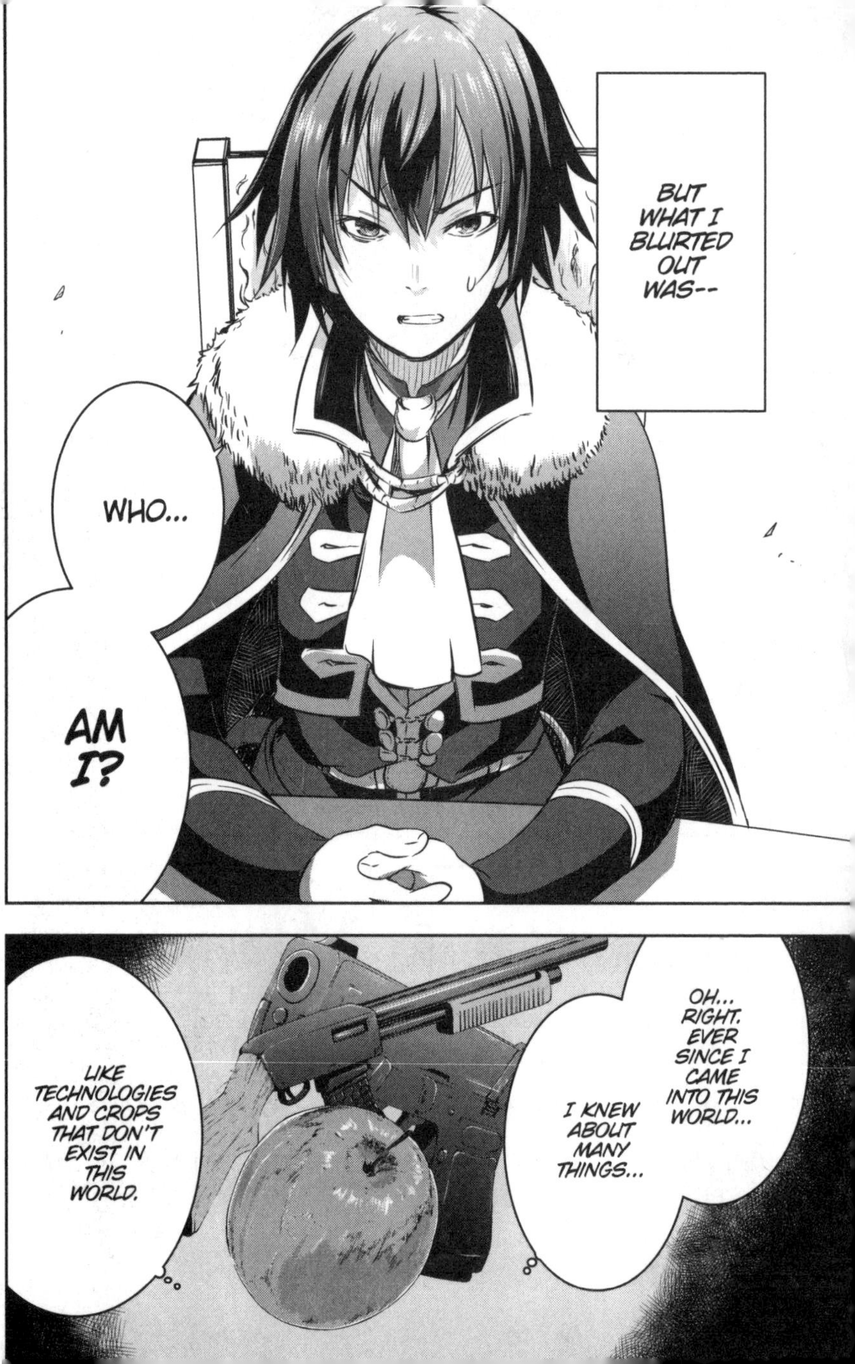
BUT WHAT I BLURTED OUT WAS--
WHO...
AM I?
OH... RIGHT. EVER SINCE I CAME INTO THIS WORLD...
I KNEW ABOUT MANY THINGS...
LIKE TECHNOLOGIES AND CROPS THAT DON'T EXIST IN THIS WORLD.

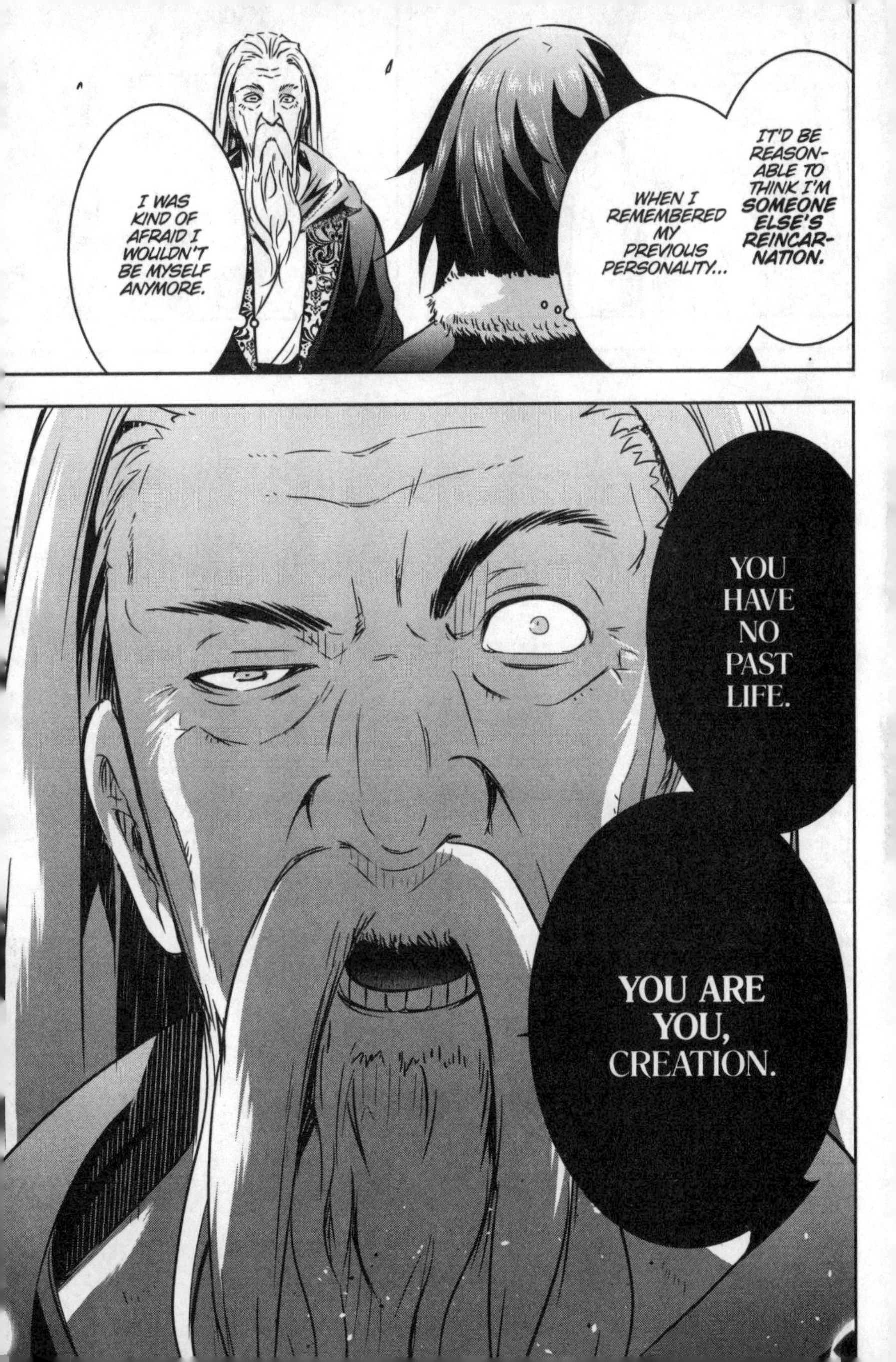
IT'D BE REASONABLE TO THINK I'M SOMEONE ELSE'S REINCARNATION.
WHEN I REMEMBERED MY PREVIOUS PERSONALITY...
I WAS KIND OF AFRAID I WOULDN'T BE MYSELF ANYMORE.
YOU HAVE NO PAST LIFE.
YOU ARE YOU, CREATION.

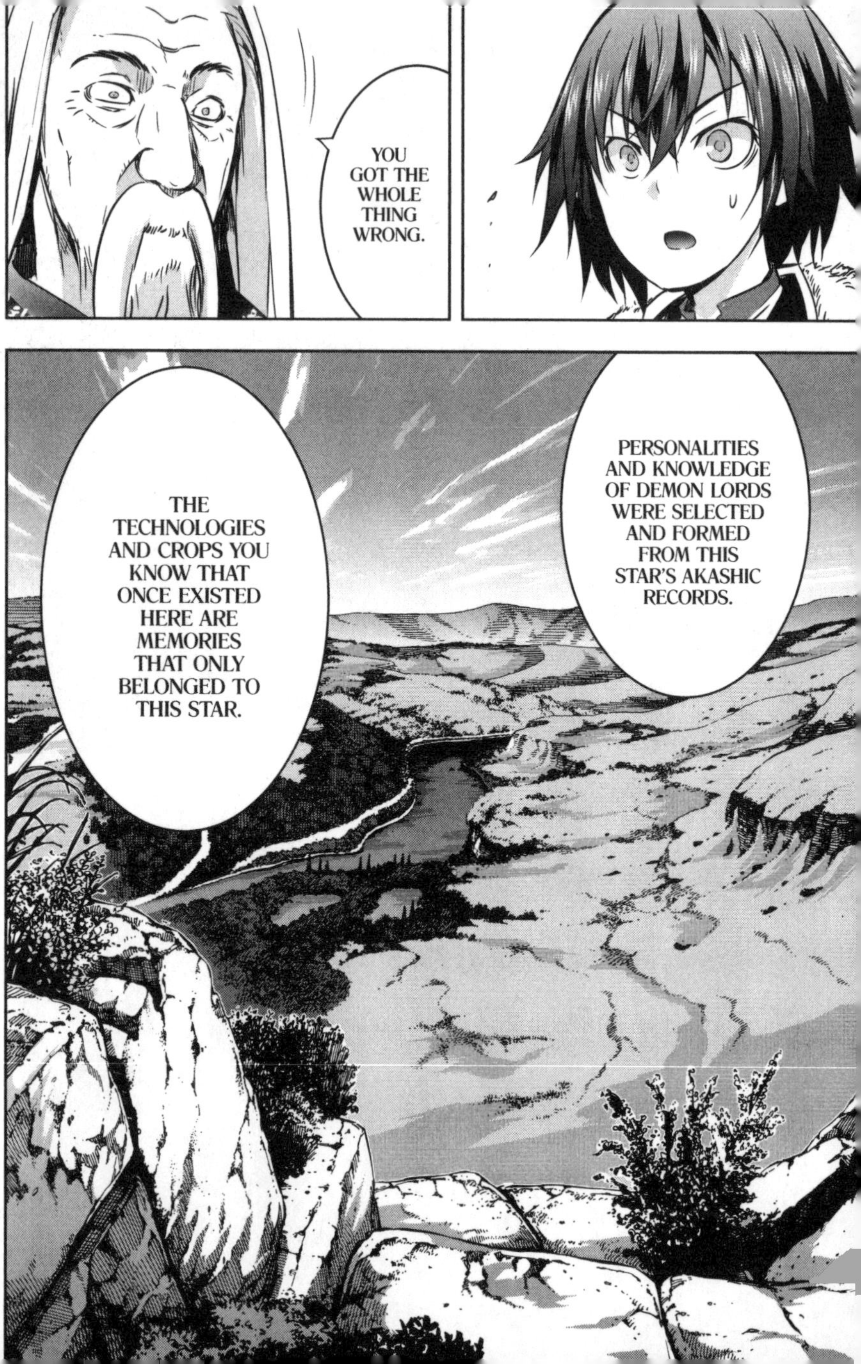
YOU GOT THE WHOLE THING WRONG.
PERSONALITIES AND KNOWLEDGE OF DEMON LORDS WERE SELECTED AND FORMED FROM THIS STAR'S AKASHIC RECORDS.
THE TECHNOLOGIES AND CROPS YOU KNOW THAT ONCE EXISTED HERE ARE MEMORIES THAT ONLY BELONGED TO THIS STAR.

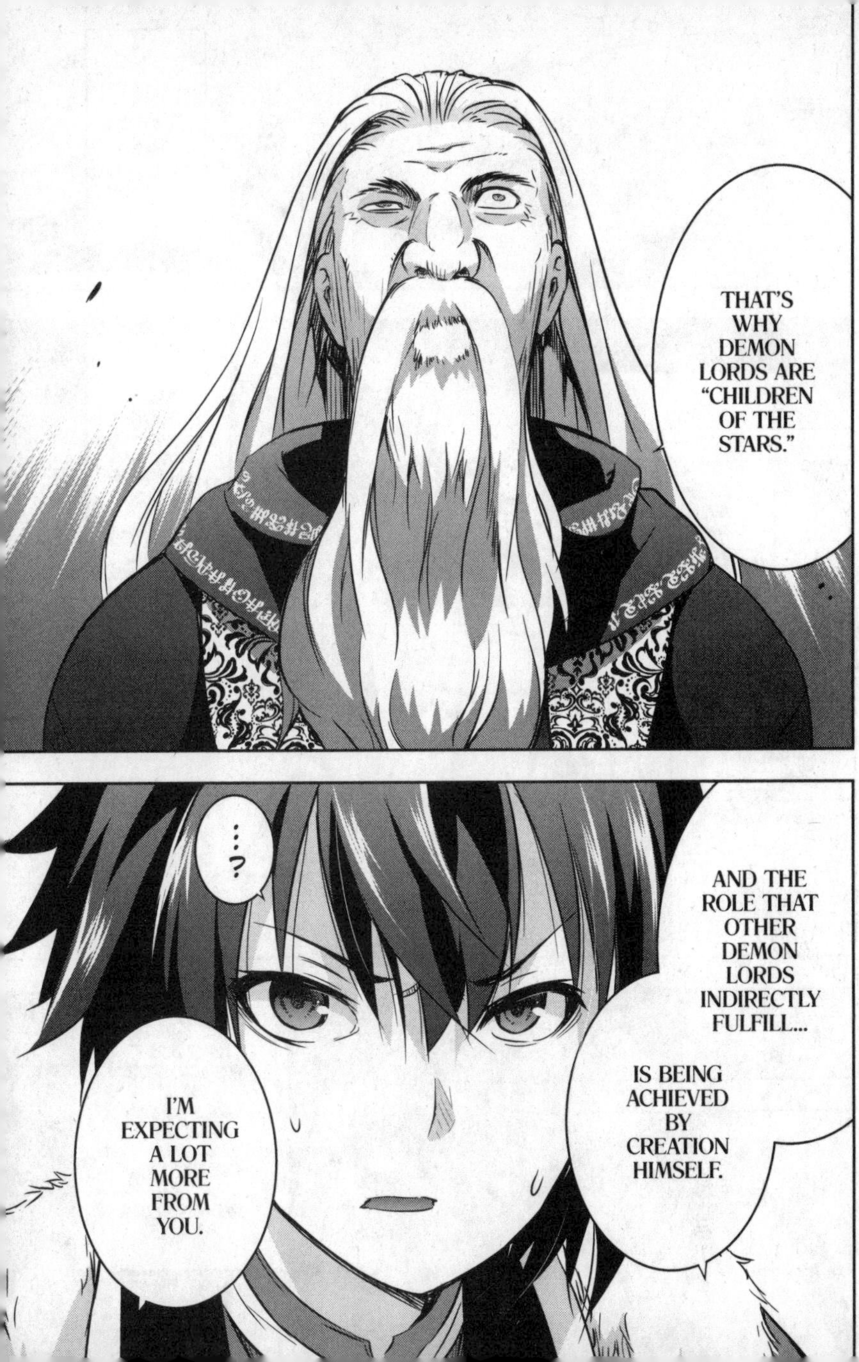
THAT'S WHY DEMON LORDS ARE "CHILDREN OF THE STARS."
AND THE ROLE THAT OTHER DEMON LORDS INDIRECTLY FULFILL...
IS BEING ACHIEVED BY CREATION HIMSELF.
...?
I'M EXPECTING A LOT MORE FROM YOU.

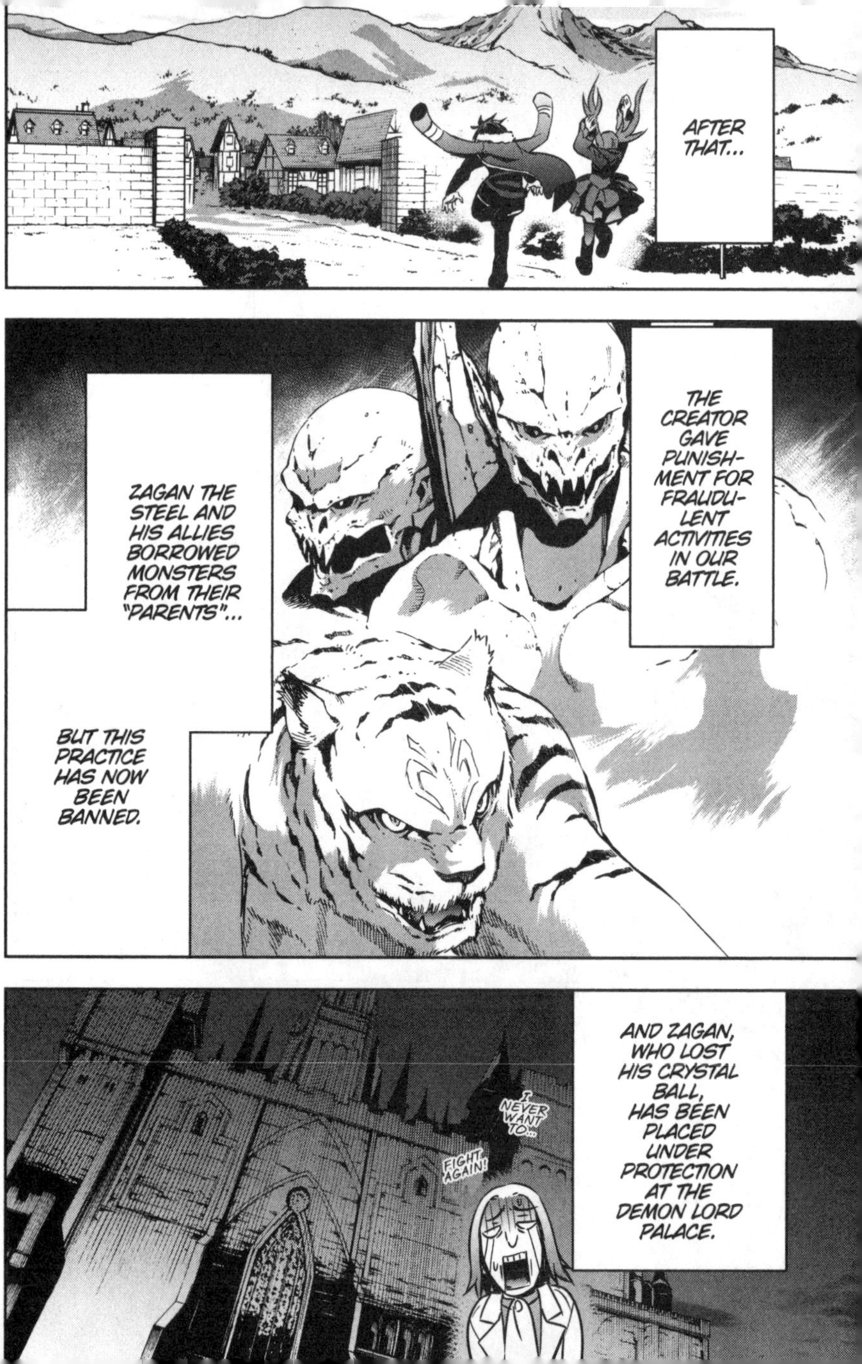
AFTER THAT...
THE CREATOR GAVE PUNISHMENT FOR FRAUDULENT ACTIVITIES IN OUR BATTLE.
ZAGAN THE STEEL AND HIS ALLIES BORROWED MONSTERS FROM THEIR "PARENTS"...
BUT THIS PRACTICE HAS NOW BEEN BANNED.
AND ZAGAN, WHO LOST HIS CRYSTAL BALL, HAS BEEN PLACED UNDER PROTECTION AT THE DEMON LORD PALACE.
I NEVER WANT TO...
FIGHT AGAIN!

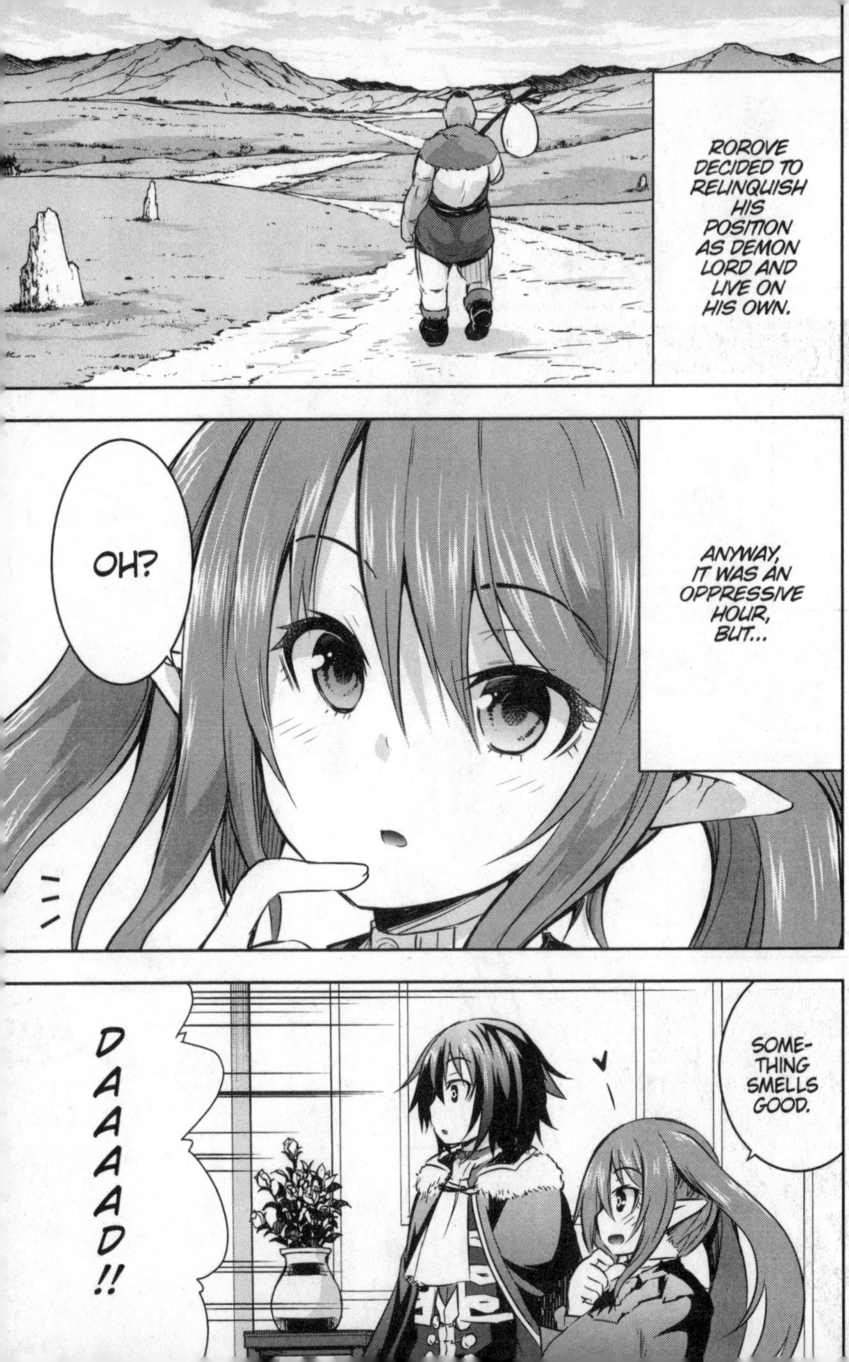
RORORVE DECIDED TO RELINQUISH HIS POSITION AS DEMON LORD AND LIVE ON HIS OWN.
ANYWAY, IT WAS AN OPPRESSIVE HOUR, BUT...
OH?
SOME-THING SMELLS GOOD.
DAAAAAD!!

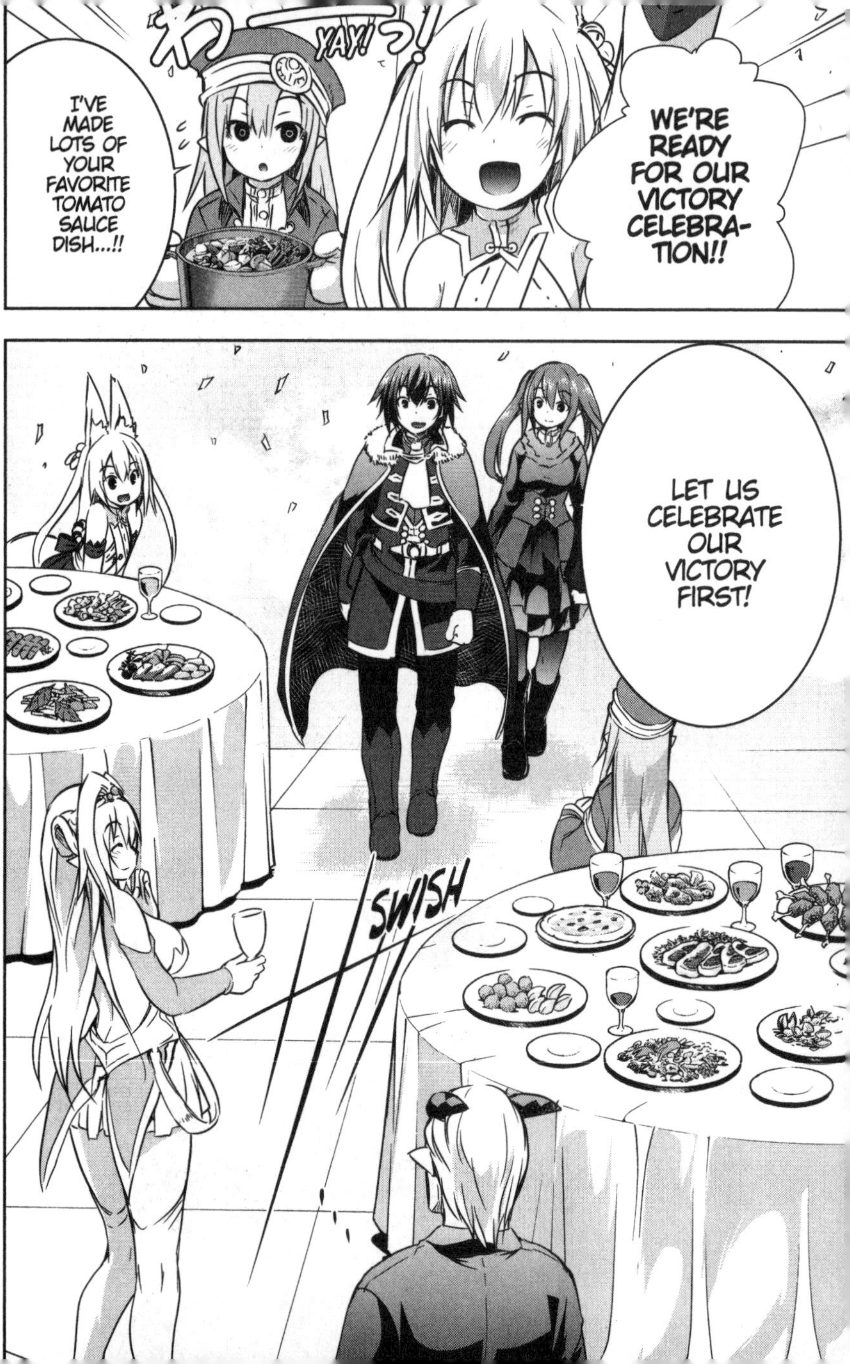

わーーーっ!
YAY!
WE'RE READY FOR OUR VICTORY CELEBRATION!!
I'VE MADE LOTS OF YOUR FAVORITE TOMATO SAUCE DISH...!!
LET US CELEBRATE OUR VICTORY FIRST!
SWISH

The Battle Actually Kept Little Stolas in Suspense

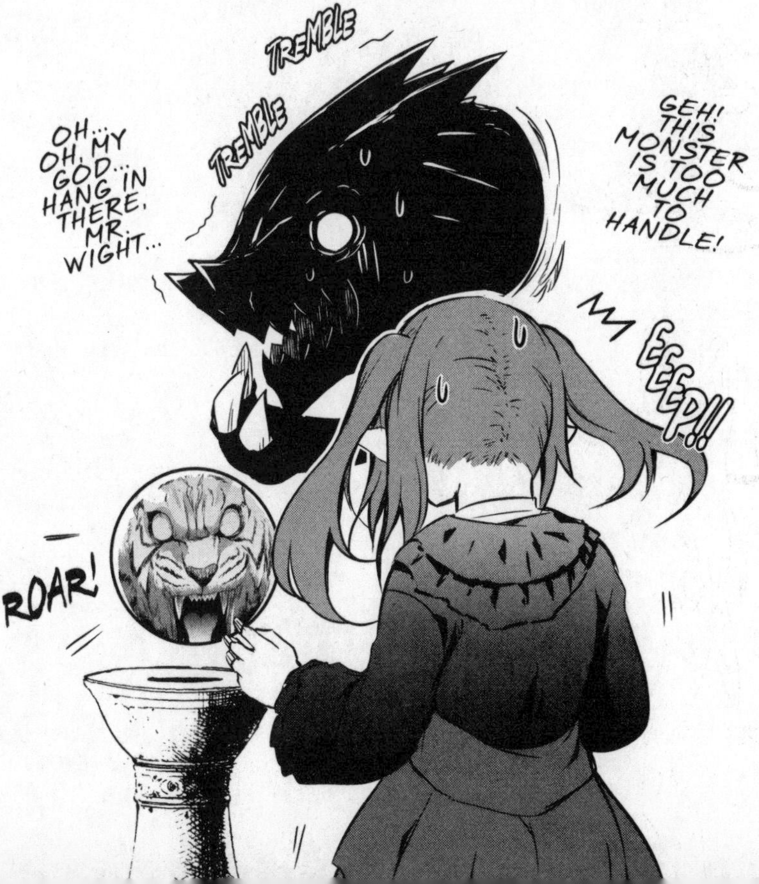
GEH! THIS MONSTER IS TOO MUCH TO HANDLE!
TREMBLE
TREMBLE
OH... OH, MY GOD... HANG IN THERE, MR. WIGHT...
EEEP!!
ROAR!

DUNGEON BUILDER:
THE DEMON KING'S LABYRINTH IS A MODERN CITY!

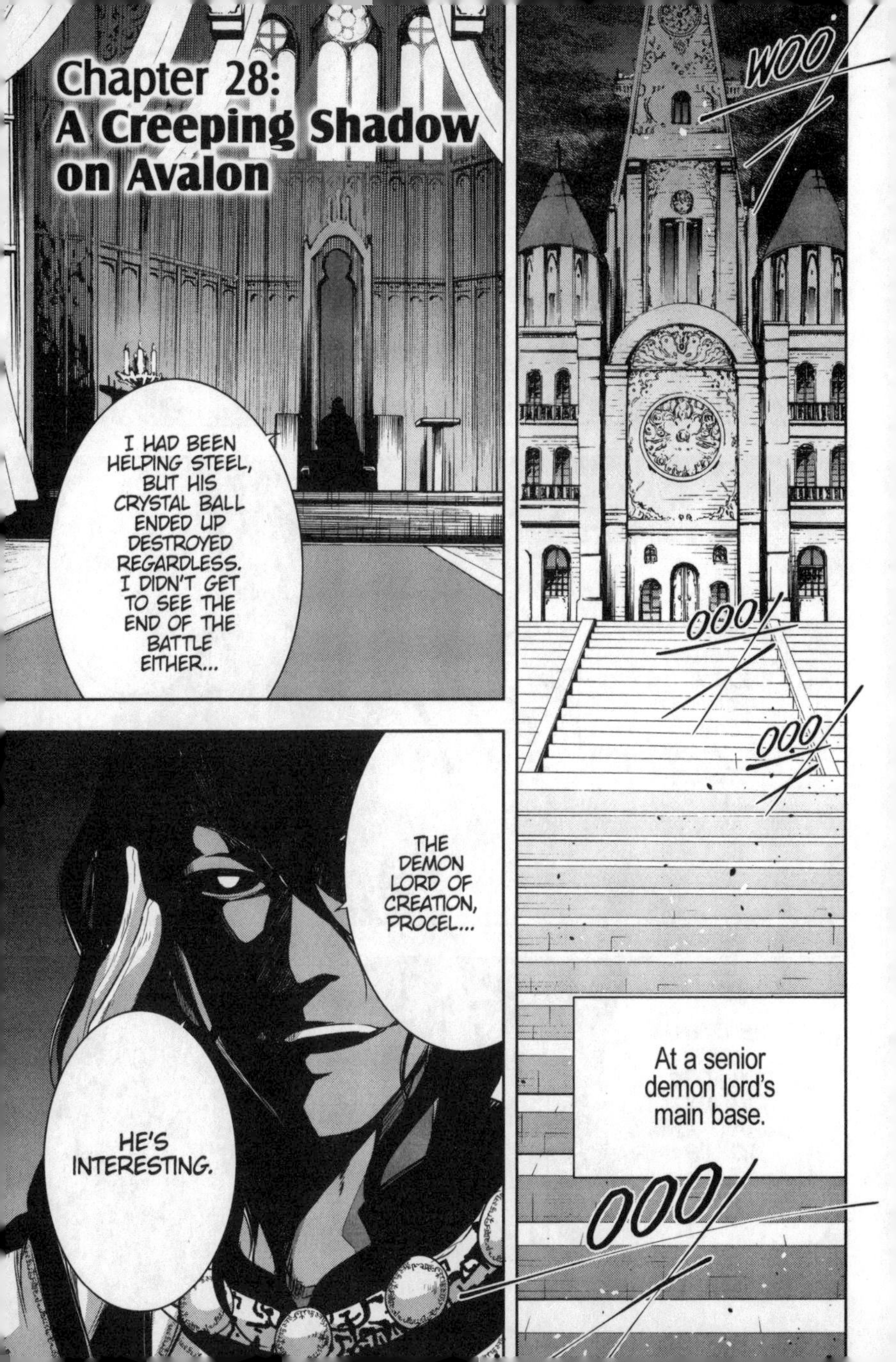
WOO
OOO
OOO
At a senior demon lord's main base.
OOO
Chapter 28: A Creeping Shadow on Avalon
I HAD BEEN HELPING STEEL, BUT HIS CRYSTAL BALL ENDED UP DESTROYED REGARDLESS. I DIDN'T GET TO SEE THE END OF THE BATTLE EITHER...
THE DEMON LORD OF CREATION, PROCEL...
HE'S INTERESTING.

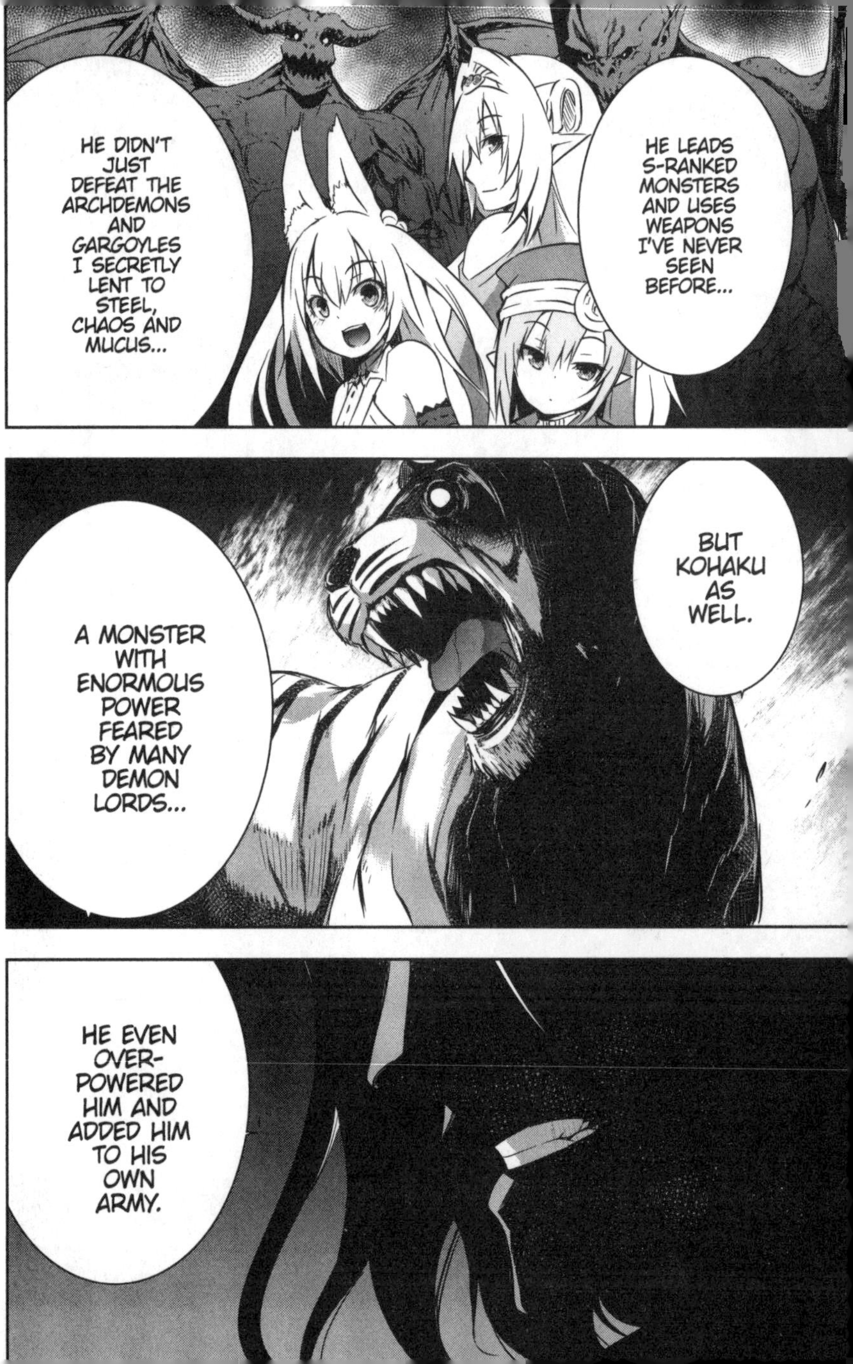
HE LEADS S-RANKED MONSTERS AND USES WEAPONS I'VE NEVER SEEN BEFORE...
HE DIDN'T JUST DEFEAT THE ARCHDEMONS AND GARGOYLES I SECRETLY LENT TO STEEL, CHAOS AND MUCUS...
BUT KOHAKU AS WELL.
A MONSTER WITH ENORMOUS POWER FEARED BY MANY DEMON LORDS...
HE EVEN OVER-POWERED HIM AND ADDED HIM TO HIS OWN ARMY.

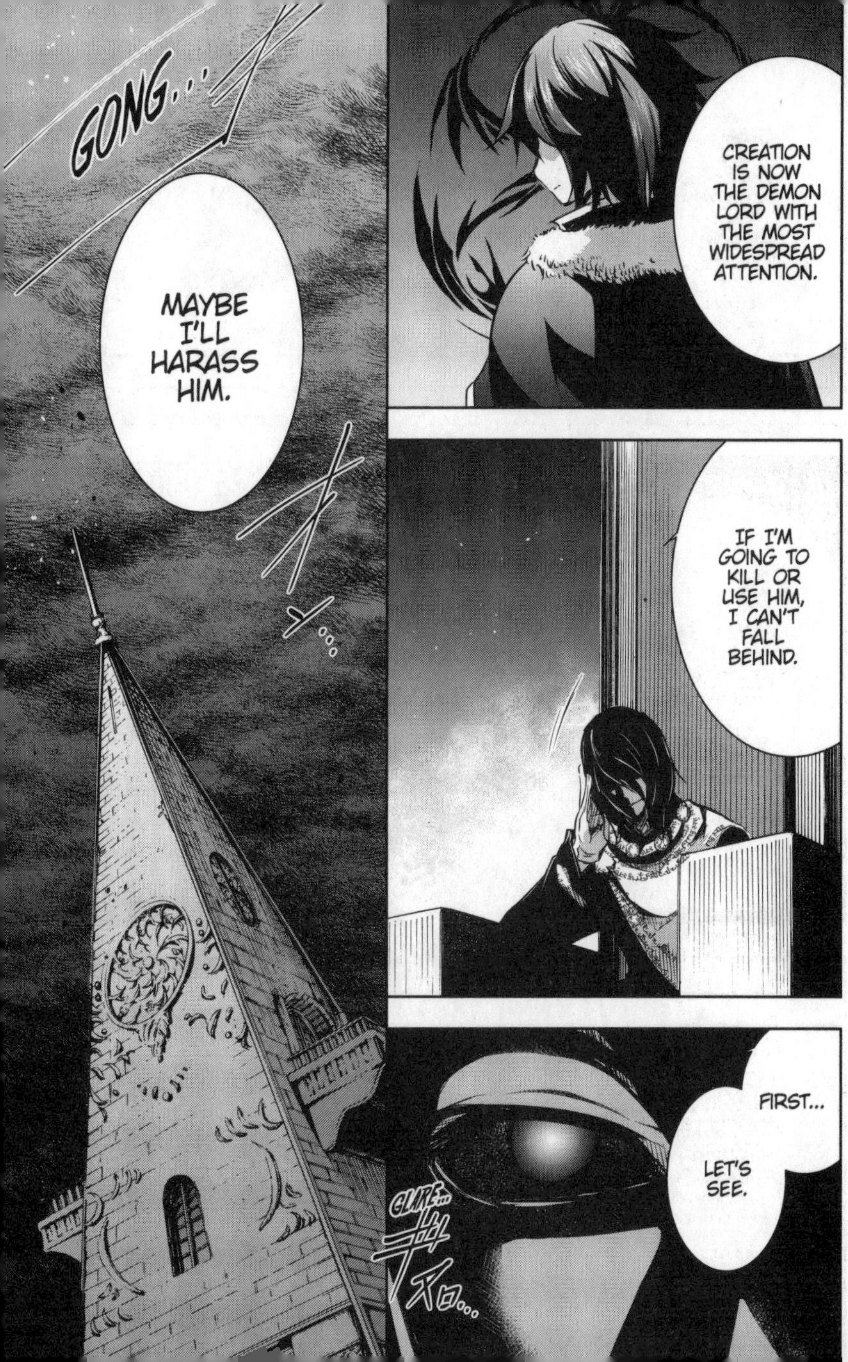
CREATION IS NOW THE DEMON LORD WITH THE MOST WIDESPREAD ATTENTION.
IF I'M GOING TO KILL OR USE HIM, I CAN'T FALL BEHIND.
FIRST...
LET'S SEE.
GLARE...
GONG...
MAYBE I'LL HARASS HIM.

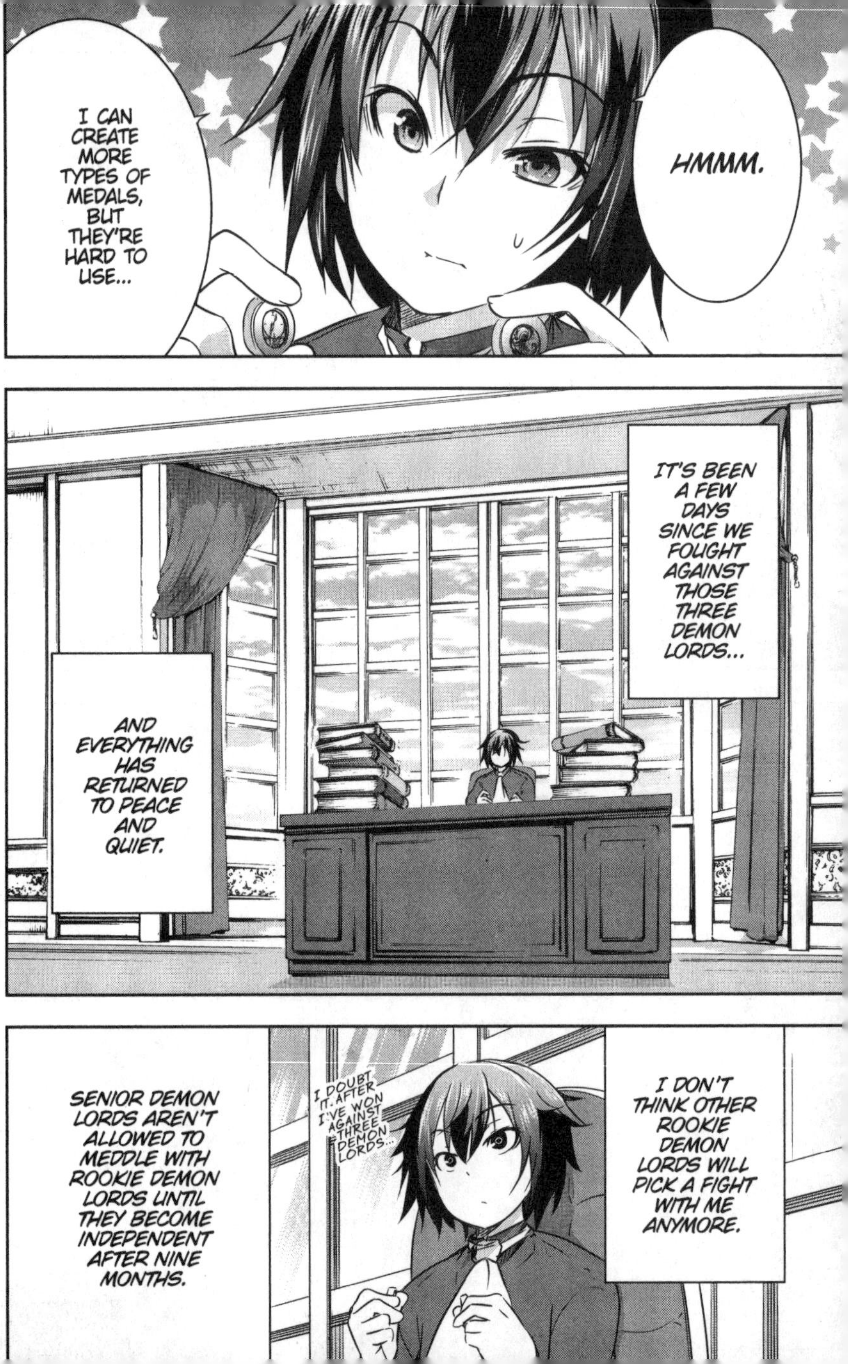
HMMM.
I CAN CREATE MORE TYPES OF MEDALS, BUT THEY'RE HARD TO USE...
IT'S BEEN A FEW DAYS SINCE WE FOUGHT AGAINST THOSE THREE DEMON LORDS...
AND EVERYTHING HAS RETURNED TO PEACE AND QUIET.
I DON'T THINK OTHER ROOKIE DEMON LORDS WILL PICK A FIGHT WITH ME ANYMORE.
I DOUBT IT. AFTER I'VE WON AGAINST THREE DEMON LORDS...
SENIOR DEMON LORDS AREN'T ALLOWED TO MEDDLE WITH ROOKIE DEMON LORDS UNTIL THEY BECOME INDEPENDENT AFTER NINE MONTHS.

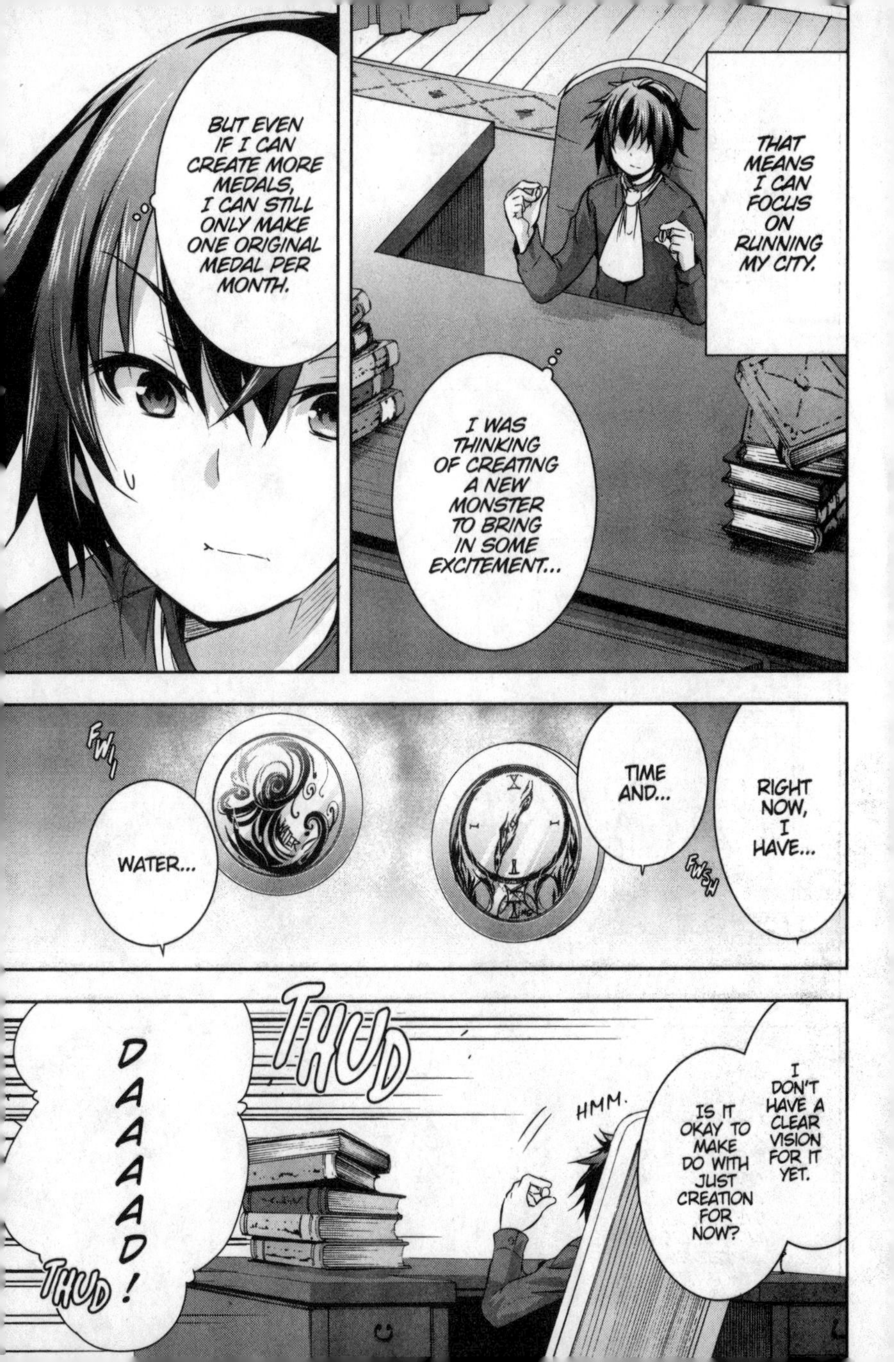
THAT MEANS I CAN FOCUS ON RUNNING MY CITY.
I WAS THINKING OF CREATING A NEW MONSTER TO BRING IN SOME EXCITEMENT...
BUT EVEN IF I CAN CREATE MORE MEDALS, I CAN STILL ONLY MAKE ONE ORIGINAL MEDAL PER MONTH.
RIGHT NOW, I HAVE...
FWSH
TIME AND...
WATER...
I DON'T HAVE A CLEAR VISION FOR IT YET.
IS IT OKAY TO MAKE DO WITH JUST CREATION FOR NOW?
HMM.
THUD
DAAAAAD!
THUD

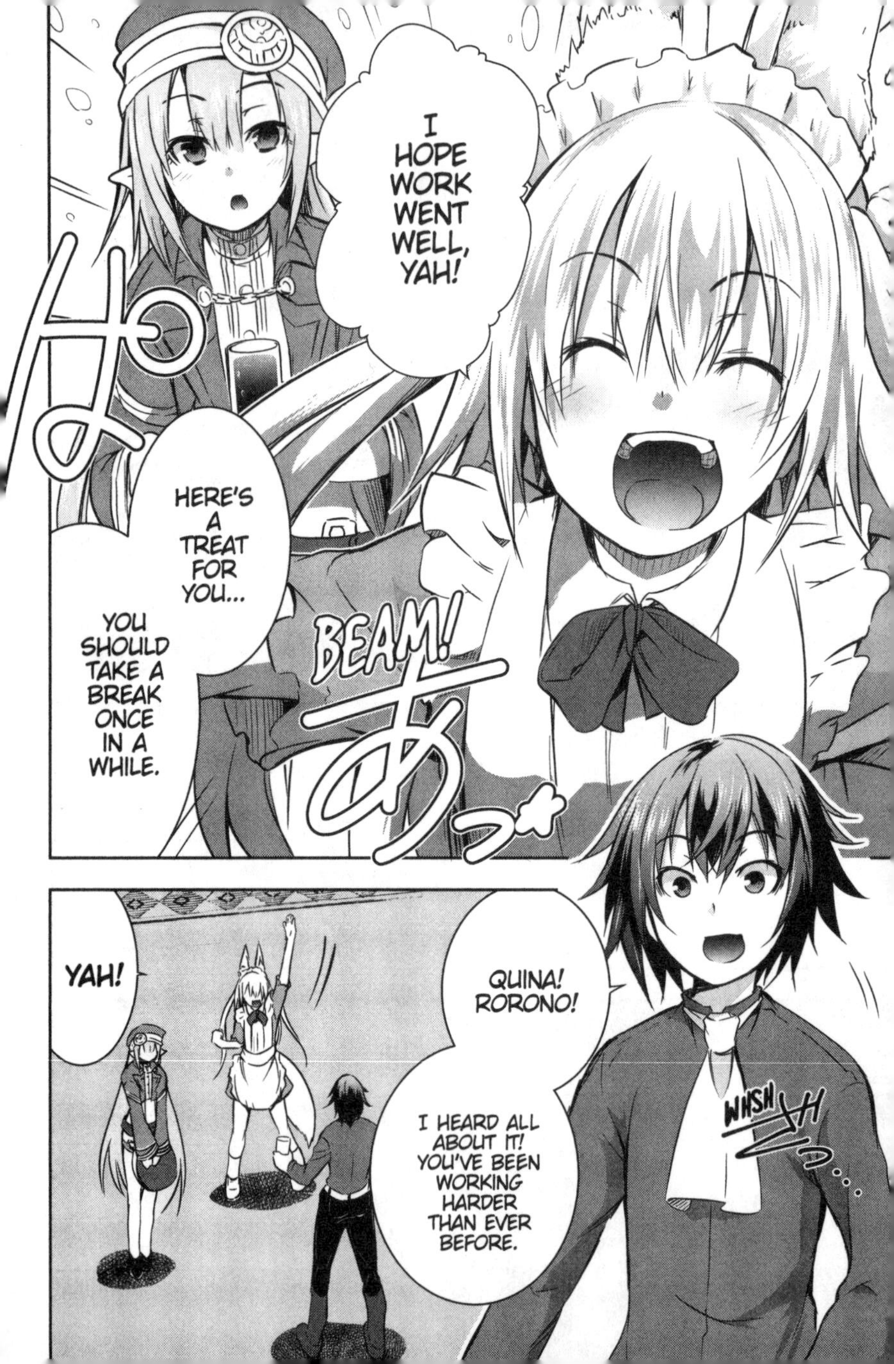
I HOPE WORK WENT WELL, YAH!
HERE'S A TREAT FOR YOU...
YOU SHOULD TAKE A BREAK ONCE IN A WHILE.
BEAM!
あっ
QUINA! RORONO!
I HEARD ALL ABOUT IT! YOU'VE BEEN WORKING HARDER THAN EVER BEFORE.
WHSH
YAH!

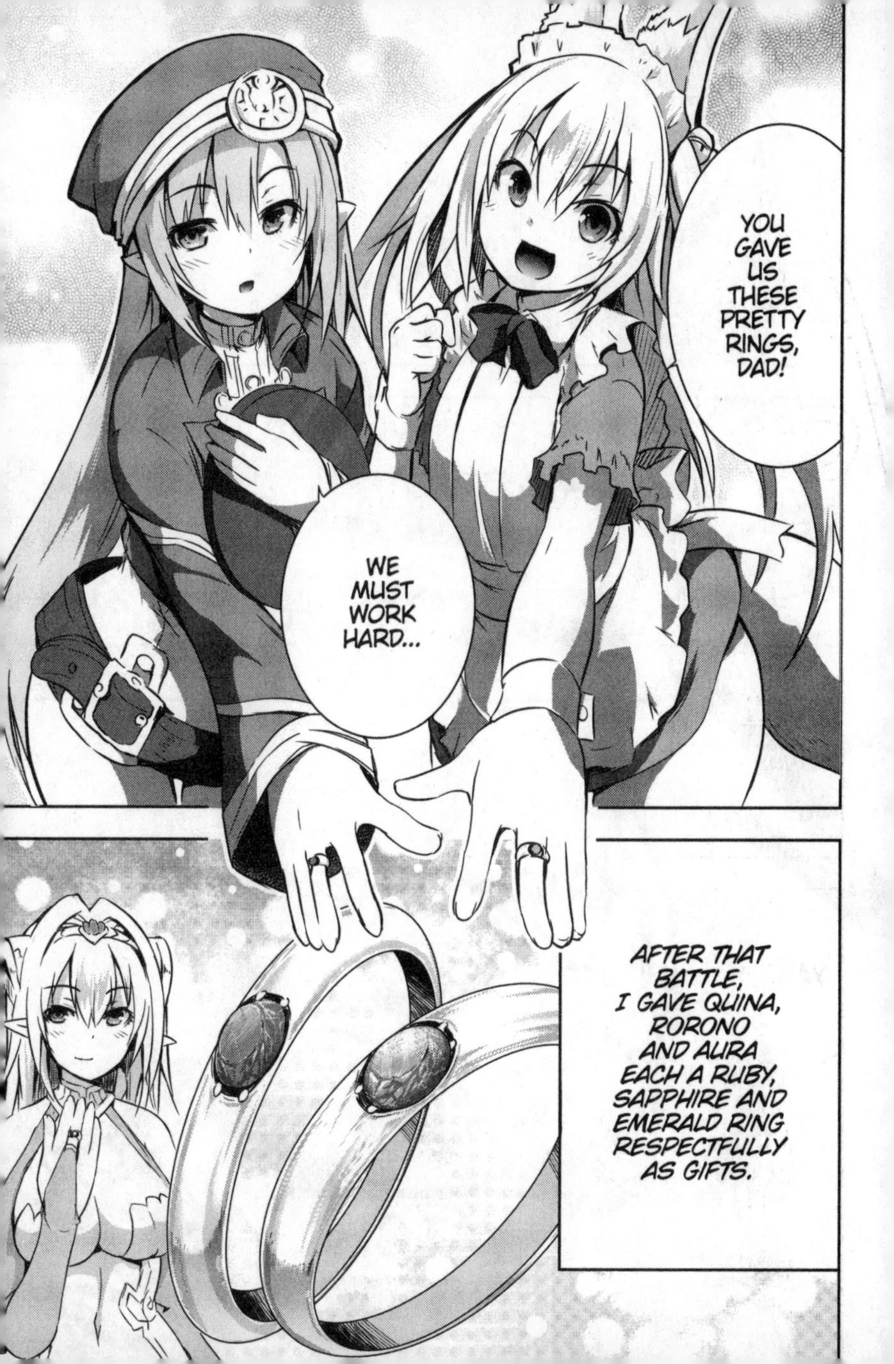
YOU GAVE US THESE PRETTY RINGS, DAD!
WE MUST WORK HARD...
AFTER THAT BATTLE, I GAVE QUINA, RORONO AND AURA EACH A RUBY, SAPPHIRE AND EMERALD RING RESPECTFULLY AS GIFTS.

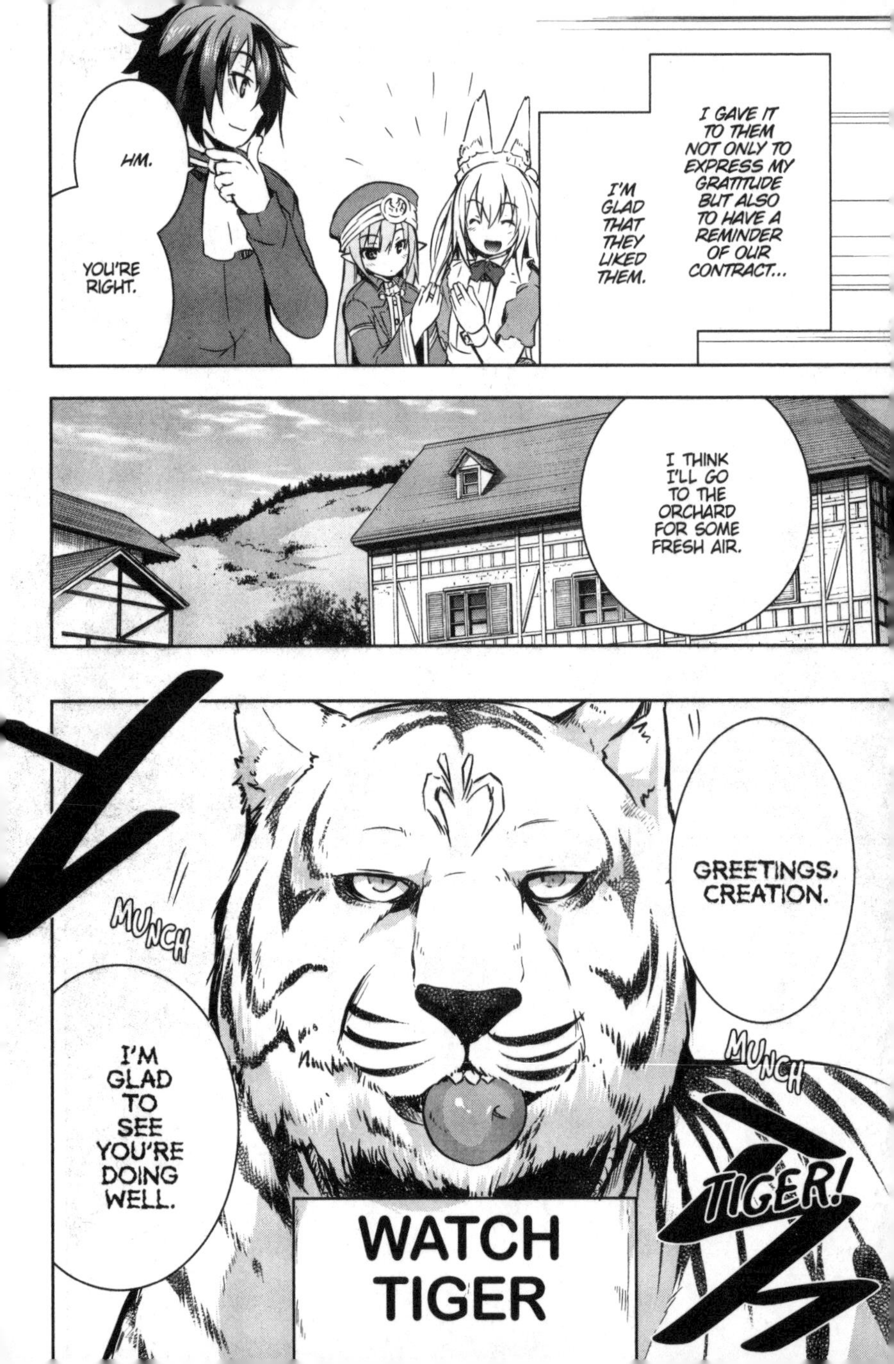
I GAVE IT TO THEM NOT ONLY TO EXPRESS MY GRATITUDE BUT ALSO TO HAVE A REMINDER OF OUR CONTRACT...
I'M GLAD THAT THEY LIKED THEM.
HM.
YOU'RE RIGHT.
I THINK I'LL GO TO THE ORCHARD FOR SOME FRESH AIR.
GREETINGS, CREATION.
MUNCH
MUNCH
I'M GLAD TO SEE YOU'RE DOING WELL.
TIGER!
WATCH TIGER

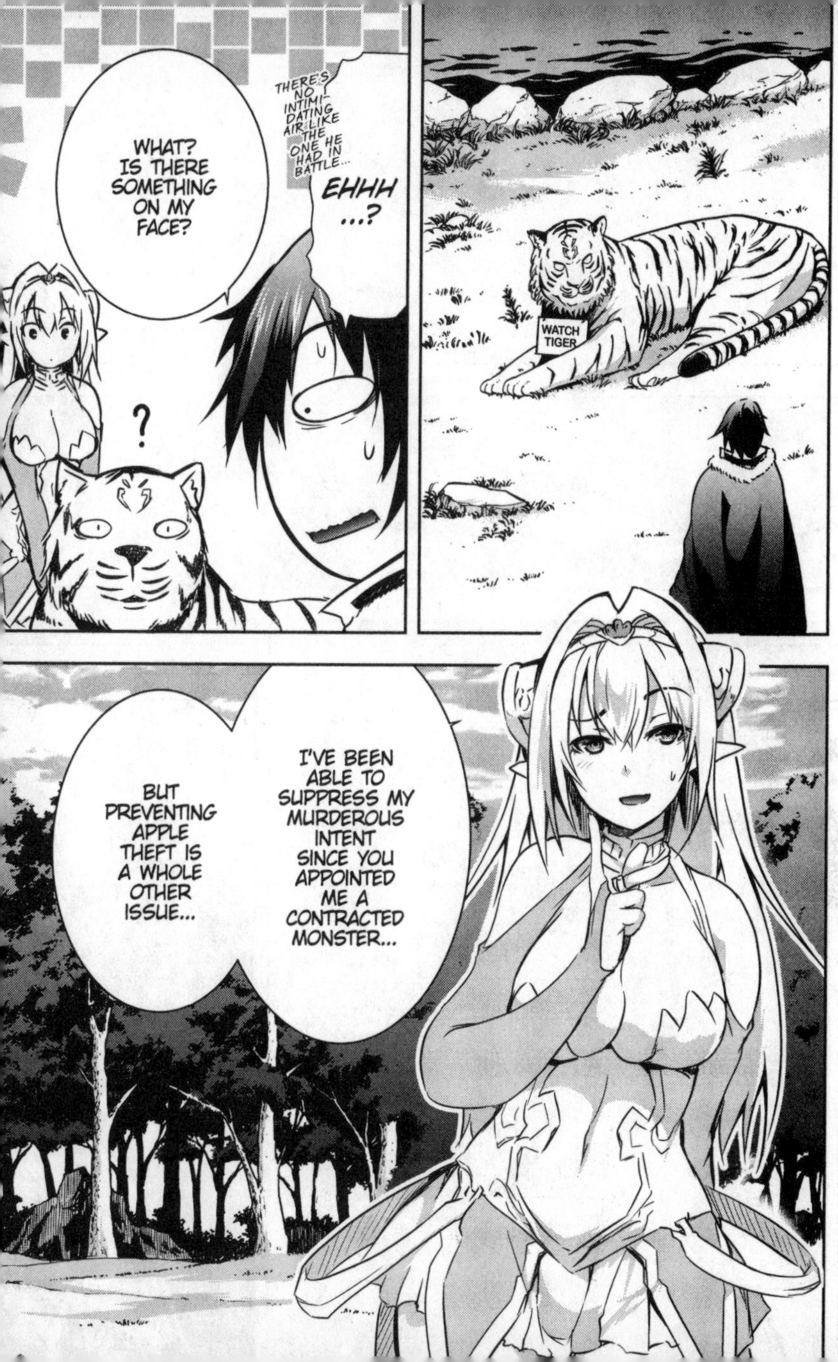
WATCH TIGER
THERE'S NO INTIMI-DATING AIR LIKE THE ONE HE HAD IN BATTLE...
EHHH ...?
WHAT? IS THERE SOMETHING ON MY FACE?
?
I'VE BEEN ABLE TO SUPPRESS MY MURDEROUS INTENT SINCE YOU APPOINTED ME A CONTRACTED MONSTER...
BUT PREVENTING APPLE THEFT IS A WHOLE OTHER ISSUE...

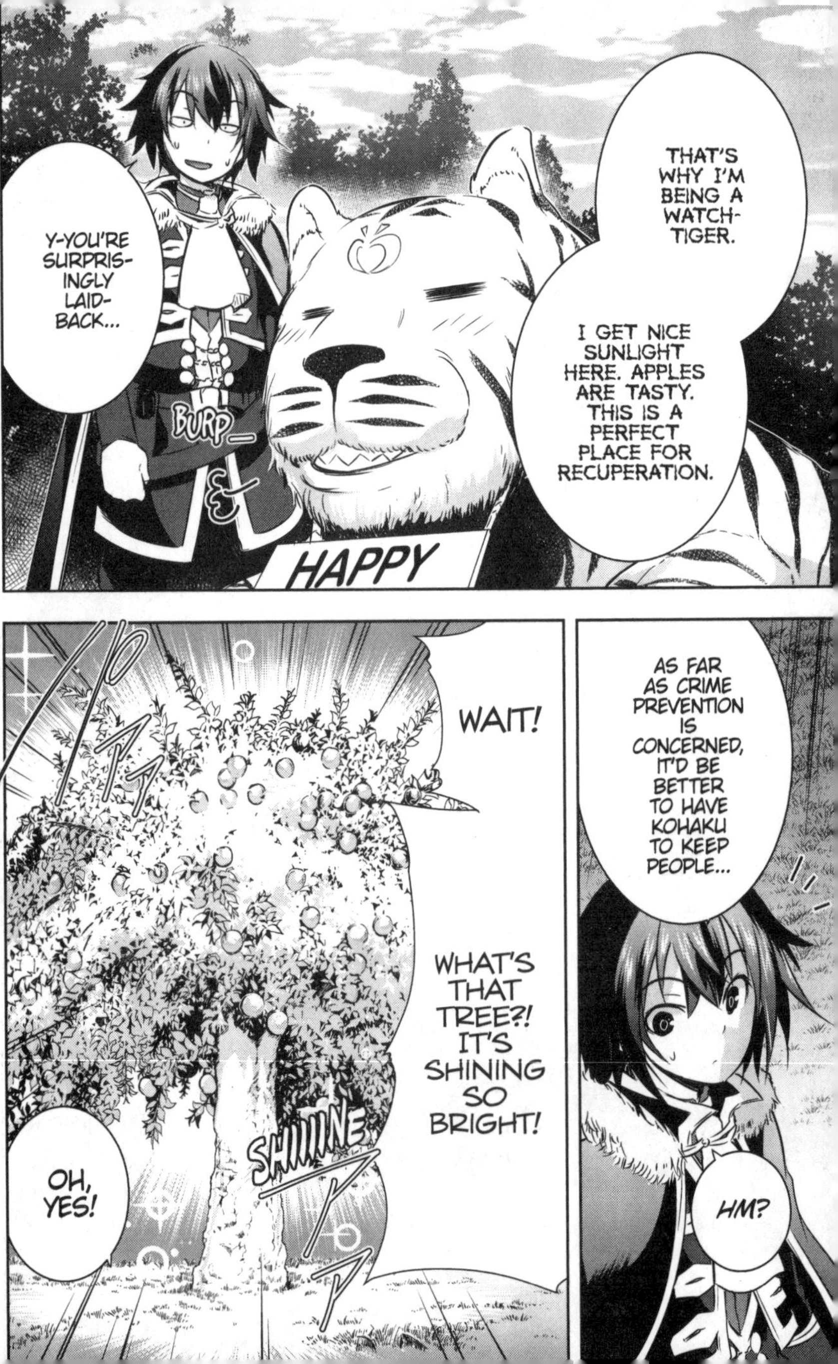
THAT'S WHY I'M BEING A WATCH-TIGER.
I GET NICE SUNLIGHT HERE. APPLES ARE TASTY. THIS IS A PERFECT PLACE FOR RECUPERATION.
Y-YOU'RE SURPRISINGLY LAID-BACK...
BURP
HAPPY
AS FAR AS CRIME PREVENTION IS CONCERNED, IT'D BE BETTER TO HAVE KOHAKU TO KEEP PEOPLE...
HM?
WAIT!
WHAT'S THAT TREE?! IT'S SHINING SO BRIGHT!
SHIIINE
OH, YES!

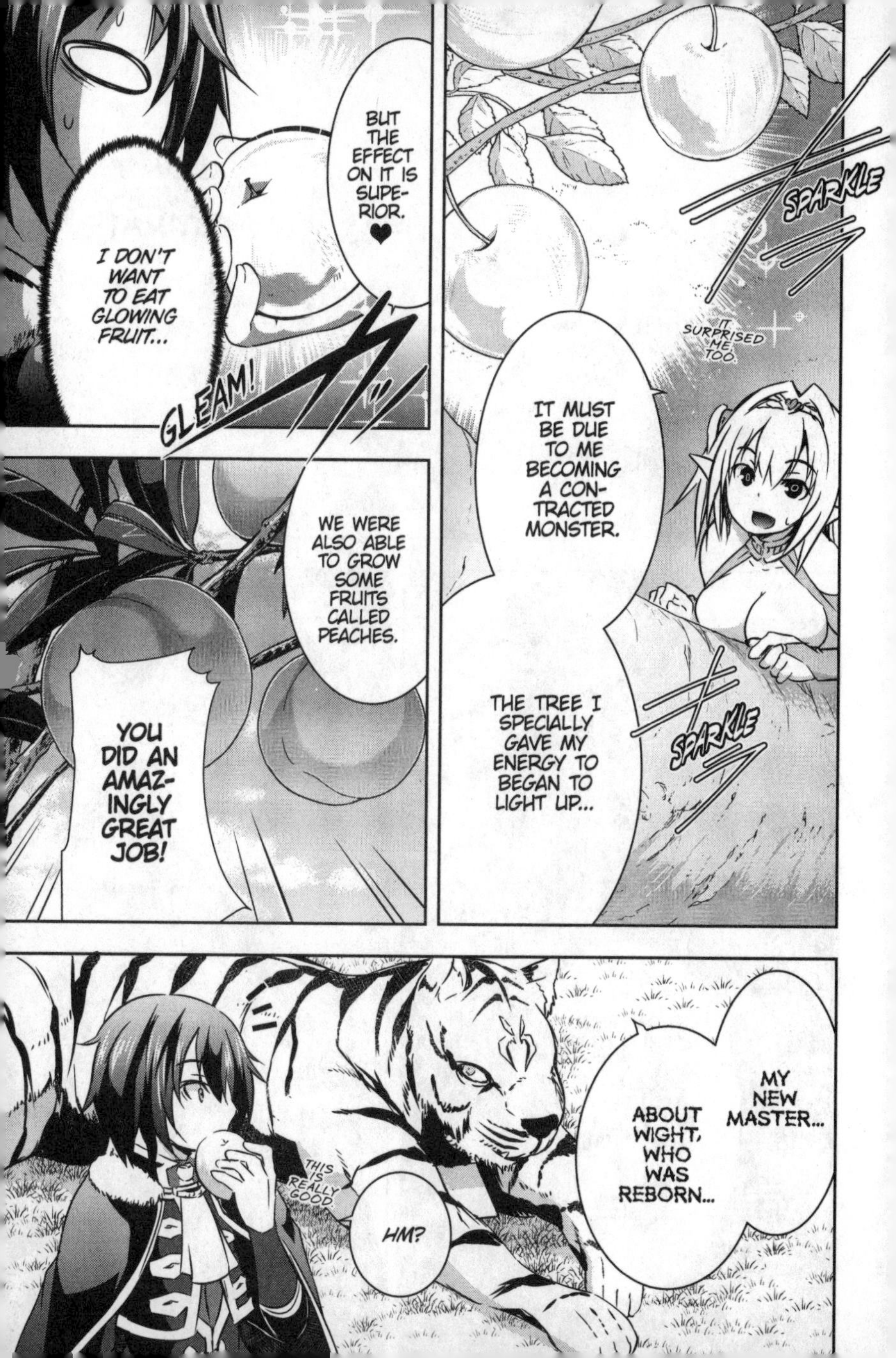
SPARKLE
IT SURPRISED ME TOO.
IT MUST BE DUE TO ME BECOMING A CONTRACTED MONSTER.
THE TREE I SPECIALLY GAVE MY ENERGY TO BEGAN TO LIGHT UP...
SPARKLE
BUT THE EFFECT ON IT IS SUPERIOR. ♥
I DON'T WANT TO EAT GLOWING FRUIT...
GLEAM!
WE WERE ALSO ABLE TO GROW SOME FRUITS CALLED PEACHES.
YOU DID AN AMAZINGLY GREAT JOB!
MY NEW MASTER...
ABOUT WIGHT, WHO WAS REBORN...
HM?
THIS IS REALLY GOOD.

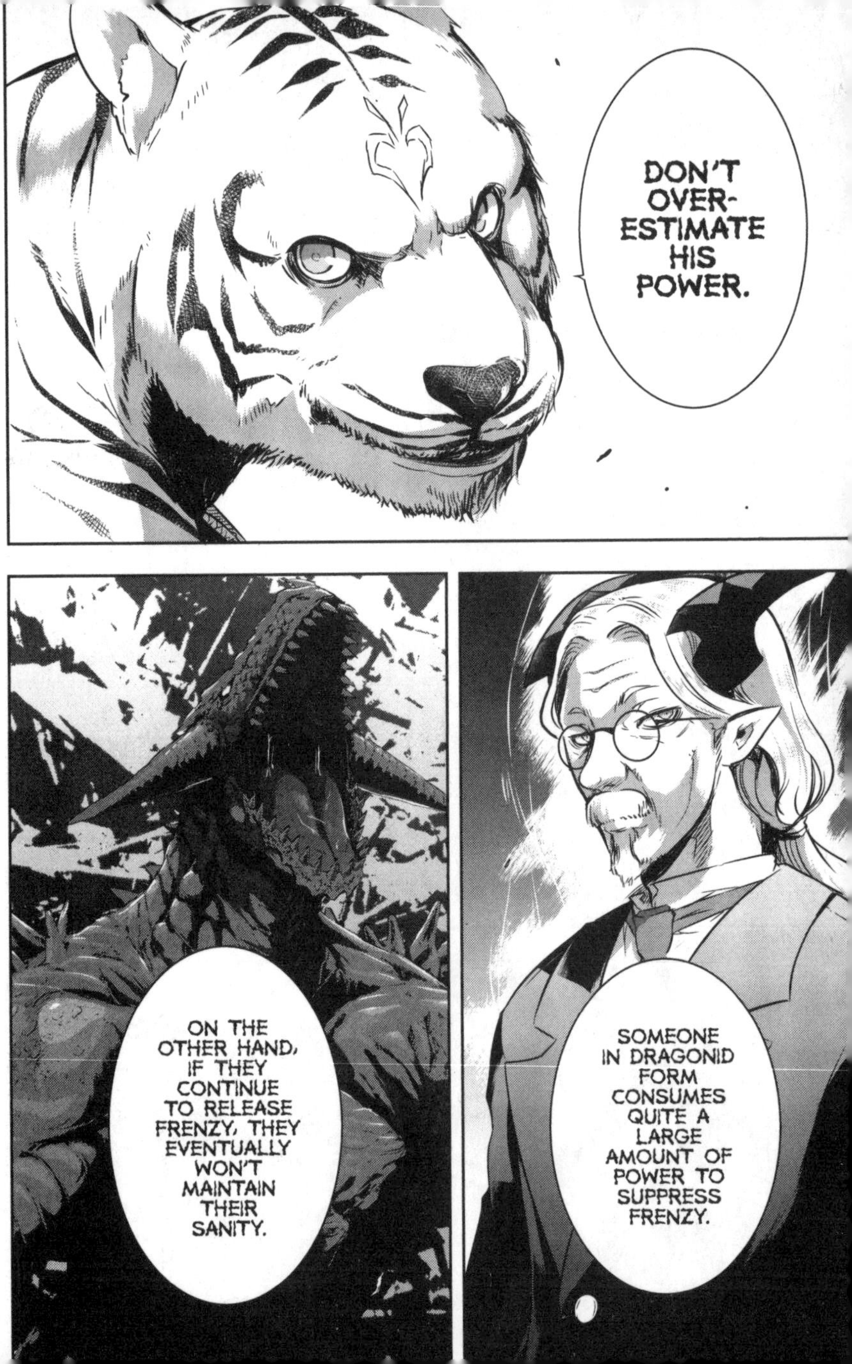
DON'T OVER-ESTIMATE HIS POWER.
SOMEONE IN DRAGONID FORM CONSUMES QUITE A LARGE AMOUNT OF POWER TO SUPPRESS FRENZY.
ON THE OTHER HAND, IF THEY CONTINUE TO RELEASE FRENZY, THEY EVENTUALLY WON'T MAINTAIN THEIR SANITY.

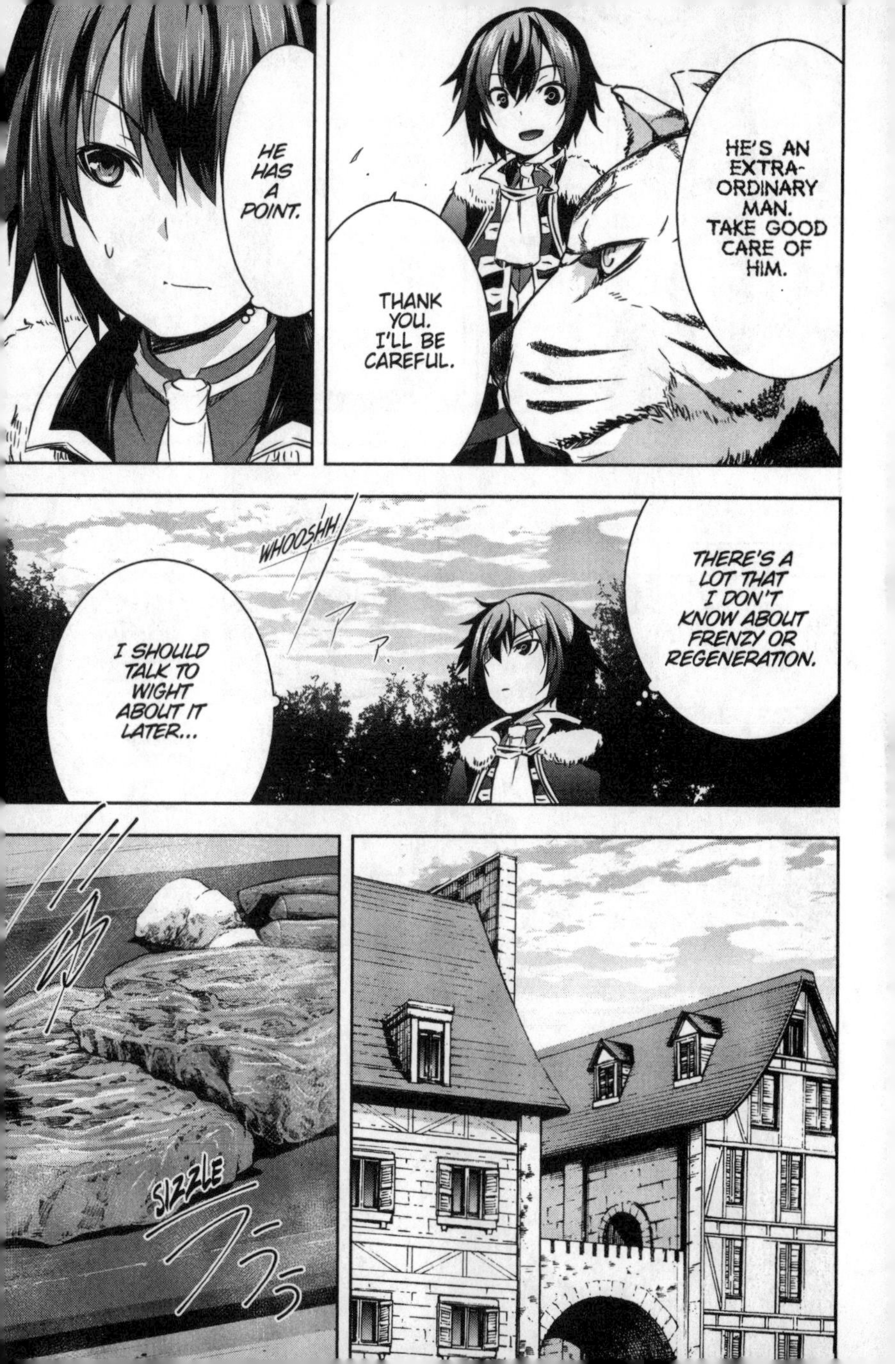
HE'S AN EXTRA-ORDINARY MAN. TAKE GOOD CARE OF HIM.
THANK YOU. I'LL BE CAREFUL.
HE HAS A POINT.
WHOOSHH
THERE'S A LOT THAT I DON'T KNOW ABOUT FRENZY OR REGENERATION.
I SHOULD TALK TO WIGHT ABOUT IT LATER...
SIZZLE

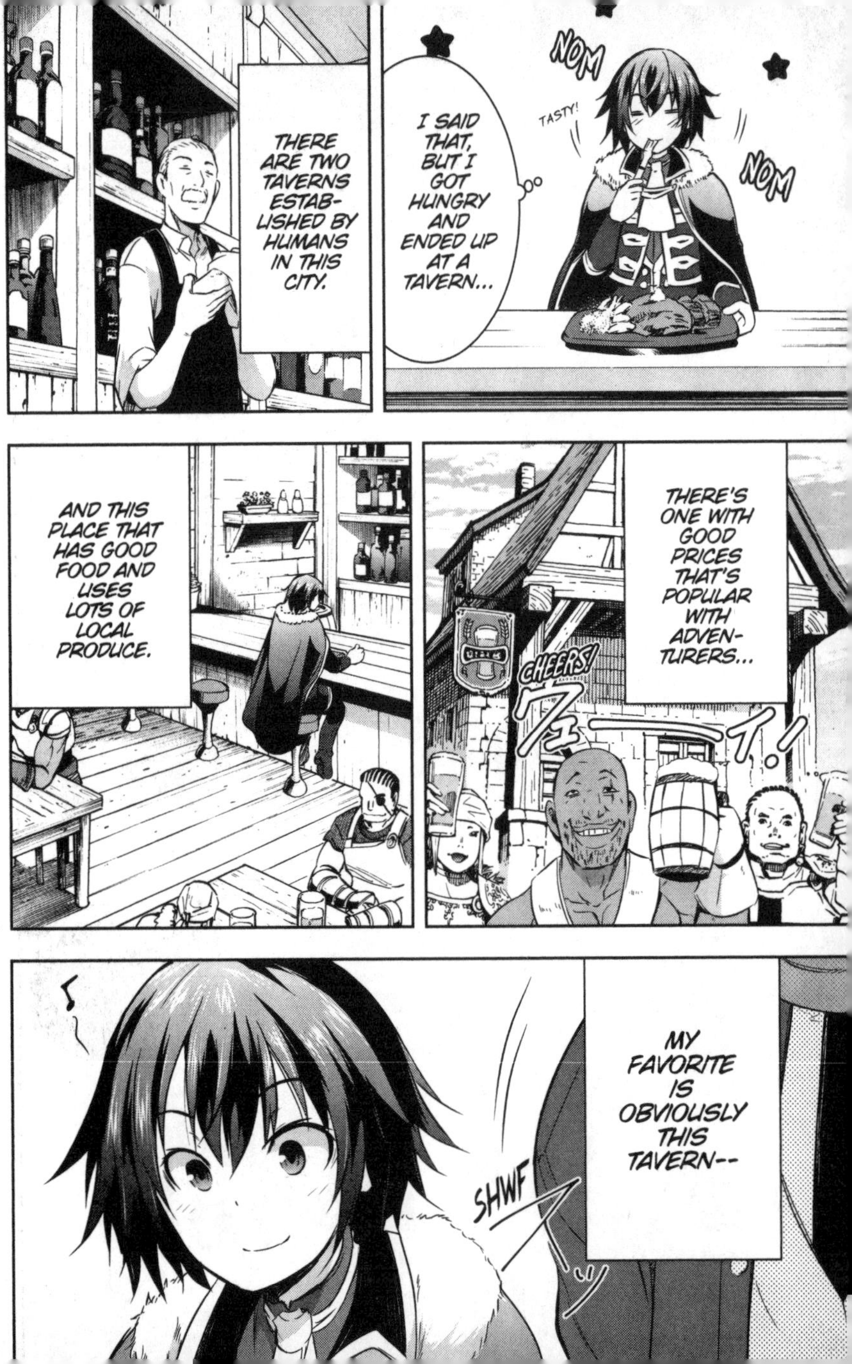
NOM
TASTY!
NOM
I SAID THAT, BUT I GOT HUNGRY AND ENDED UP AT A TAVERN...
THERE ARE TWO TAVERNS ESTAB-LISHED BY HUMANS IN THIS CITY.
THERE'S ONE WITH GOOD PRICES THAT'S POPULAR WITH ADVEN-TURERS...
CHEERS!
ウェーイ!!
AND THIS PLACE THAT HAS GOOD FOOD AND USES LOTS OF LOCAL PRODUCE.
MY FAVORITE IS OBVIOUSLY THIS TAVERN--
SHWF

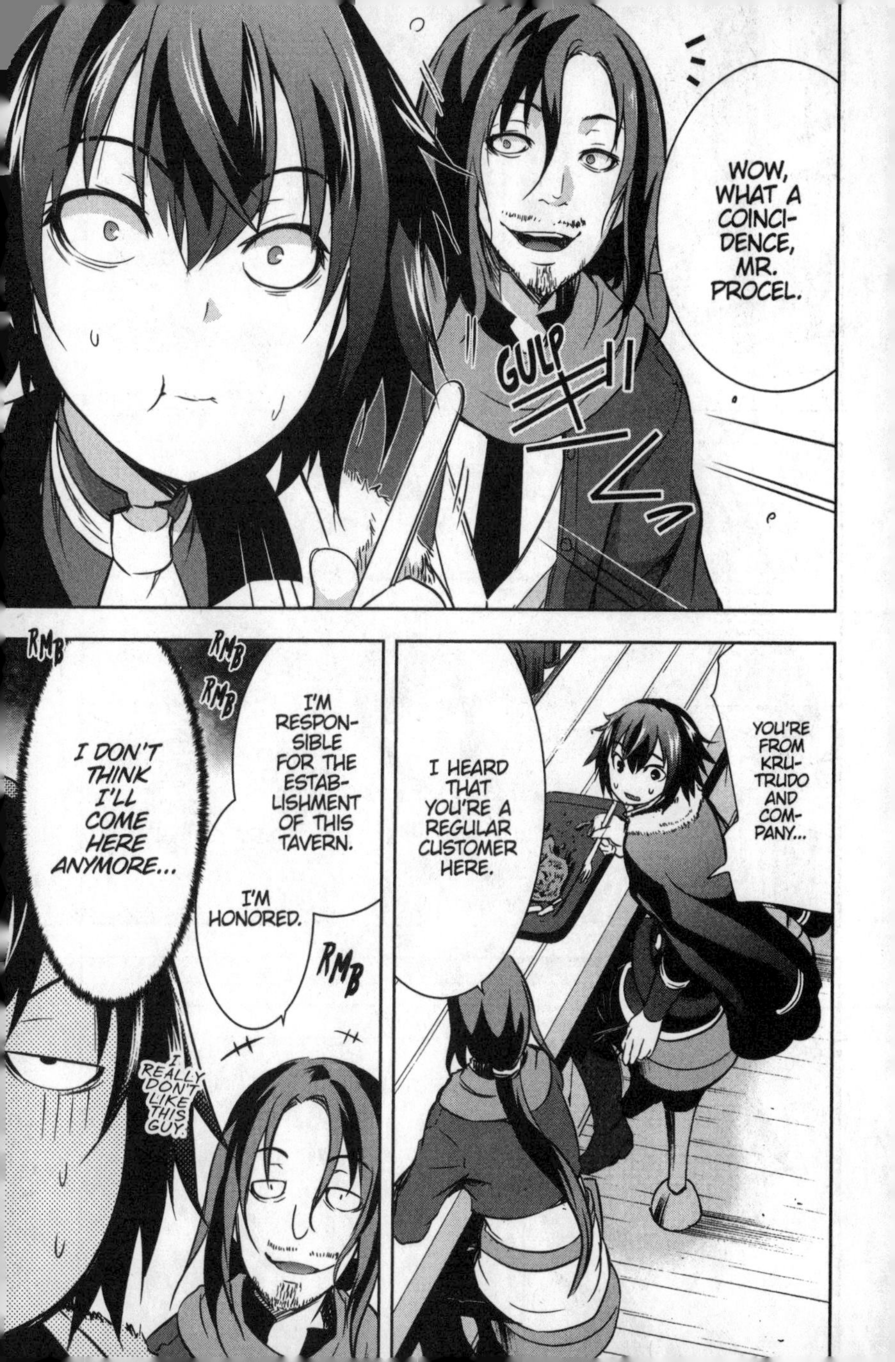
WOW, WHAT A COINCI-DENCE, MR. PROCEL.
GULP
YOU'RE FROM KRU-TRUDO AND COM-PANY...
I HEARD THAT YOU'RE A REGULAR CUSTOMER HERE.
I'M RESPON-SIBLE FOR THE ESTAB-LISHMENT OF THIS TAVERN.
I'M HONORED.
RMB
RMB
RMB
RMB
I DON'T THINK I'LL COME HERE ANYMORE...
I REALLY DON'T LIKE THIS GUY.

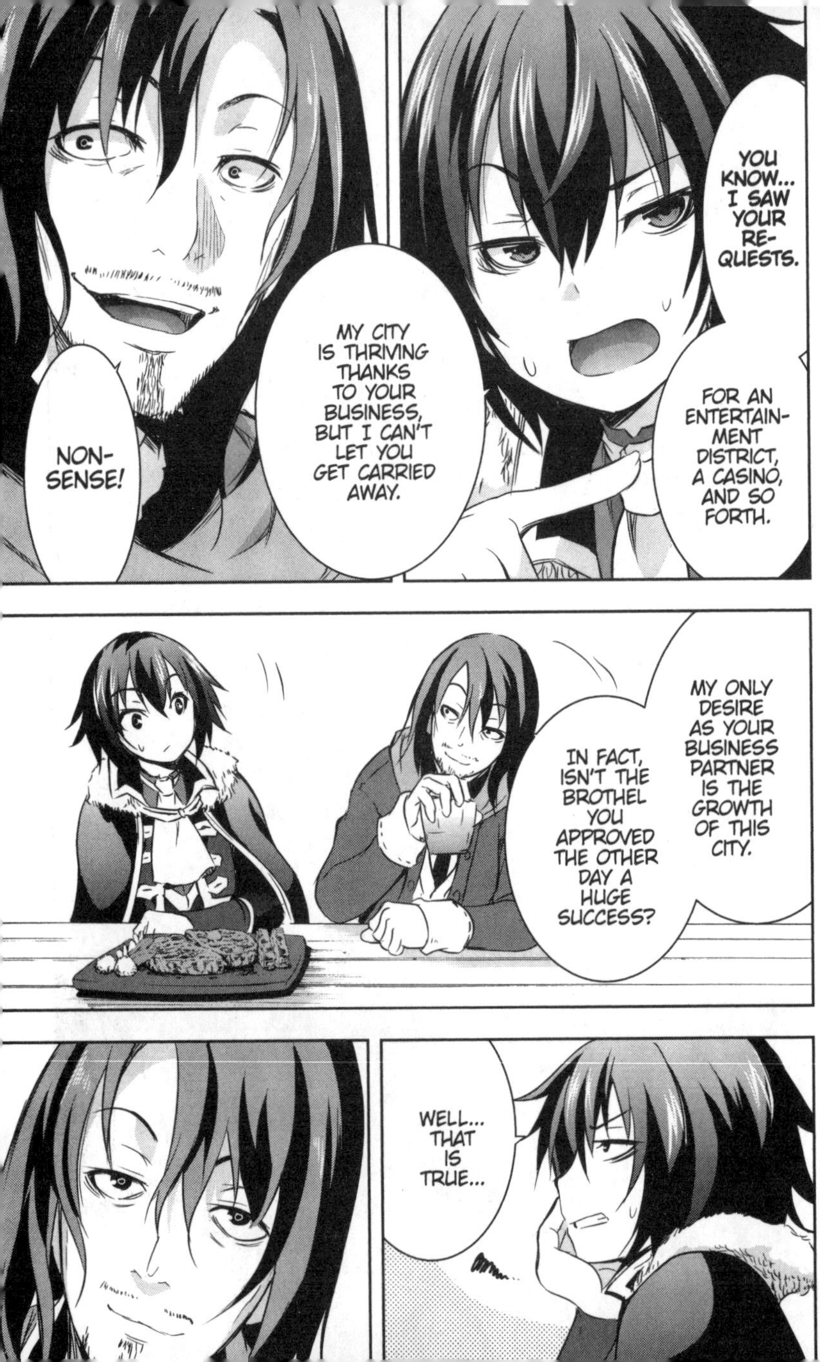
YOU KNOW... I SAW YOUR RE-QUESTS.
FOR AN ENTERTAIN-MENT DISTRICT, A CASINO, AND SO FORTH.
MY CITY IS THRIVING THANKS TO YOUR BUSINESS, BUT I CAN'T LET YOU GET CARRIED AWAY.
NON-SENSE!
MY ONLY DESIRE AS YOUR BUSINESS PARTNER IS THE GROWTH OF THIS CITY.
IN FACT, ISN'T THE BROTHEL YOU APPROVED THE OTHER DAY A HUGE SUCCESS?
WELL... THAT IS TRUE...

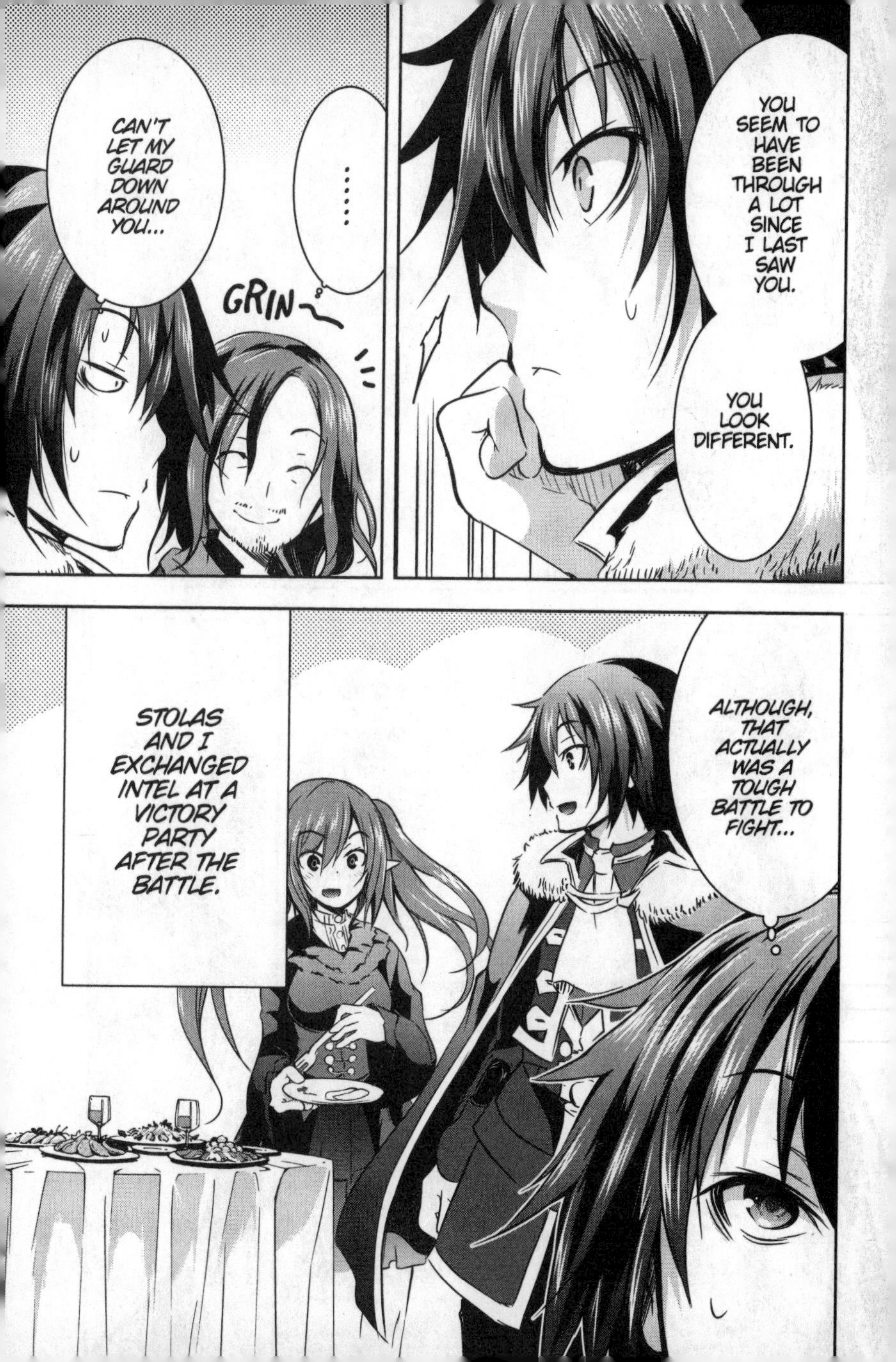
YOU SEEM TO HAVE BEEN THROUGH A LOT SINCE I LAST SAW YOU.
YOU LOOK DIFFERENT.
......
GRIN~
CAN'T LET MY GUARD DOWN AROUND YOU...
ALTHOUGH, THAT ACTUALLY WAS A TOUGH BATTLE TO FIGHT...
STOLAS AND I EXCHANGED INTEL AT A VICTORY PARTY AFTER THE BATTLE.

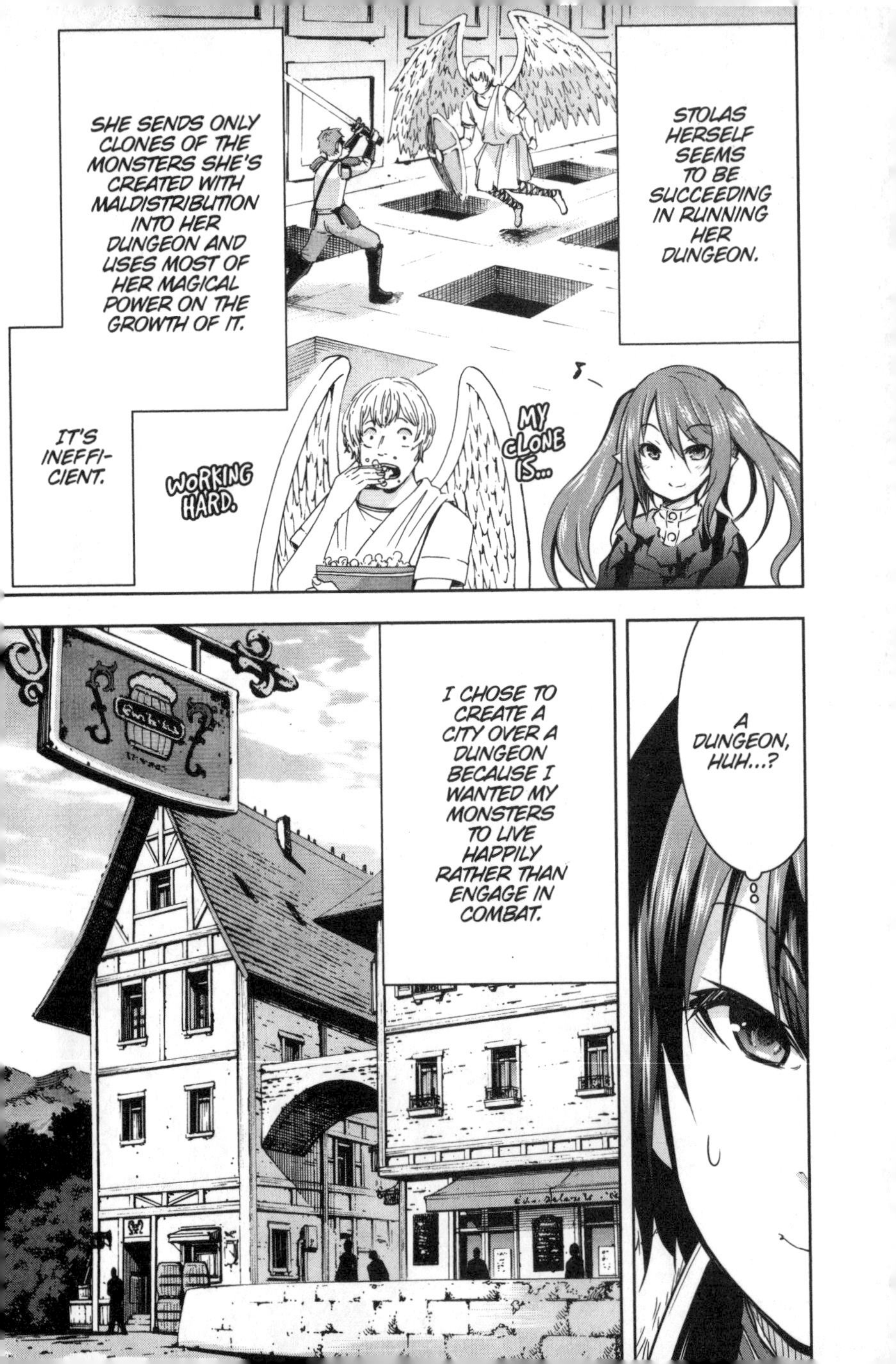
STOLAS HERSELF SEEMS TO BE SUCCEEDING IN RUNNING HER DUNGEON.
SHE SENDS ONLY CLONES OF THE MONSTERS SHE'S CREATED WITH MALDISTRIBUTION INTO HER DUNGEON AND USES MOST OF HER MAGICAL POWER ON THE GROWTH OF IT.
MY CLONE IS...
WORKING HARD.
IT'S INEFFI-CIENT.
A DUNGEON, HUH...?
I CHOSE TO CREATE A CITY OVER A DUNGEON BECAUSE I WANTED MY MONSTERS TO LIVE HAPPILY RATHER THAN ENGAGE IN COMBAT.

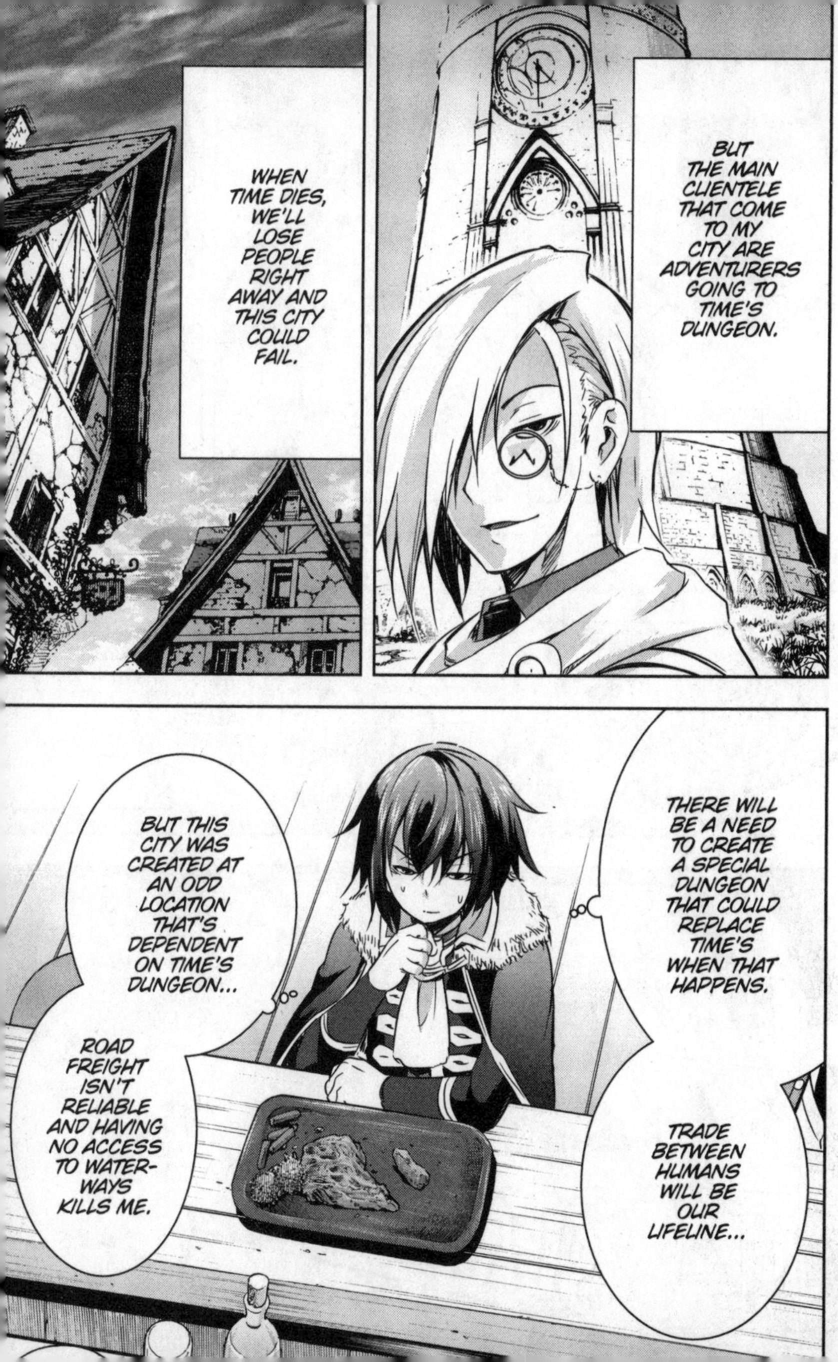
BUT THE MAIN CLIENTELE THAT COME TO MY CITY ARE ADVENTURERS GOING TO TIME'S DUNGEON.
WHEN TIME DIES, WE'LL LOSE PEOPLE RIGHT AWAY AND THIS CITY COULD FAIL.
THERE WILL BE A NEED TO CREATE A SPECIAL DUNGEON THAT COULD REPLACE TIME'S WHEN THAT HAPPENS.
BUT THIS CITY WAS CREATED AT AN ODD LOCATION THAT'S DEPENDENT ON TIME'S DUNGEON...
ROAD FREIGHT ISN'T RELIABLE AND HAVING NO ACCESS TO WATER-WAYS KILLS ME.
TRADE BETWEEN HUMANS WILL BE OUR LIFELINE...

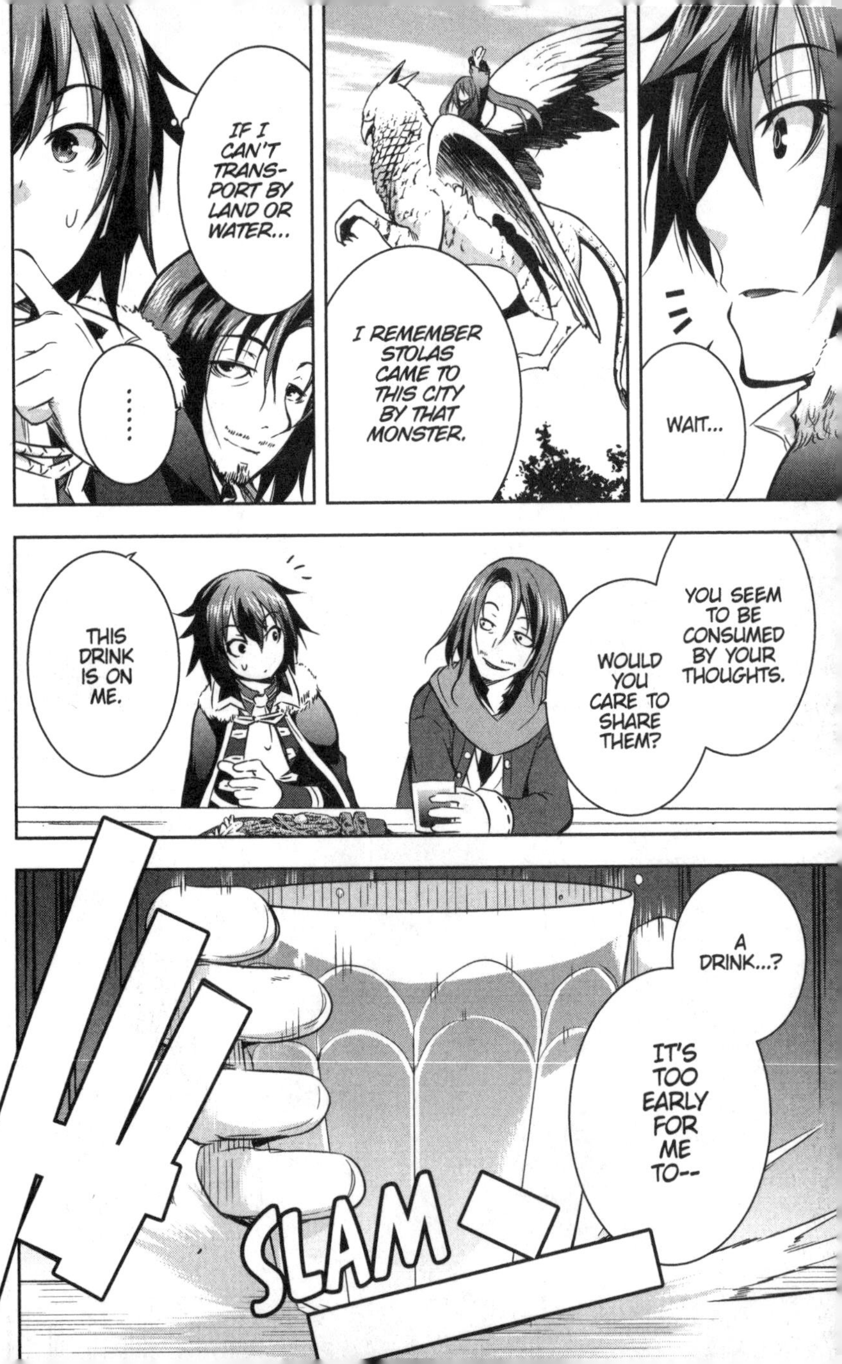
WAIT...
I REMEMBER STOLAS CAME TO THIS CITY BY THAT MONSTER.
IF I CAN'T TRANS-PORT BY LAND OR WATER...
......
YOU SEEM TO BE CONSUMED BY YOUR THOUGHTS.
WOULD YOU CARE TO SHARE THEM?
THIS DRINK IS ON ME.
A DRINK...?
IT'S TOO EARLY FOR ME TO--
SLAM

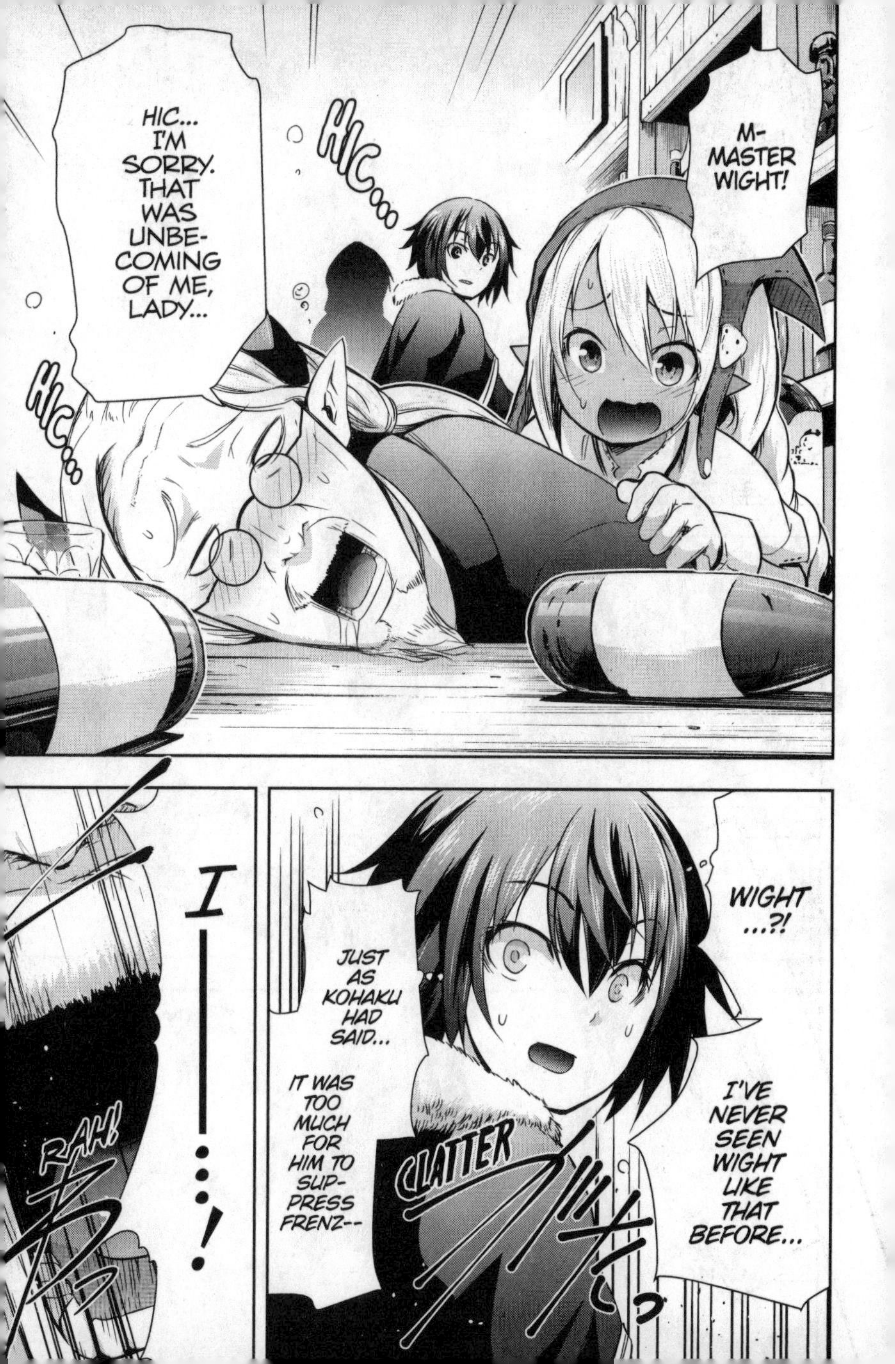
M-MASTER WIGHT!
HIC...
HIC... I'M SORRY. THAT WAS UNBECOMING OF ME, LADY...
HIC...
WIGHT ...?!
I'VE NEVER SEEN WIGHT LIKE THAT BEFORE...
JUST AS KOHAKU HAD SAID...
IT WAS TOO MUCH FOR HIM TO SUPPRESS FRENZ--
CLATTER
I------...!
RAH!

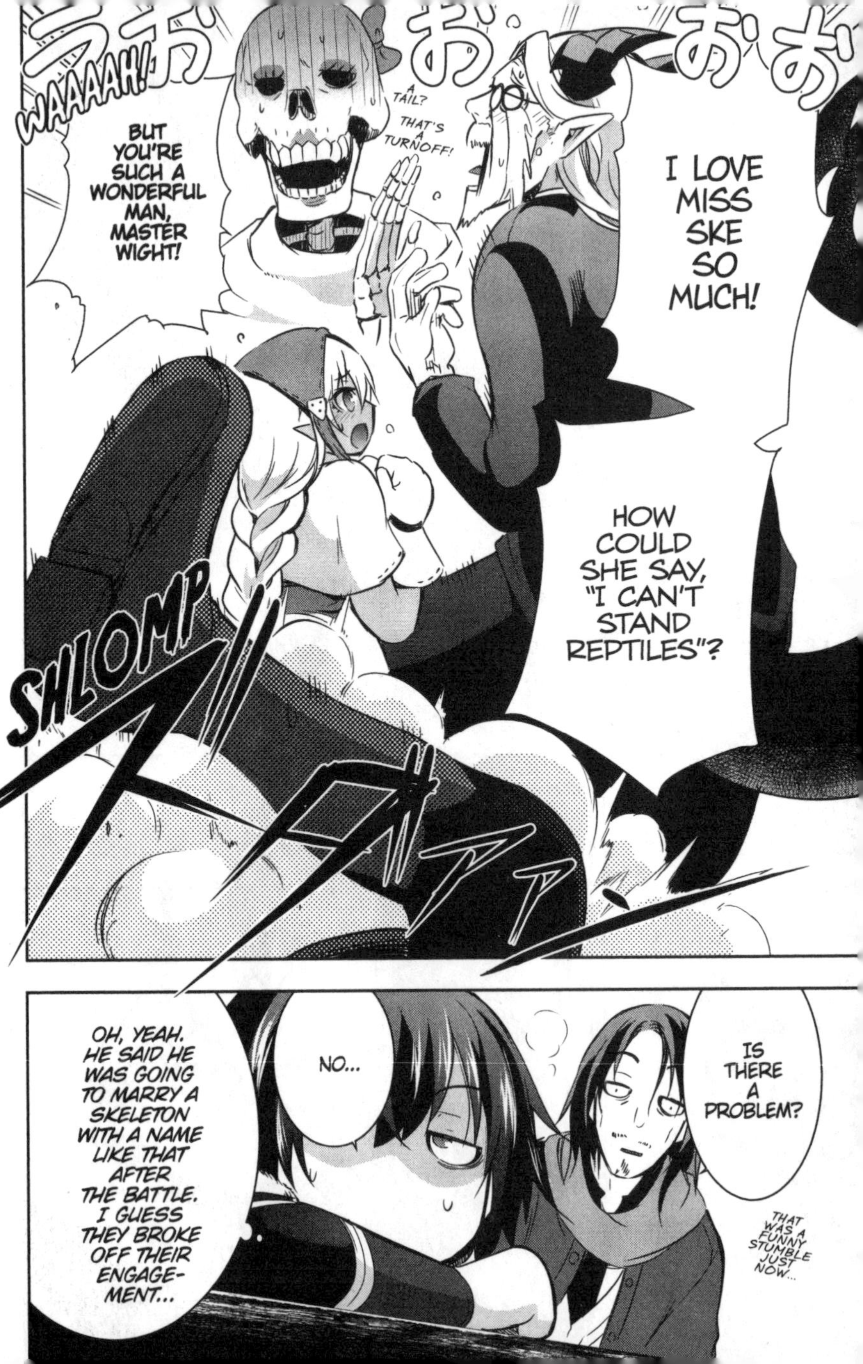
WAAAAH!
I LOVE MISS SKE SO MUCH!
A TAIL? THAT'S A TURNOFF!
BUT YOU'RE SUCH A WONDERFUL MAN, MASTER WIGHT!
HOW COULD SHE SAY, "I CAN'T STAND REPTILES"?
SHLOMP
IS THERE A PROBLEM?
THAT WAS A FUNNY STUMBLE JUST NOW...
NO...
OH, YEAH. HE SAID HE WAS GOING TO MARRY A SKELETON WITH A NAME LIKE THAT AFTER THE BATTLE. I GUESS THEY BROKE OFF THEIR ENGAGE-MENT...

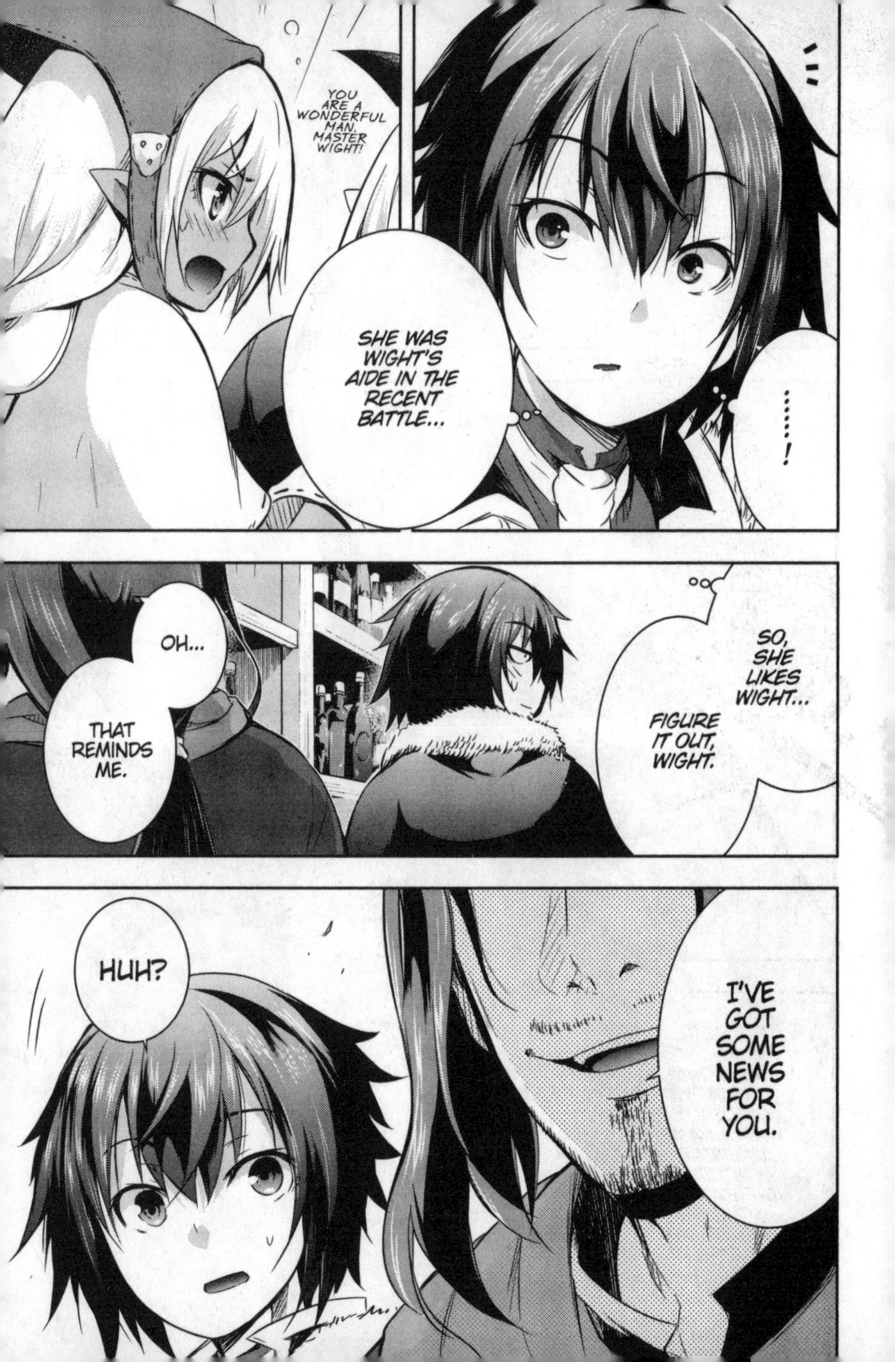
YOU ARE A WONDERFUL MAN, MASTER WIGHT!
......!
SHE WAS WIGHT'S AIDE IN THE RECENT BATTLE...
SO, SHE LIKES WIGHT...
FIGURE IT OUT, WIGHT.
OH...
THAT REMINDS ME.
I'VE GOT SOME NEWS FOR YOU.
HUH?

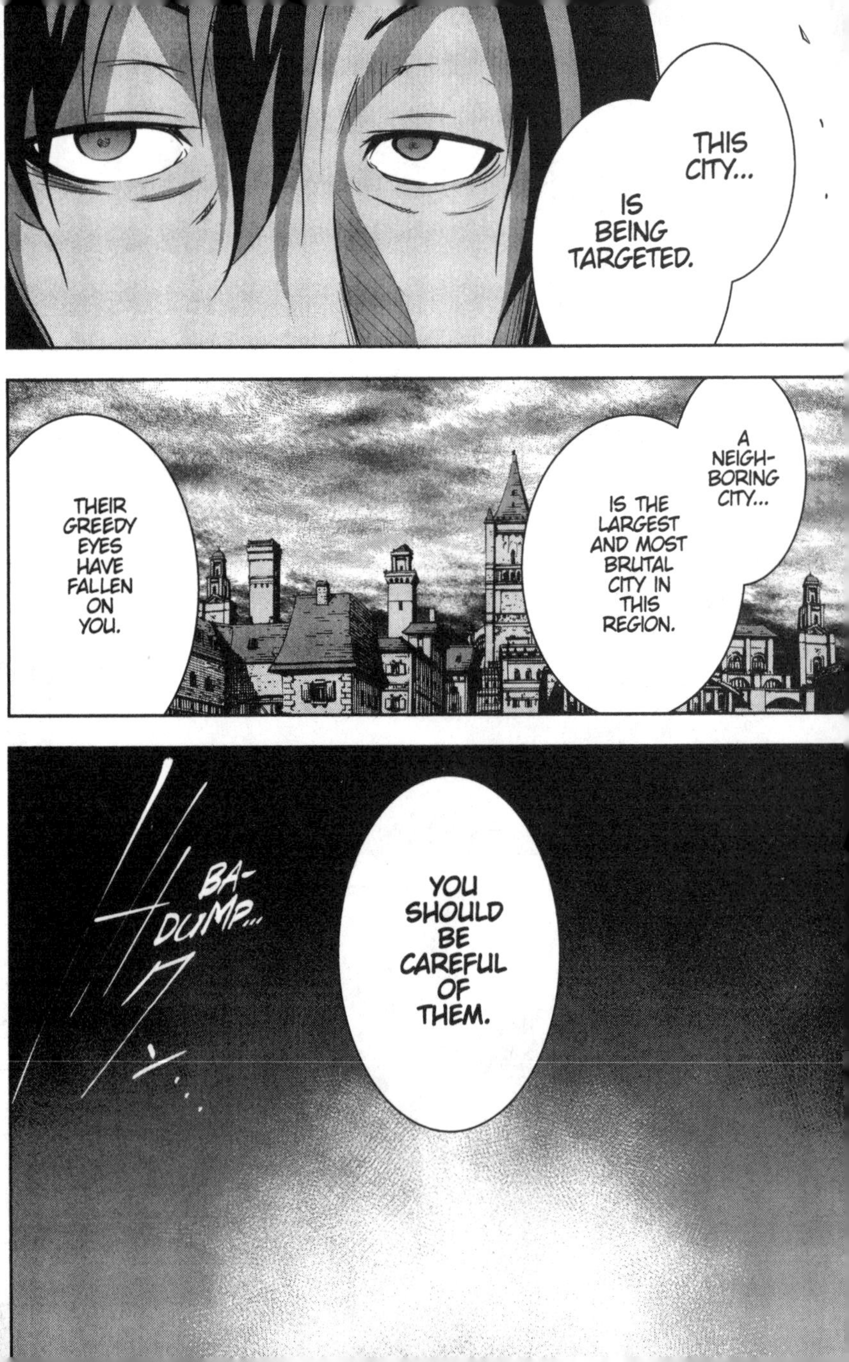
THIS CITY...
IS BEING TARGETED.
A NEIGH-BORING CITY...
IS THE LARGEST AND MOST BRUTAL CITY IN THIS REGION.
THEIR GREEDY EYES HAVE FALLEN ON YOU.
YOU SHOULD BE CAREFUL OF THEM.
BA-DUMP...

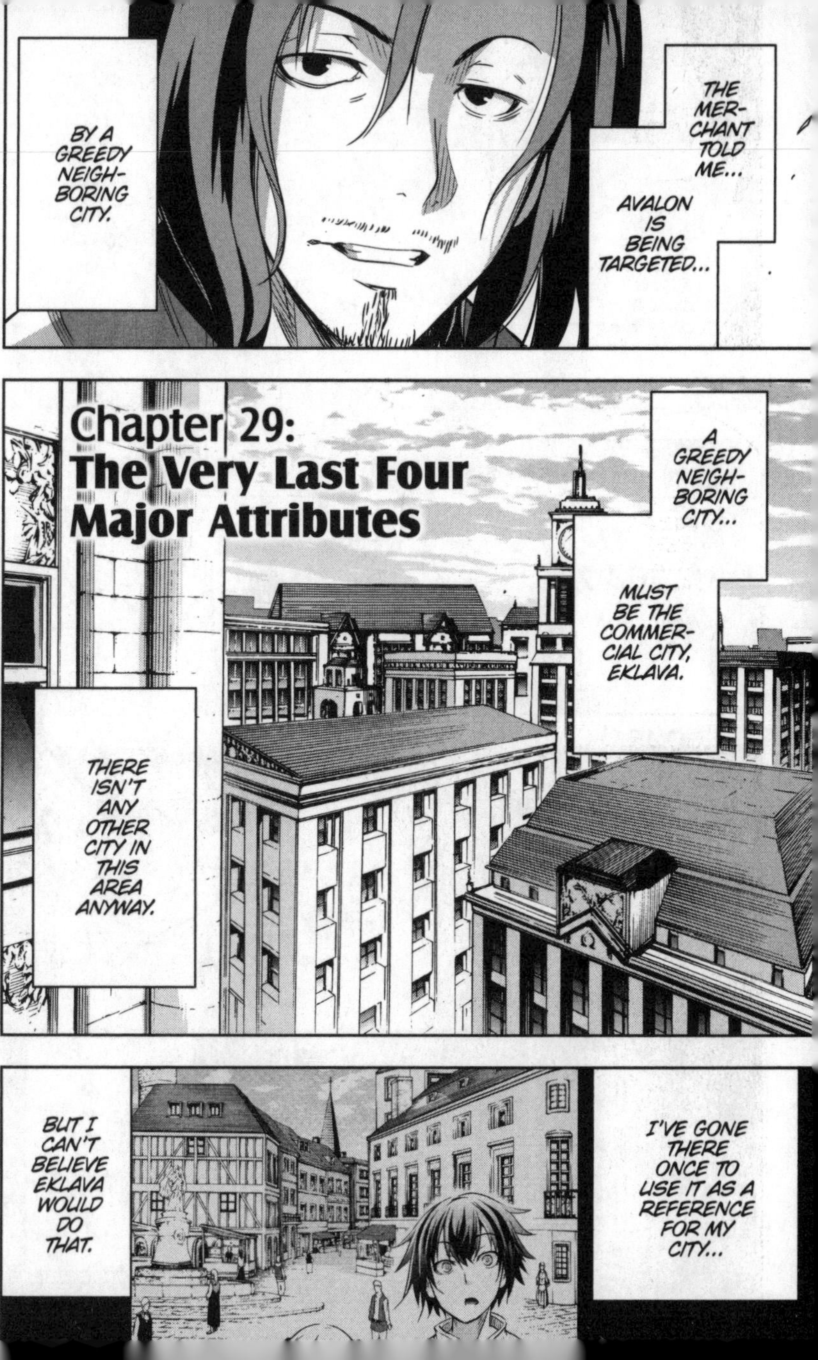
THE MERCHANT TOLD ME...
AVALON IS BEING TARGETED...
BY A GREEDY NEIGHBORING CITY.
Chapter 29: The Very Last Four Major Attributes
A GREEDY NEIGHBORING CITY...
MUST BE THE COMMERCIAL CITY, EKLAVA.
THERE ISN'T ANY OTHER CITY IN THIS AREA ANYWAY.
I'VE GONE THERE ONCE TO USE IT AS A REFERENCE FOR MY CITY...
BUT I CAN'T BELIEVE EKLAVA WOULD DO THAT.

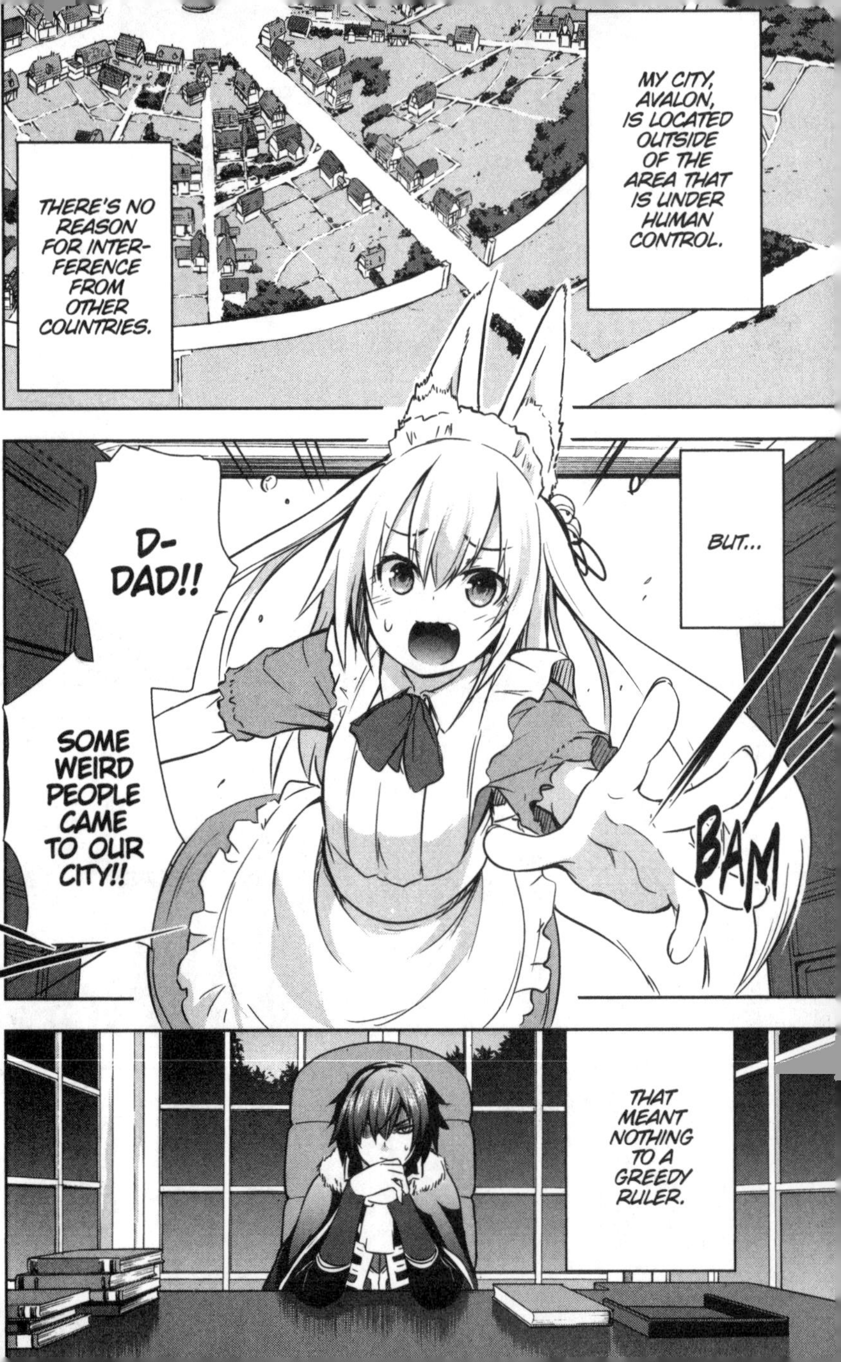
MY CITY, AVALON, IS LOCATED OUTSIDE OF THE AREA THAT IS UNDER HUMAN CONTROL.
THERE'S NO REASON FOR INTER-FERENCE FROM OTHER COUNTRIES.
BUT...
BAM
D-DAD!!
SOME WEIRD PEOPLE CAME TO OUR CITY!!
THAT MEANT NOTHING TO A GREEDY RULER.

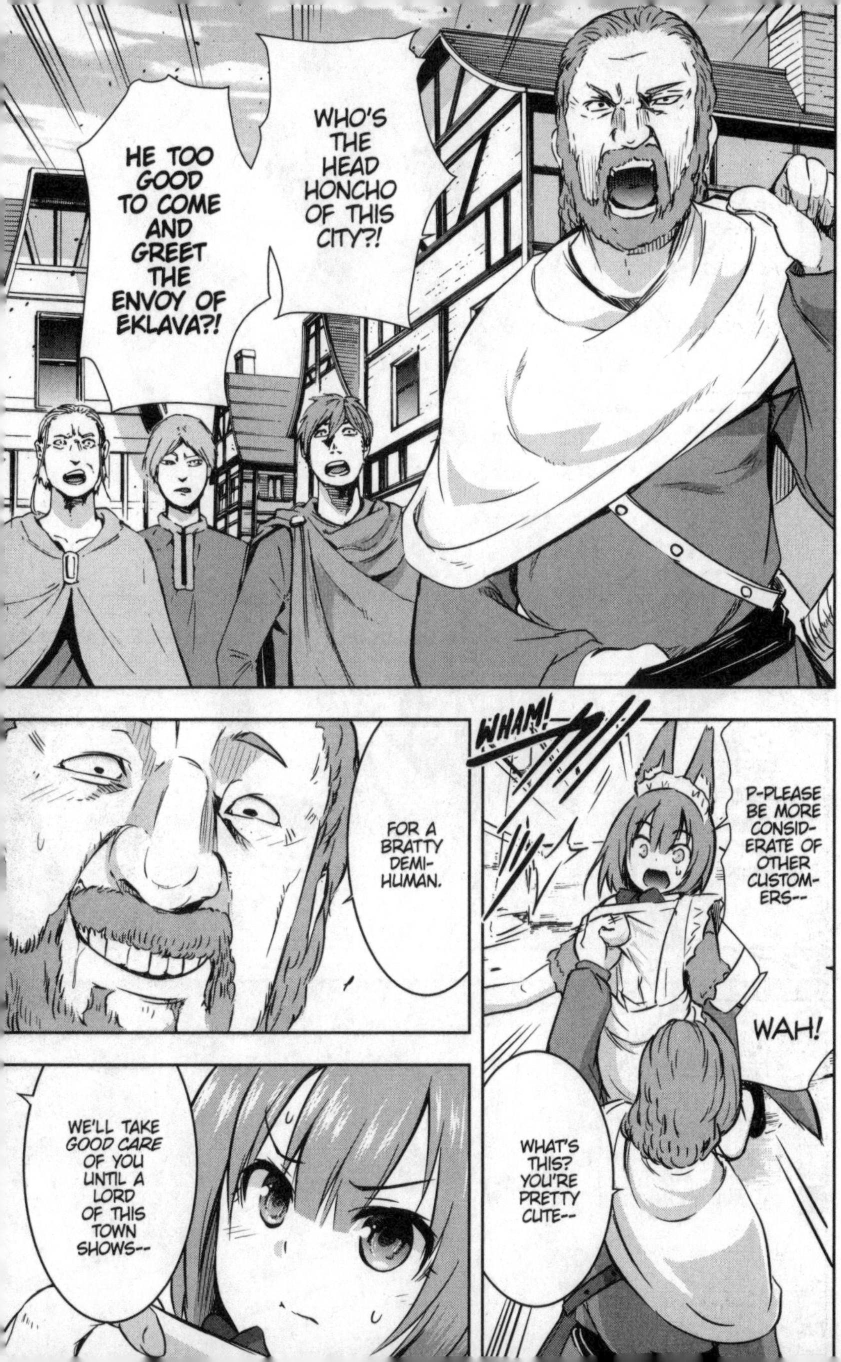
WHO'S THE HEAD HONCHO OF THIS CITY?!
HE TOO GOOD TO COME AND GREET THE ENVOY OF EKLAVA?!
WHAM!
P-PLEASE BE MORE CONSID-ERATE OF OTHER CUSTOME-ERS--
WAH!
WHAT'S THIS? YOU'RE PRETTY CUTE--
FOR A BRATTY DEMI-HUMAN.
WE'LL TAKE GOOD CARE OF YOU UNTIL A LORD OF THIS TOWN SHOWS--

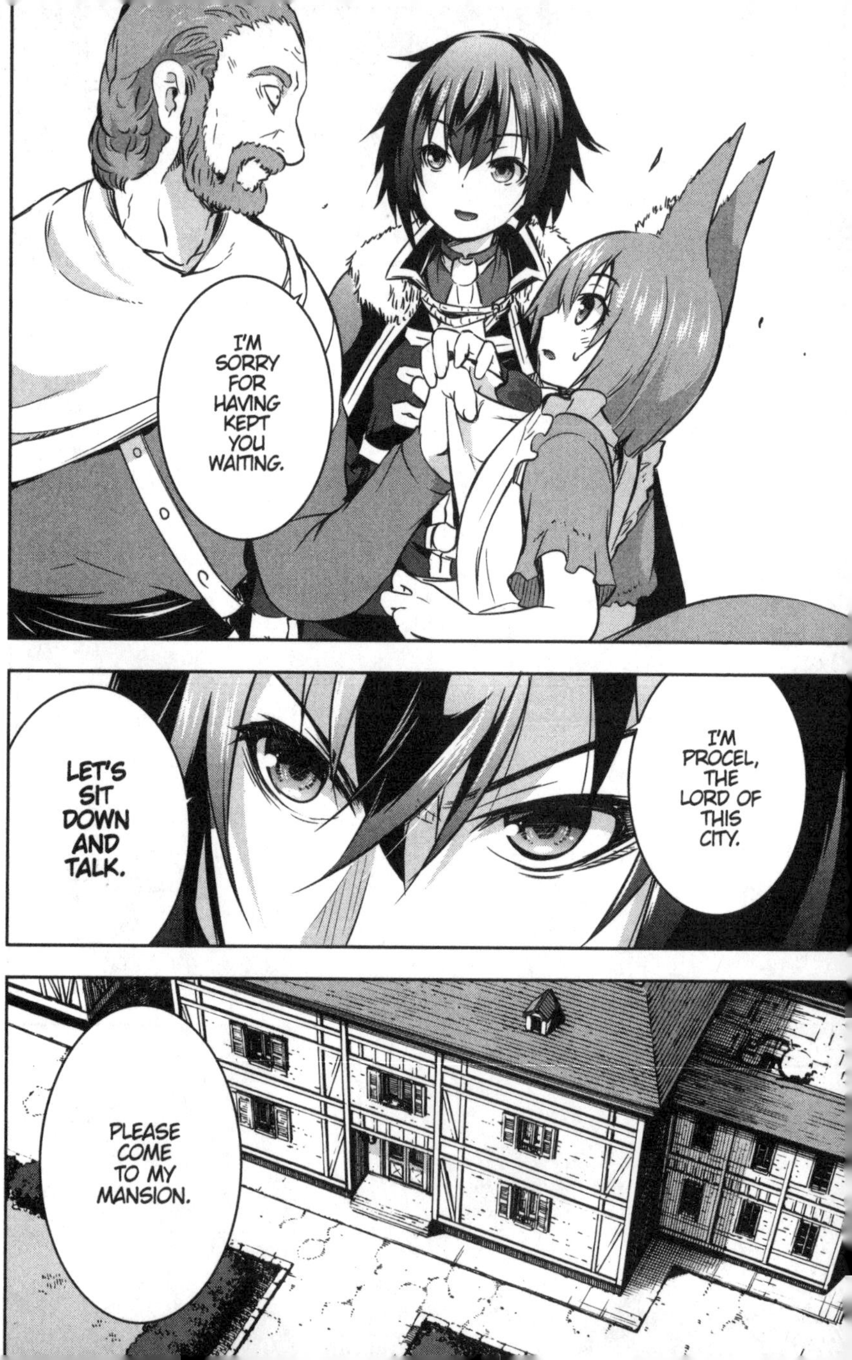
I'M SORRY FOR HAVING KEPT YOU WAITING.
I'M PROCEL, THE LORD OF THIS CITY.
LET'S SIT DOWN AND TALK.
PLEASE COME TO MY MANSION.

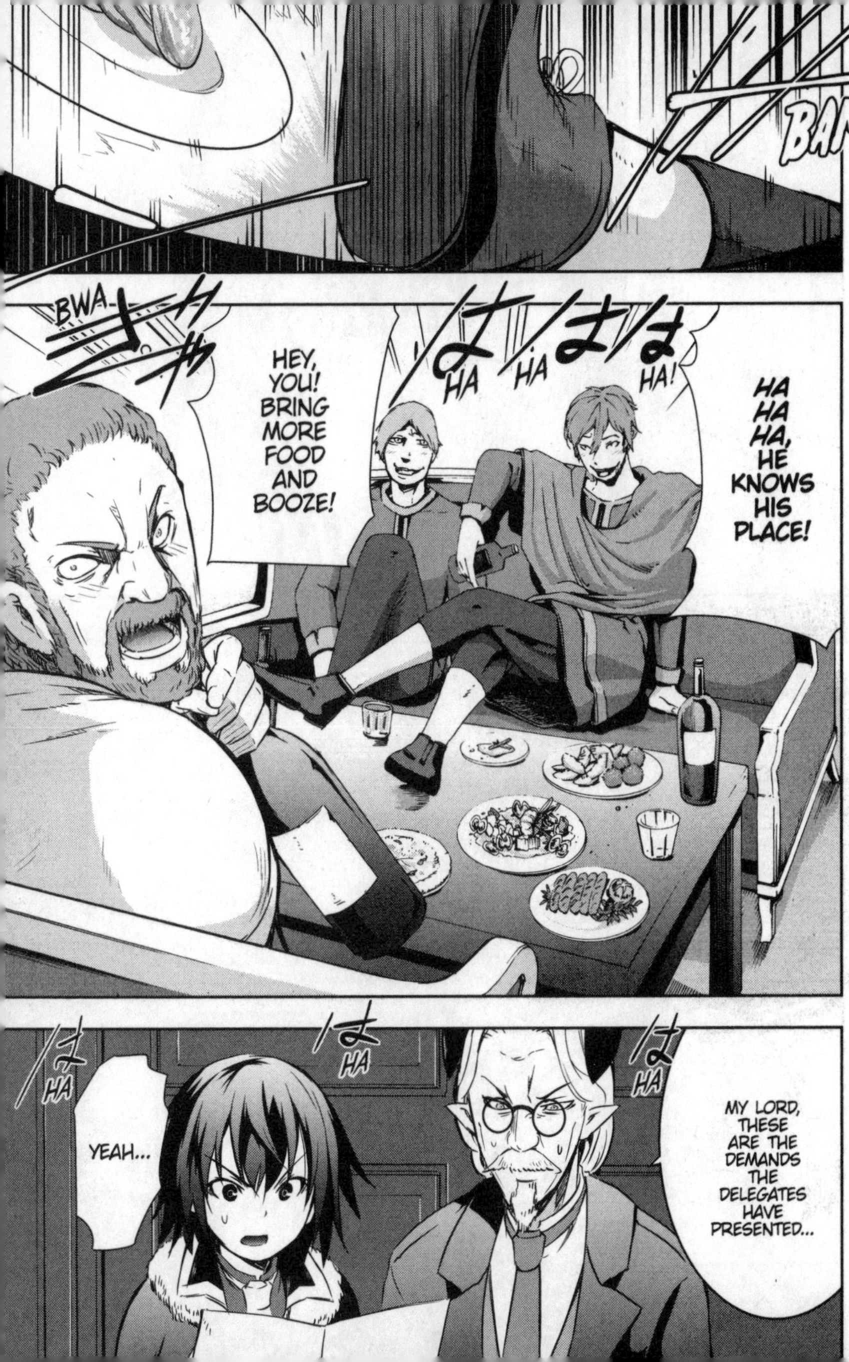
BAM
HA HA HA, HE KNOWS HIS PLACE!
HA HA HA!
HEY, YOU! BRING MORE FOOD AND BOOZE!
BWA
HA
HA
MY LORD, THESE ARE THE DEMANDS THE DELEGATES HAVE PRESENTED...
YEAH...
HA

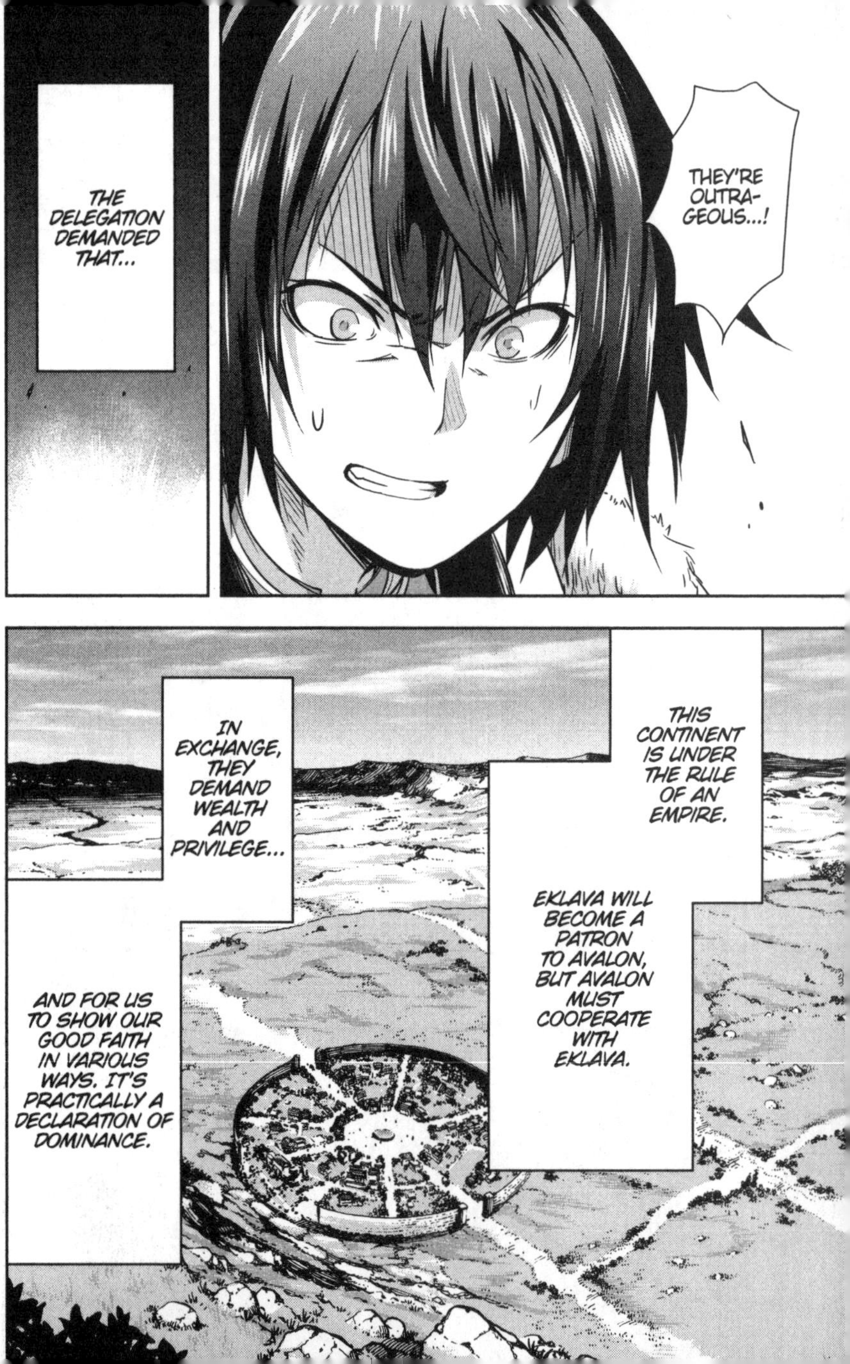
THEY'RE OUTRA-GEOUS...!
THE DELEGATION DEMANDED THAT...
THIS CONTINENT IS UNDER THE RULE OF AN EMPIRE.
EKLAVA WILL BECOME A PATRON TO AVALON, BUT AVALON MUST COOPERATE WITH EKLAVA.
IN EXCHANGE, THEY DEMAND WEALTH AND PRIVILEGE...
AND FOR US TO SHOW OUR GOOD FAITH IN VARIOUS WAYS. IT'S PRACTICALLY A DECLARATION OF DOMINANCE.

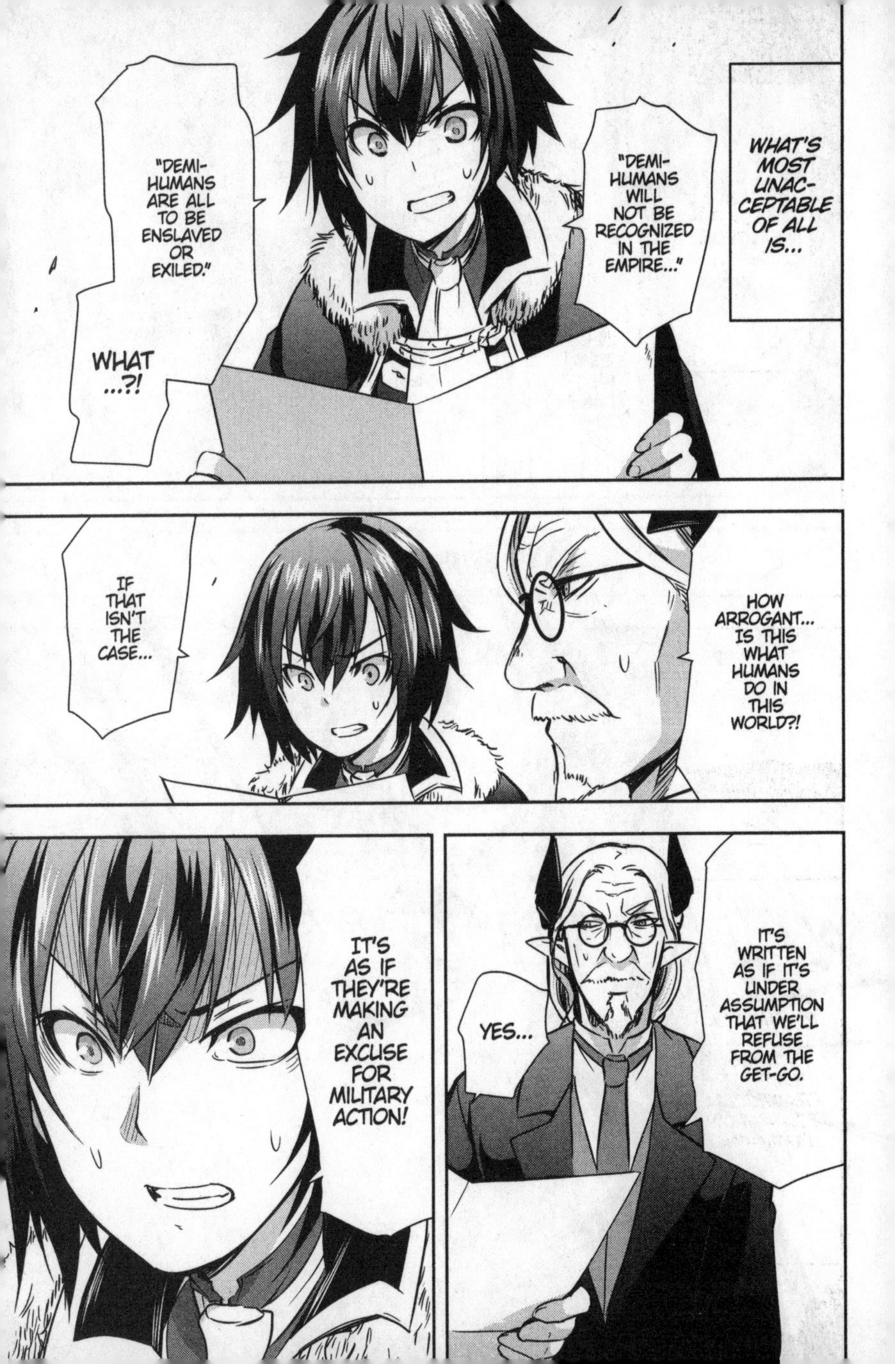
WHAT'S MOST UNACCEPTABLE OF ALL IS...
"DEMI-HUMANS WILL NOT BE RECOGNIZED IN THE EMPIRE..."
"DEMI-HUMANS ARE ALL TO BE ENSLAVED OR EXILED."
WHAT ...?!
HOW ARROGANT... IS THIS WHAT HUMANS DO IN THIS WORLD?!
IF THAT ISN'T THE CASE...
IT'S WRITTEN AS IF IT'S UNDER ASSUMPTION THAT WE'LL REFUSE FROM THE GET-GO.
YES...
IT'S AS IF THEY'RE MAKING AN EXCUSE FOR MILITARY ACTION!

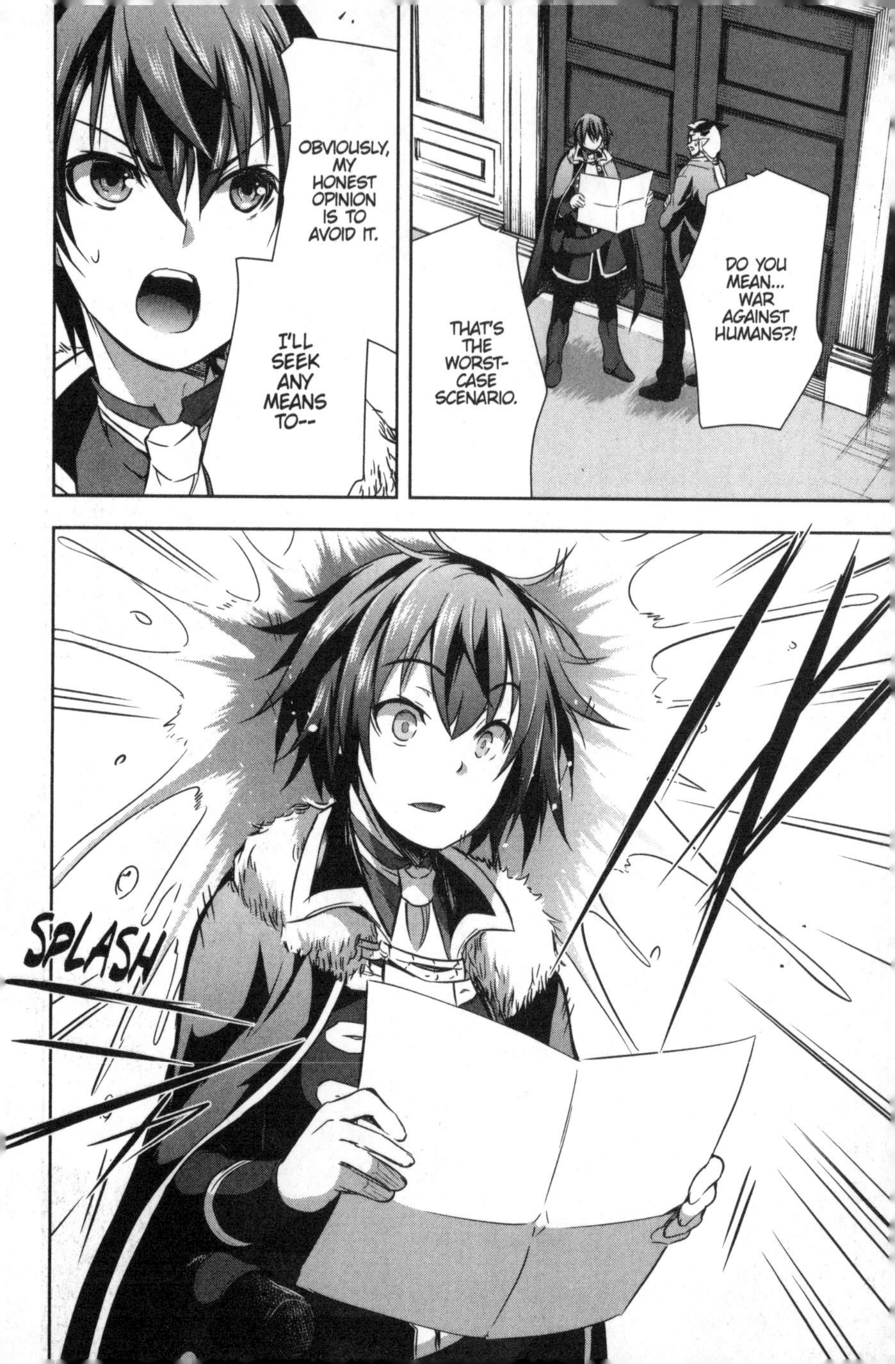
DO YOU MEAN... WAR AGAINST HUMANS?!
THAT'S THE WORST-CASE SCENARIO.
OBVIOUSLY, MY HONEST OPINION IS TO AVOID IT.
I'LL SEEK ANY MEANS TO--
SPLASH

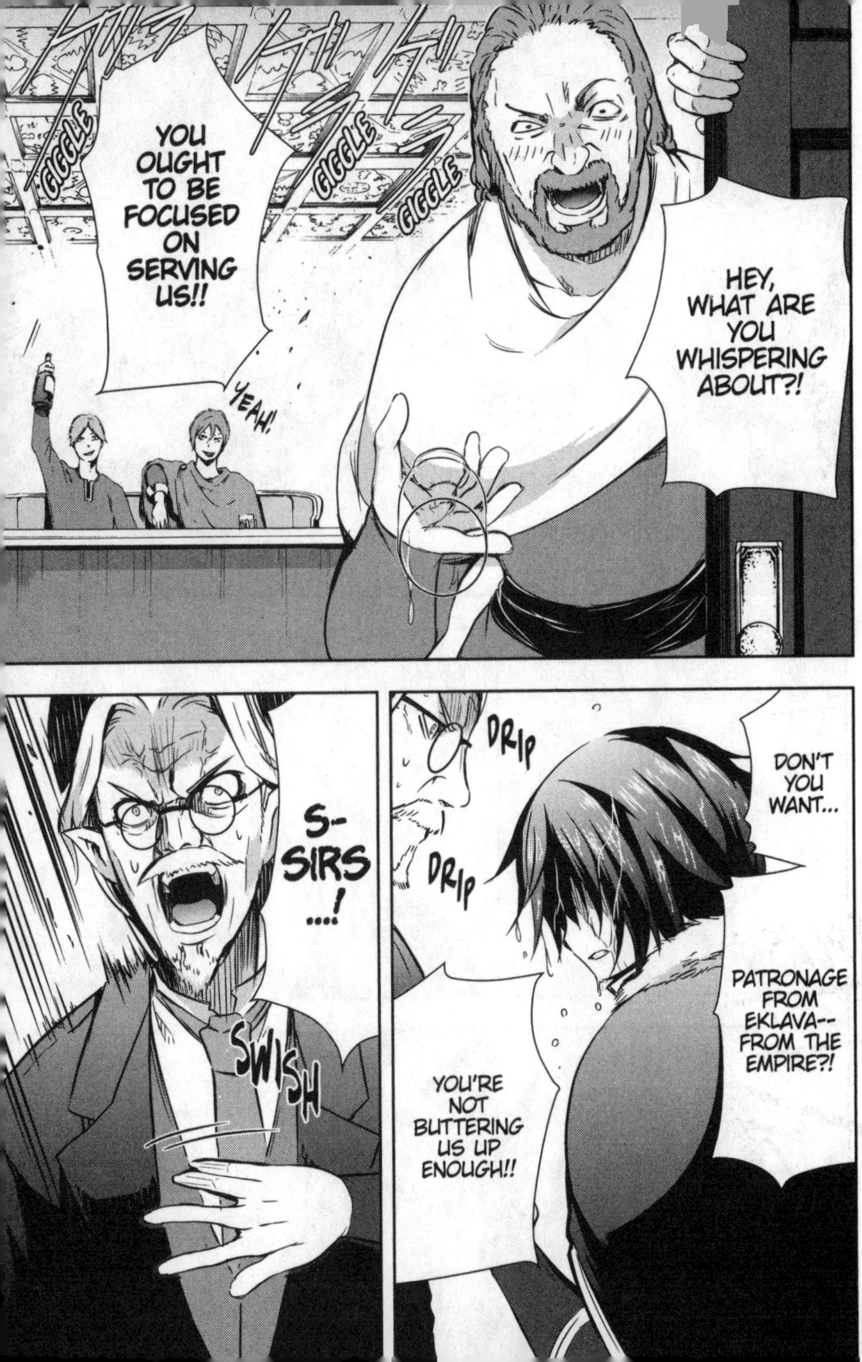
HEY, WHAT ARE YOU WHISPERING ABOUT?!
GIGGLE
GIGGLE
GIGGLE
YOU OUGHT TO BE FOCUSED ON SERVING US!!
YEAH!
DON'T YOU WANT...
DRIP
DRIP
PATRONAGE FROM EKLAVA-- FROM THE EMPIRE?!
YOU'RE NOT BUTTERING US UP ENOUGH!!
S-SIRS ...!
SWISH

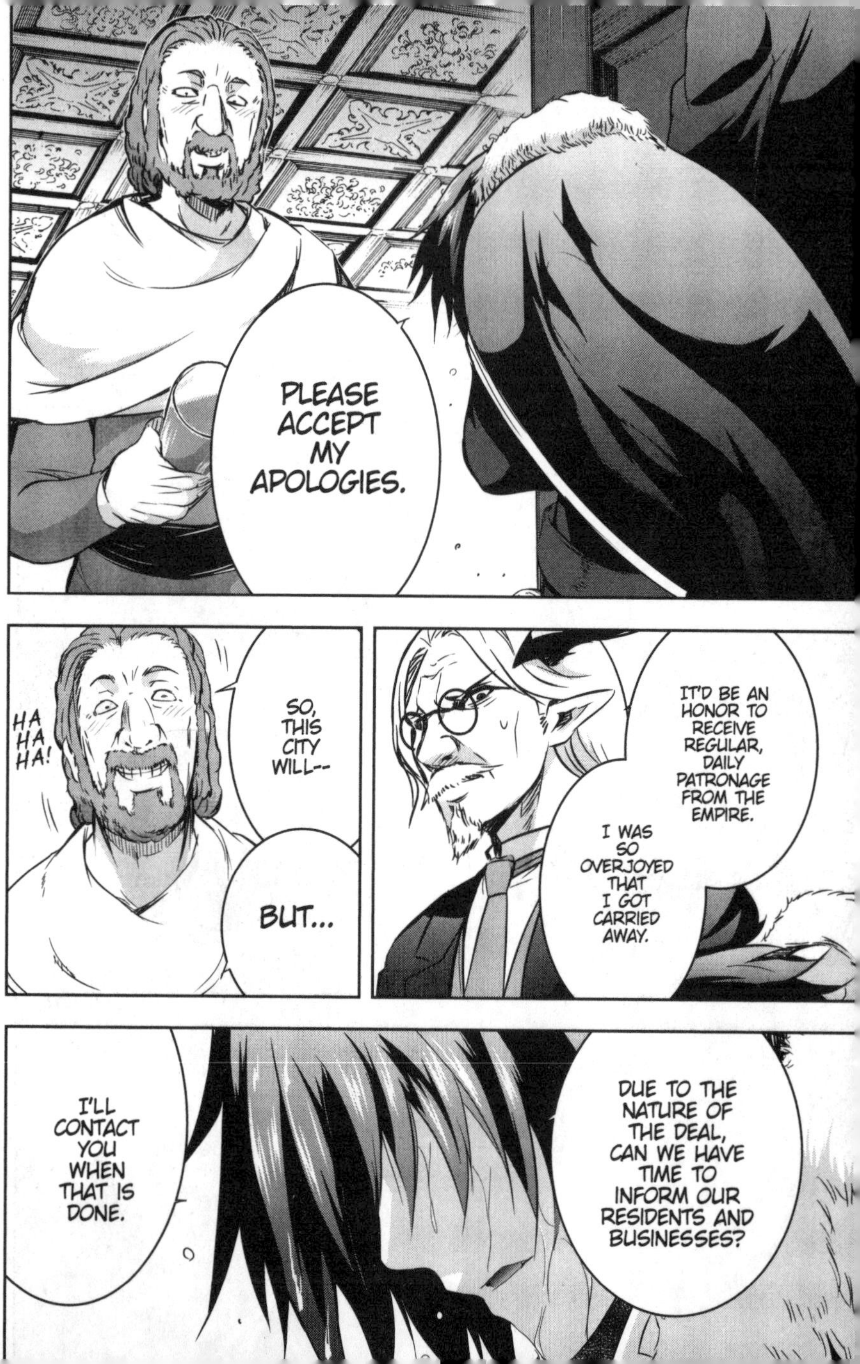
PLEASE ACCEPT MY APOLOGIES.
IT'D BE AN HONOR TO RECEIVE REGULAR, DAILY PATRONAGE FROM THE EMPIRE.
I WAS SO OVERJOYED THAT I GOT CARRIED AWAY.
HA HA HA!
SO, THIS CITY WILL--
BUT...
DUE TO THE NATURE OF THE DEAL, CAN WE HAVE TIME TO INFORM OUR RESIDENTS AND BUSINESSES?
I'LL CONTACT YOU WHEN THAT IS DONE.

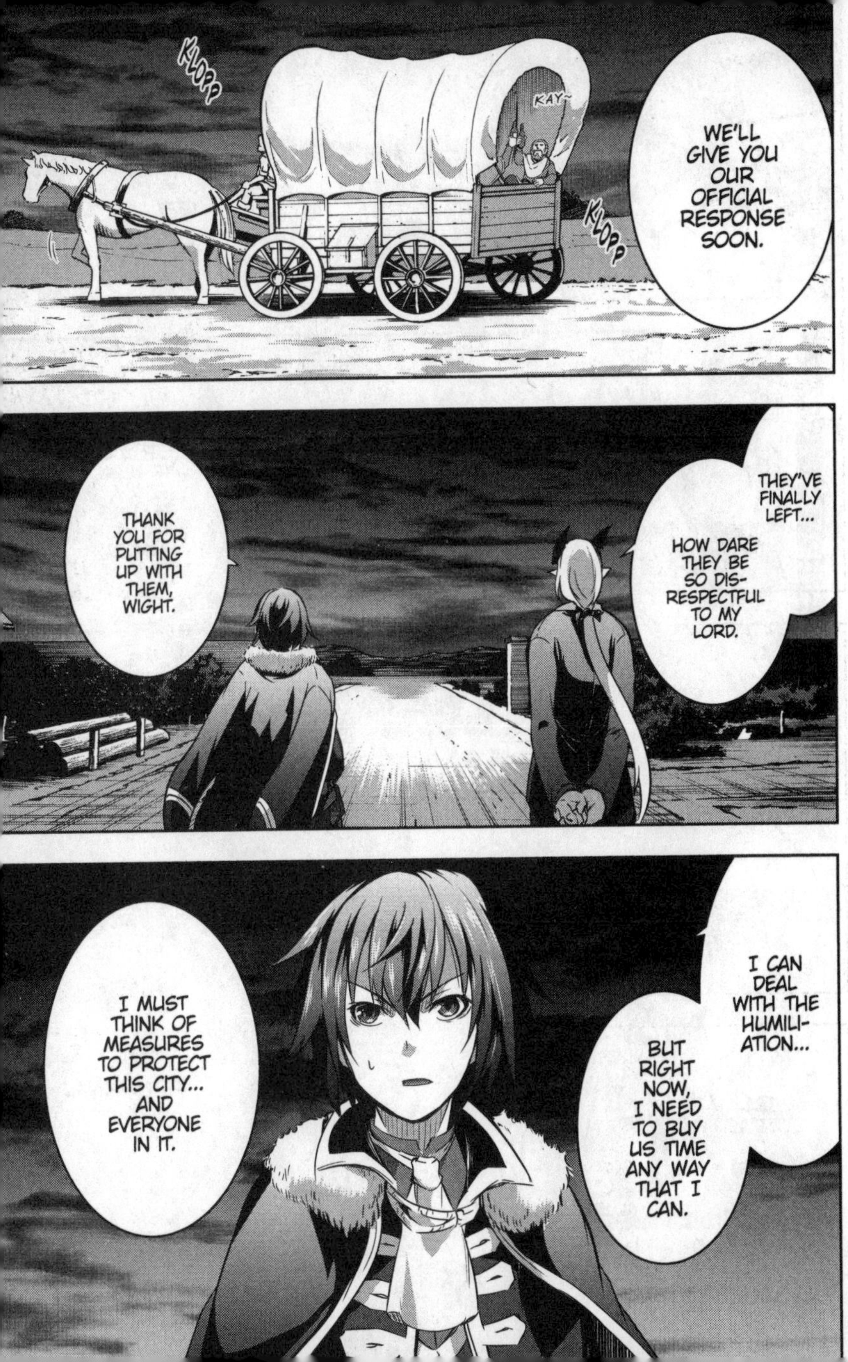
KLOPP
KAY~
KLOPP
WE'LL GIVE YOU OUR OFFICIAL RESPONSE SOON.
THEY'VE FINALLY LEFT...
HOW DARE THEY BE SO DIS-RESPECTFUL TO MY LORD.
THANK YOU FOR PUTTING UP WITH THEM, WIGHT.
I CAN DEAL WITH THE HUMILI-ATION...
BUT RIGHT NOW, I NEED TO BUY US TIME ANY WAY THAT I CAN.
I MUST THINK OF MEASURES TO PROTECT THIS CITY... AND EVERYONE IN IT.

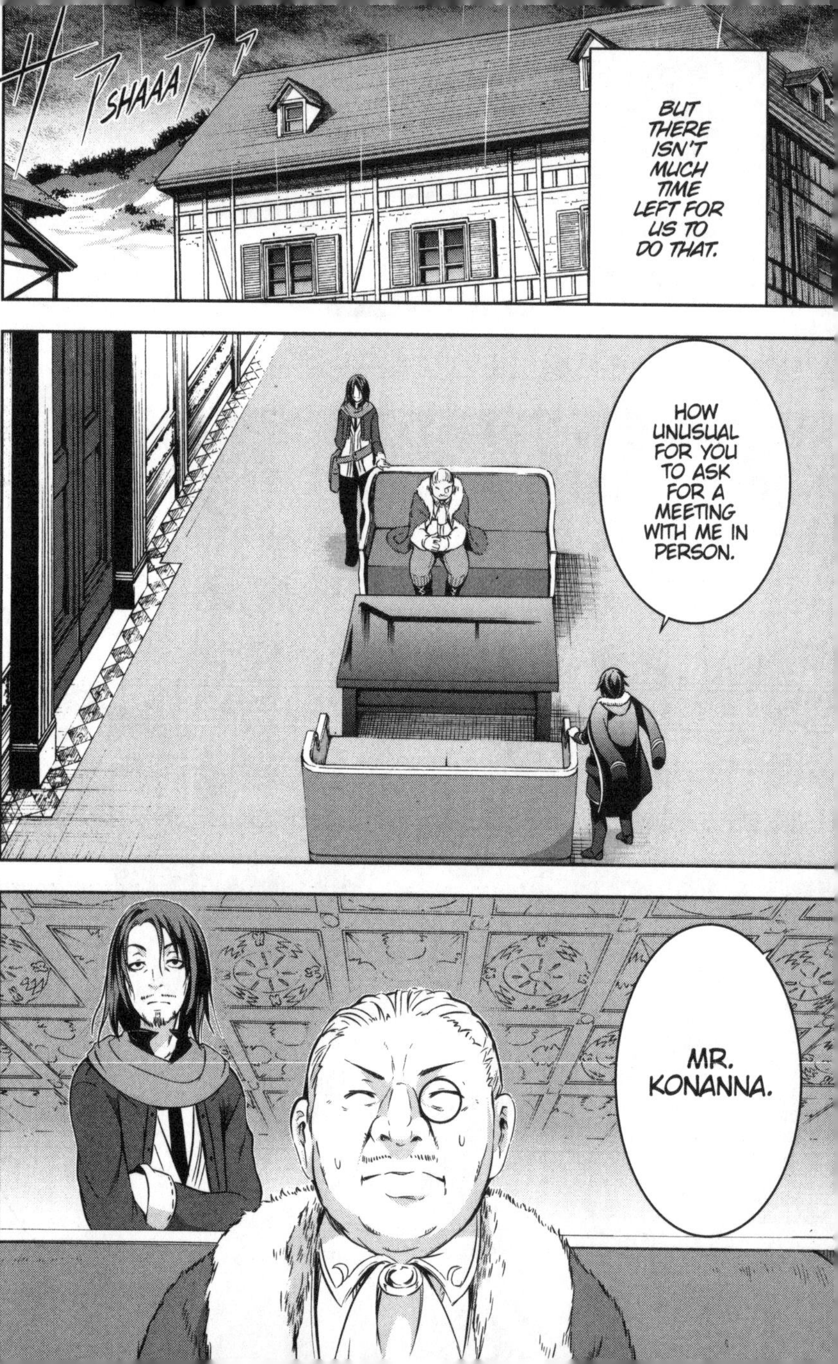
SHAAA
BUT THERE ISN'T MUCH TIME LEFT FOR US TO DO THAT.
HOW UNUSUAL FOR YOU TO ASK FOR A MEETING WITH ME IN PERSON.
MR. KONANNA.

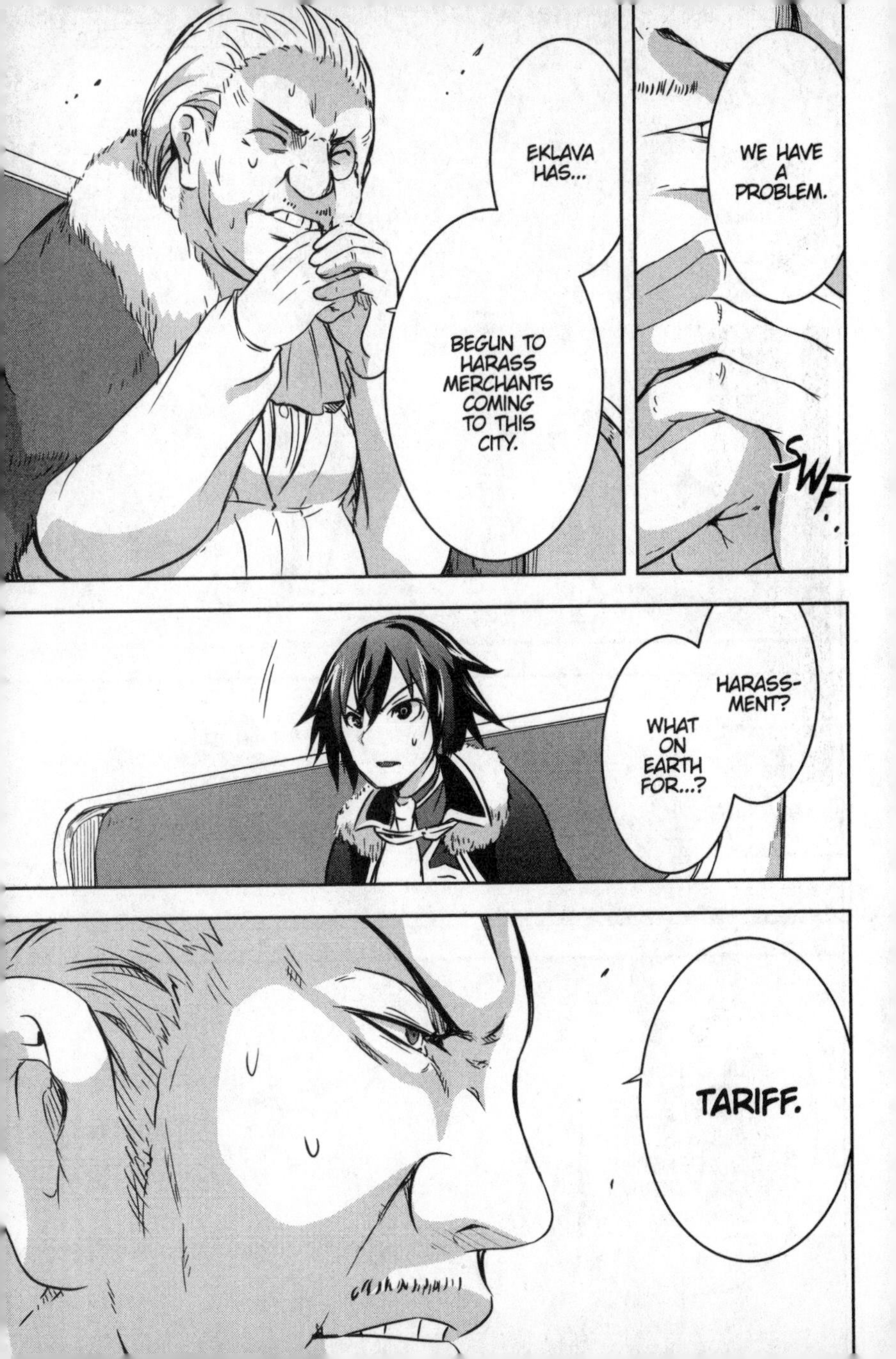
WE HAVE A PROBLEM.
SWF...
EKLAVA HAS...
BEGUN TO HARASS MERCHANTS COMING TO THIS CITY.
HARASS-MENT?
WHAT ON EARTH FOR...?
TARIFF.

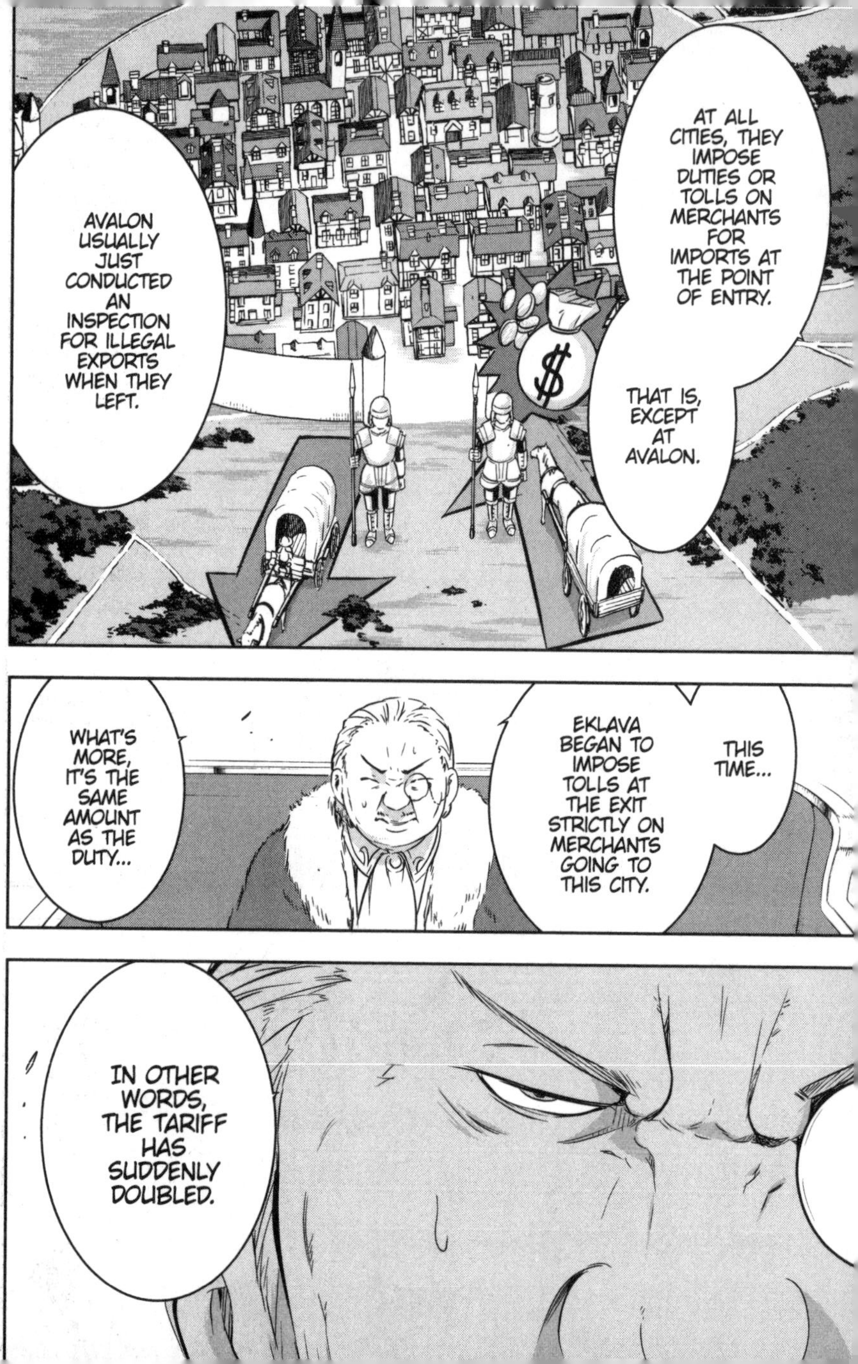
AT ALL CITIES, THEY IMPOSE DUTIES OR TOLLS ON MERCHANTS FOR IMPORTS AT THE POINT OF ENTRY.
THAT IS, EXCEPT AT AVALON.
AVALON USUALLY JUST CONDUCTED AN INSPECTION FOR ILLEGAL EXPORTS WHEN THEY LEFT.
$
THIS TIME...
EKLAVA BEGAN TO IMPOSE TOLLS AT THE EXIT STRICTLY ON MERCHANTS GOING TO THIS CITY.
WHAT'S MORE, IT'S THE SAME AMOUNT AS THE DUTY...
IN OTHER WORDS, THE TARIFF HAS SUDDENLY DOUBLED.

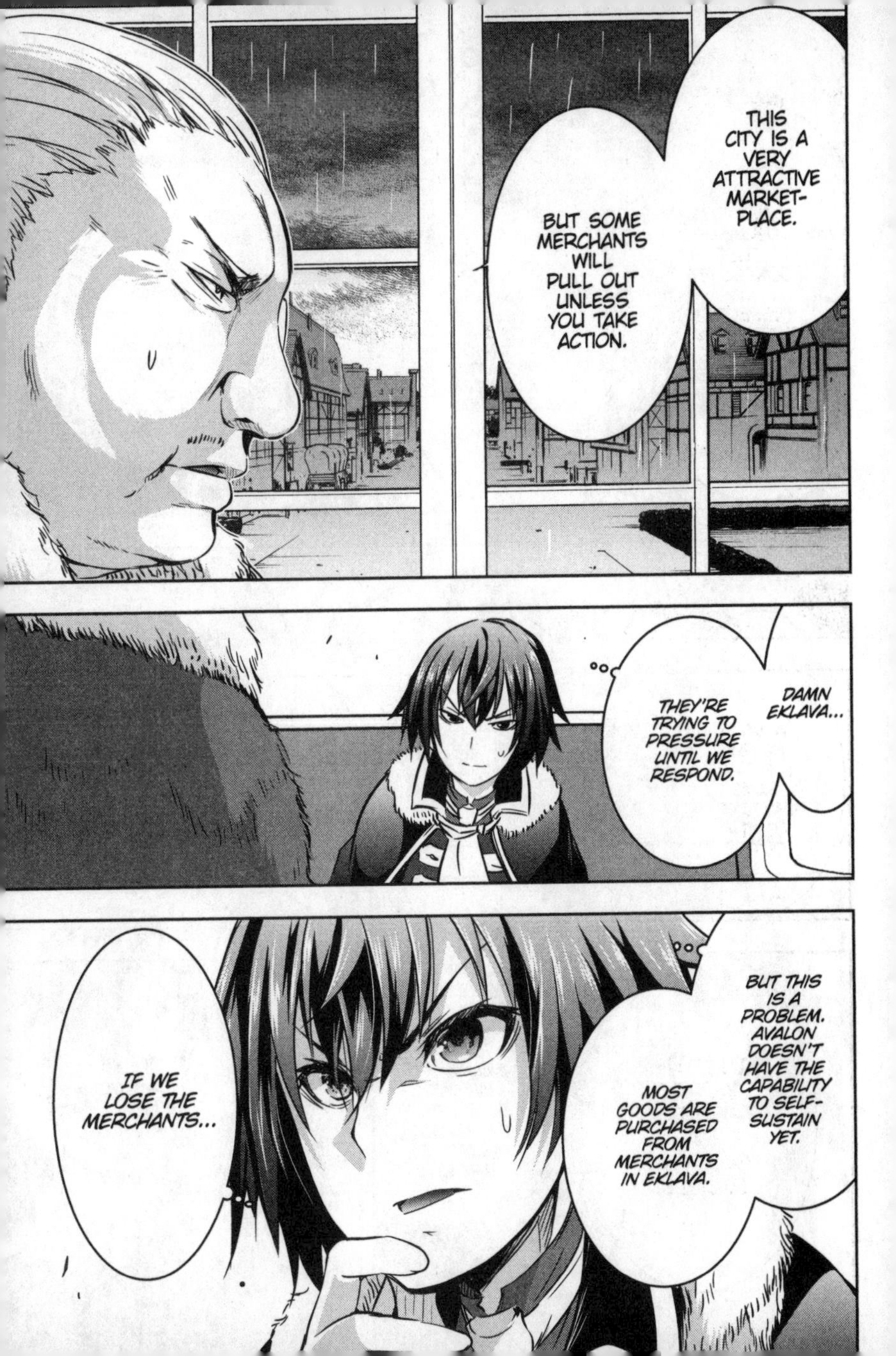
THIS CITY IS A VERY ATTRACTIVE MARKET-PLACE.
BUT SOME MERCHANTS WILL PULL OUT UNLESS YOU TAKE ACTION.
DAMN EKLAVA...
THEY'RE TRYING TO PRESSURE UNTIL WE RESPOND.
BUT THIS IS A PROBLEM. AVALON DOESN'T HAVE THE CAPABILITY TO SELF-SUSTAIN YET.
MOST GOODS ARE PURCHASED FROM MERCHANTS IN EKLAVA.
IF WE LOSE THE MERCHANTS...

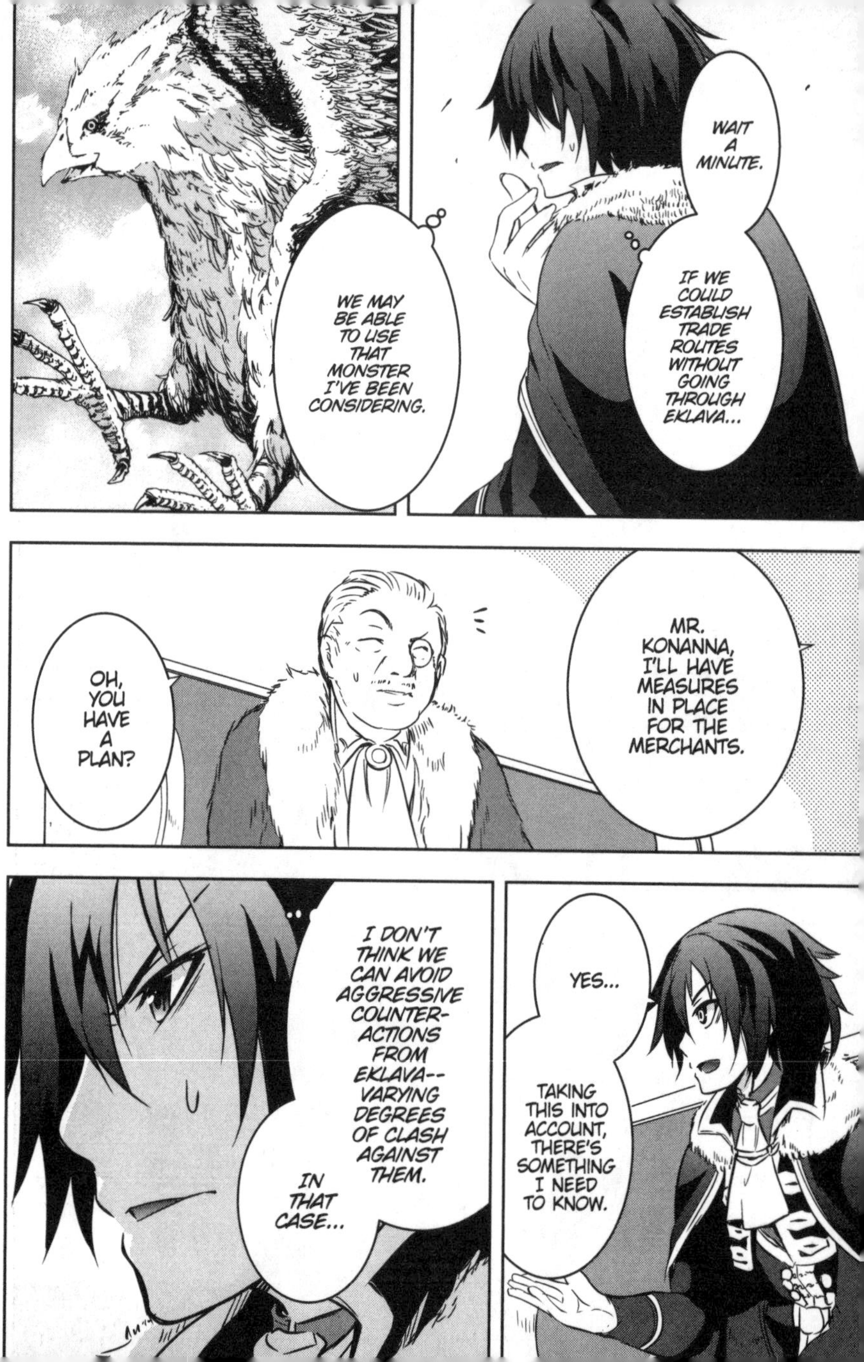
WAIT A MINUTE.
IF WE COULD ESTABLISH TRADE ROUTES WITHOUT GOING THROUGH EKLAVA...
WE MAY BE ABLE TO USE THAT MONSTER I'VE BEEN CONSIDERING.
MR. KONANNA, I'LL HAVE MEASURES IN PLACE FOR THE MERCHANTS.
OH, YOU HAVE A PLAN?
YES...
TAKING THIS INTO ACCOUNT, THERE'S SOMETHING I NEED TO KNOW.
...
I DON'T THINK WE CAN AVOID AGGRESSIVE COUNTER-ACTIONS FROM EKLAVA--VARYING DEGREES OF CLASH AGAINST THEM.
IN THAT CASE...

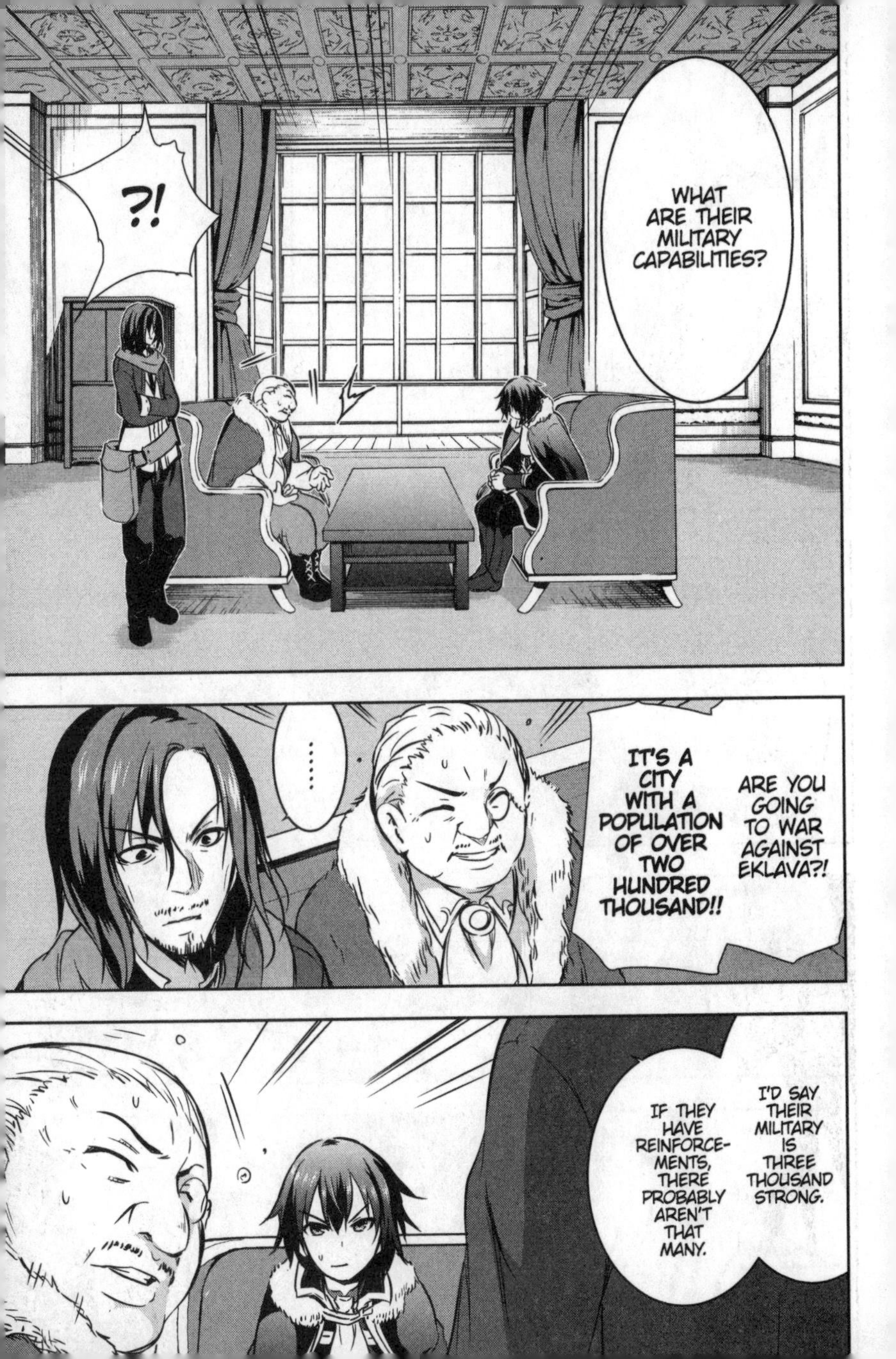
WHAT ARE THEIR MILITARY CAPABILITIES?
?!
ARE YOU GOING TO WAR AGAINST EKLAVA?!
IT'S A CITY WITH A POPULATION OF OVER TWO HUNDRED THOUSAND!!
......
I'D SAY THEIR MILITARY IS THREE THOUSAND STRONG.
IF THEY HAVE REINFORCE-MENTS, THERE PROBABLY AREN'T THAT MANY.

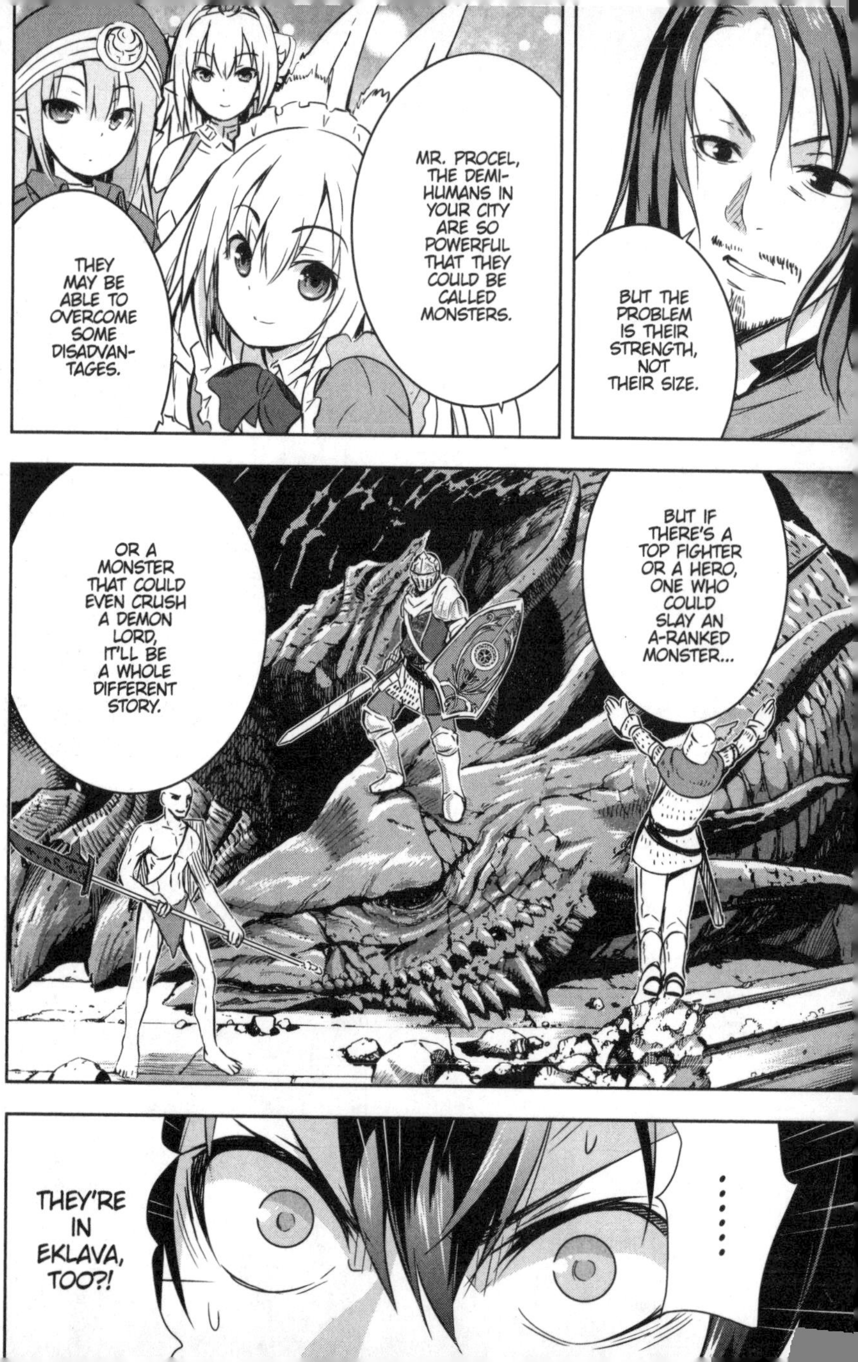
BUT THE PROBLEM IS THEIR STRENGTH, NOT THEIR SIZE.
MR. PROCEL, THE DEMI-HUMANS IN YOUR CITY ARE SO POWERFUL THAT THEY COULD BE CALLED MONSTERS.
THEY MAY BE ABLE TO OVERCOME SOME DISADVANTAGES.
BUT IF THERE'S A TOP FIGHTER OR A HERO, ONE WHO COULD SLAY AN A-RANKED MONSTER...
OR A MONSTER THAT COULD EVEN CRUSH A DEMON LORD, IT'LL BE A WHOLE DIFFERENT STORY.
......
THEY'RE IN EKLAVA, TOO?!

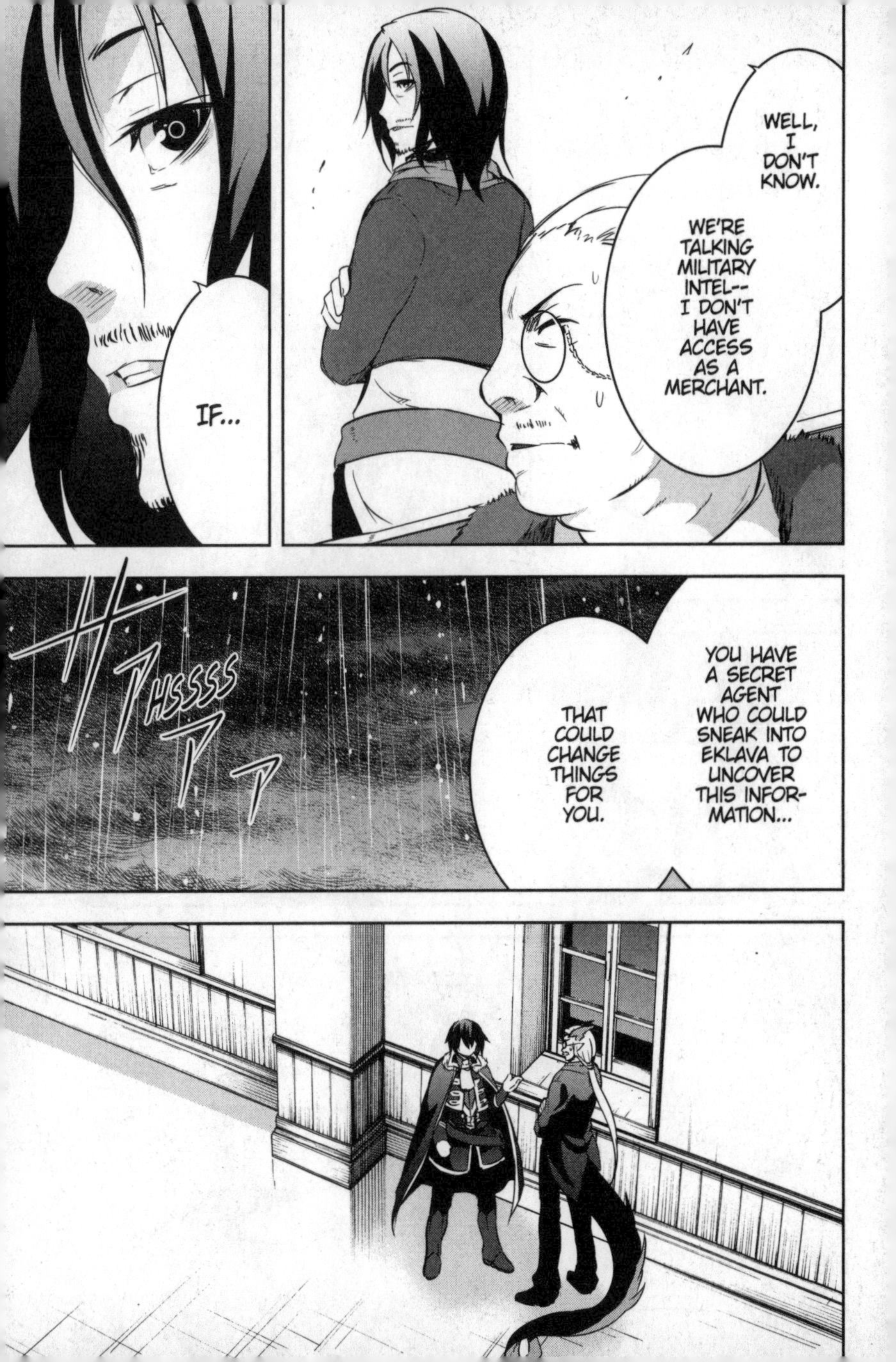
WELL, I DON'T KNOW.
WE'RE TALKING MILITARY INTEL-- I DON'T HAVE ACCESS AS A MERCHANT.
IF...
HSSSSS
YOU HAVE A SECRET AGENT WHO COULD SNEAK INTO EKLAVA TO UNCOVER THIS INFOR-MATION...
THAT COULD CHANGE THINGS FOR YOU.

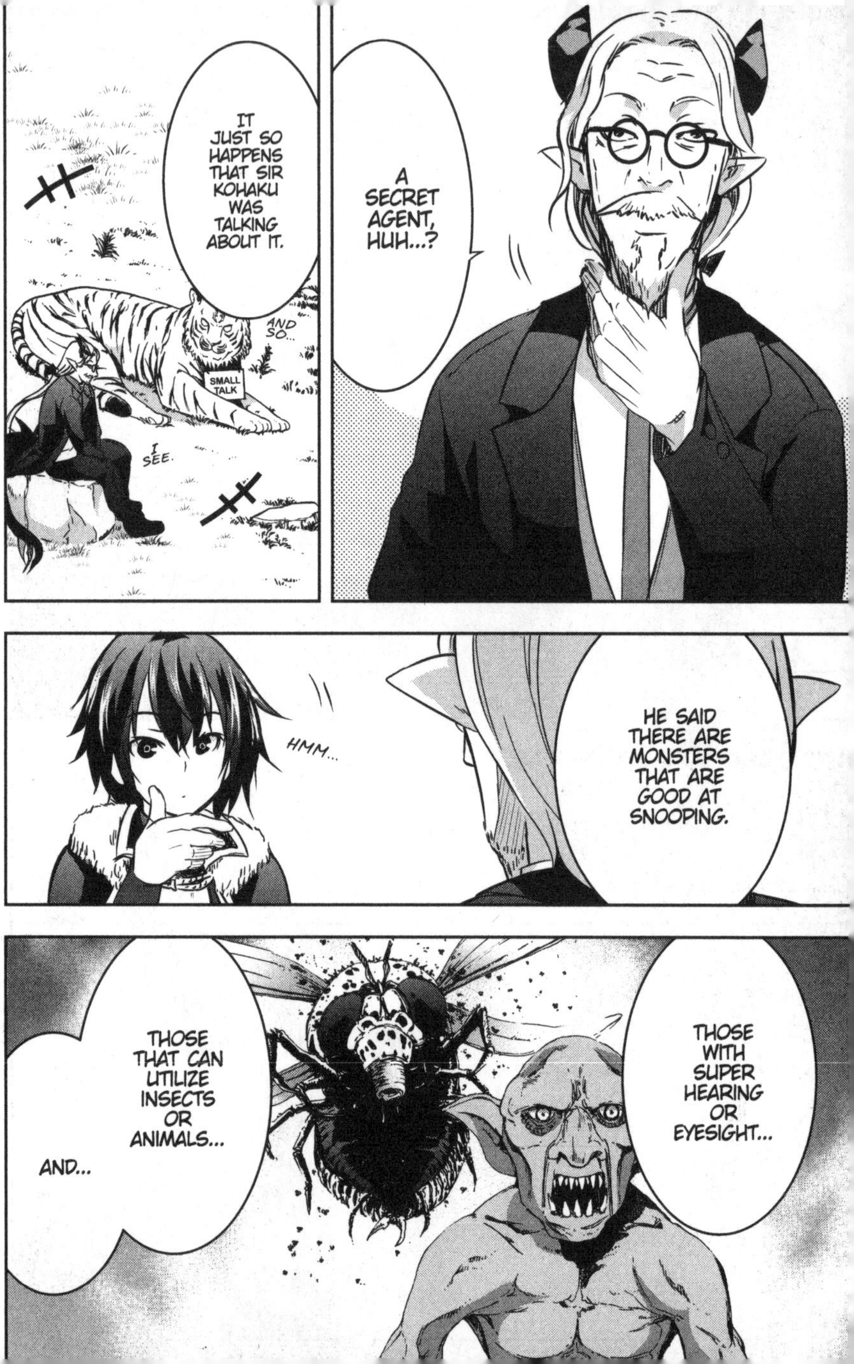
A SECRET AGENT, HUH...?
IT JUST SO HAPPENS THAT SIR KOHAKU WAS TALKING ABOUT IT.
AND SO...
SMALL TALK
I SEE.
HE SAID THERE ARE MONSTERS THAT ARE GOOD AT SNOOPING.
HMM...
THOSE WITH SUPER HEARING OR EYESIGHT...
THOSE THAT CAN UTILIZE INSECTS OR ANIMALS...
AND...

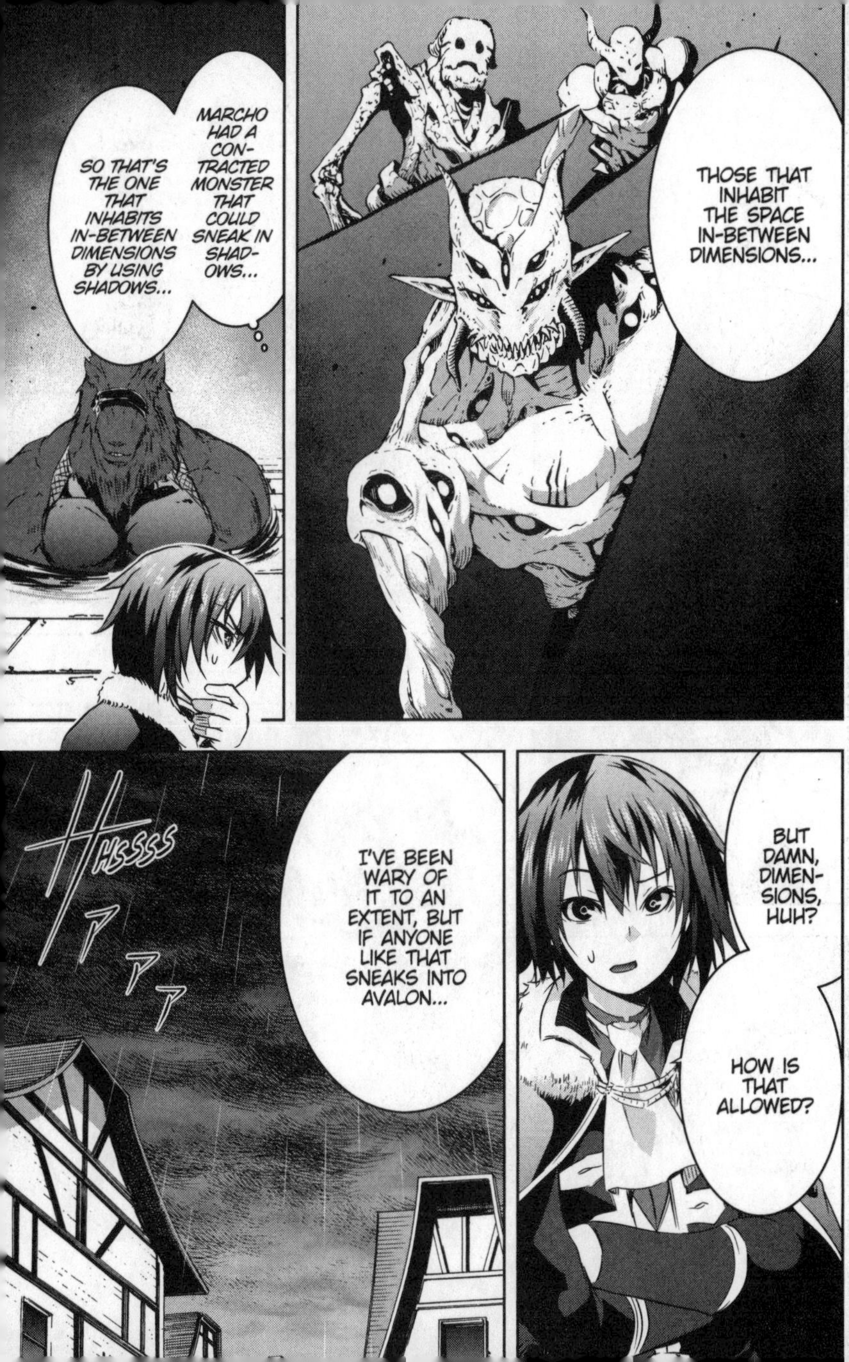
THOSE THAT INHABIT THE SPACE IN-BETWEEN DIMENSIONS...
MARCHO HAD A CONTRACTED MONSTER THAT COULD SNEAK IN SHADOWS...
SO THAT'S THE ONE THAT INHABITS IN-BETWEEN DIMENSIONS BY USING SHADOWS...
BUT DAMN, DIMENSIONS, HUH?
HOW IS THAT ALLOWED?
I'VE BEEN WARY OF IT TO AN EXTENT, BUT IF ANYONE LIKE THAT SNEAKS INTO AVALON...
HSSSS
アアア

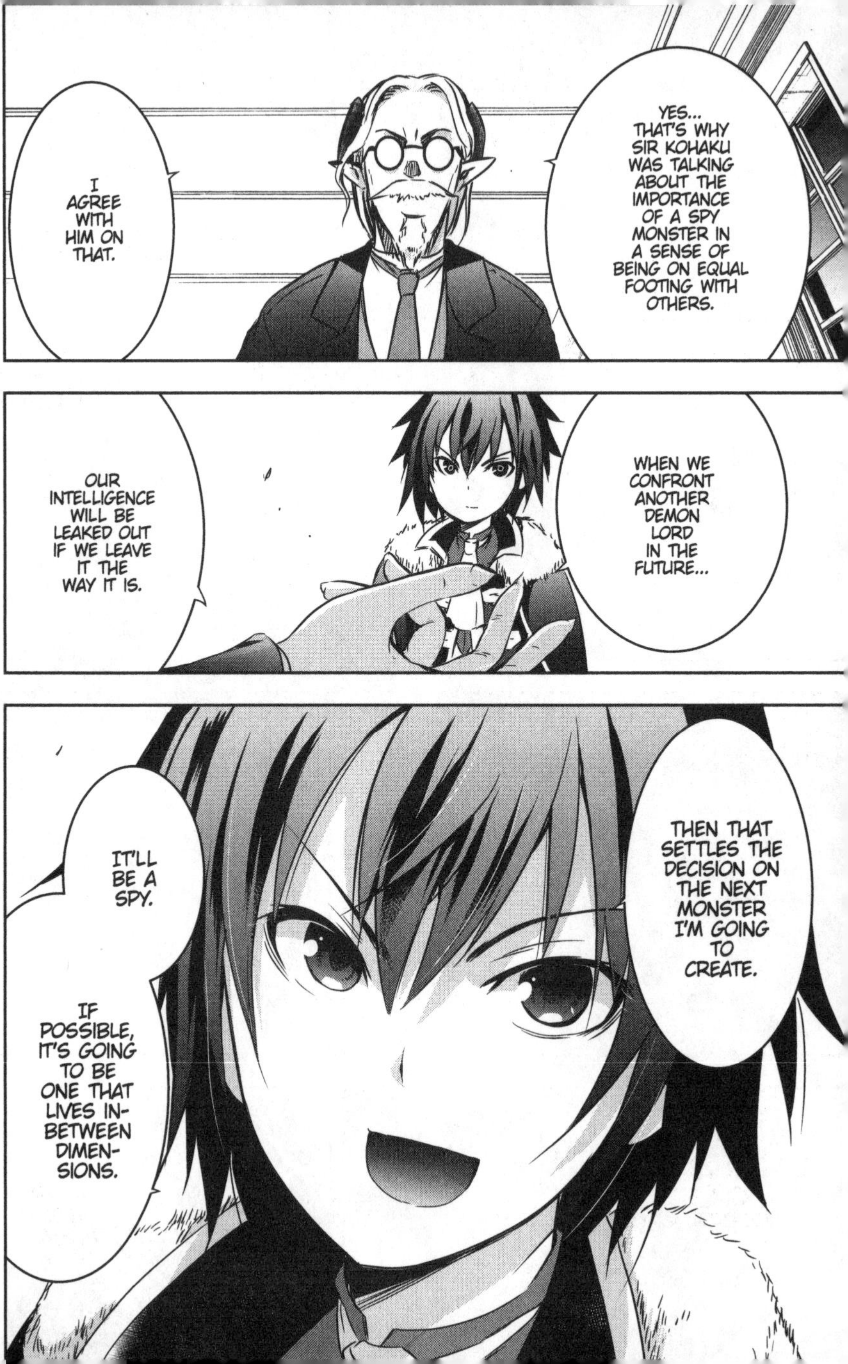
YES... THAT'S WHY SIR KOHAKU WAS TALKING ABOUT THE IMPORTANCE OF A SPY MONSTER IN A SENSE OF BEING ON EQUAL FOOTING WITH OTHERS.
I AGREE WITH HIM ON THAT.
WHEN WE CONFRONT ANOTHER DEMON LORD IN THE FUTURE...
OUR INTELLIGENCE WILL BE LEAKED OUT IF WE LEAVE IT THE WAY IT IS.
THEN THAT SETTLES THE DECISION ON THE NEXT MONSTER I'M GOING TO CREATE.
IT'LL BE A SPY.
IF POSSIBLE, IT'S GOING TO BE ONE THAT LIVES IN-BETWEEN DIMEN-SIONS.

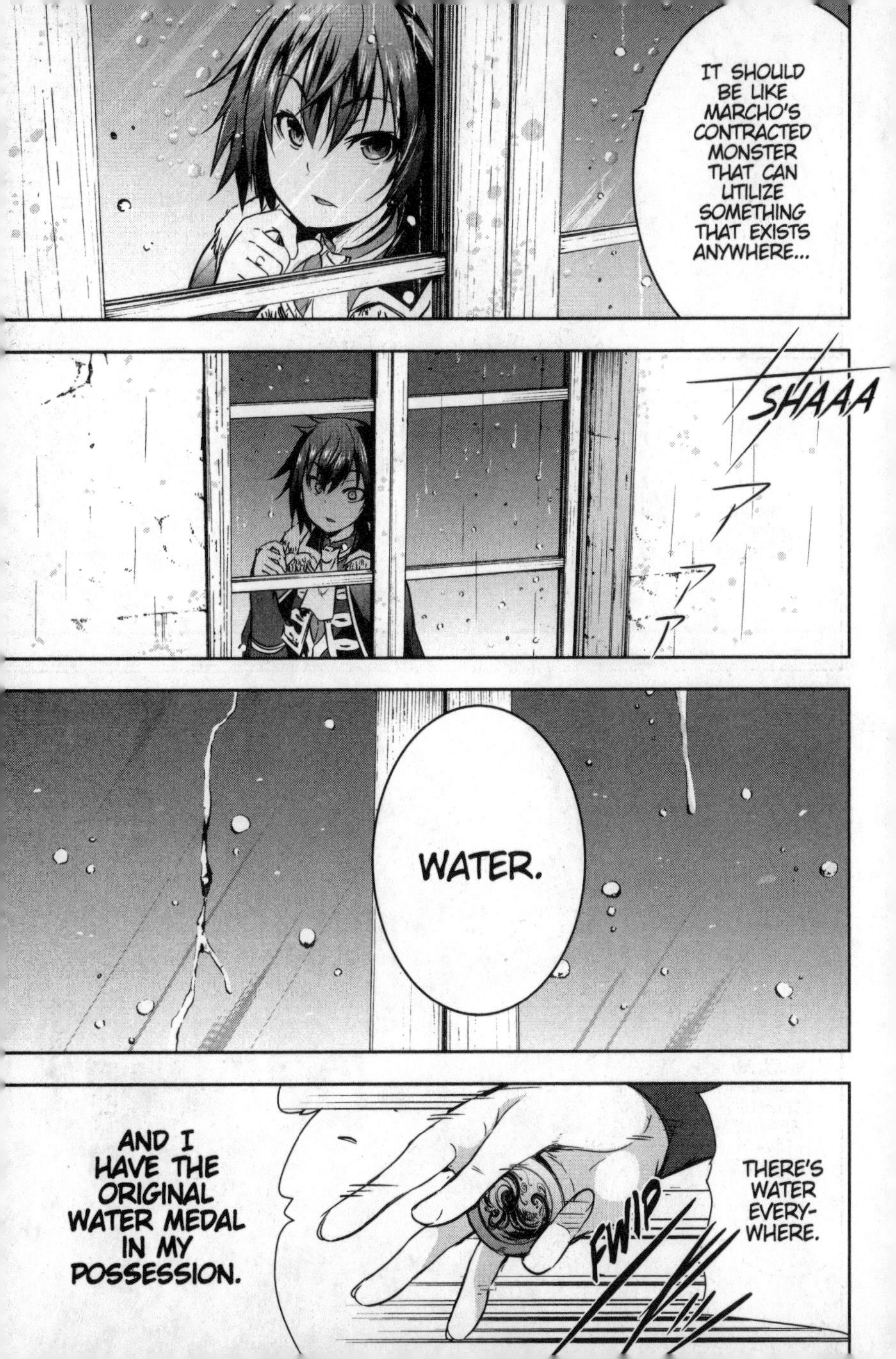
IT SHOULD BE LIKE MARCHO'S CONTRACTED MONSTER THAT CAN UTILIZE SOMETHING THAT EXISTS ANYWHERE...
SHAAA
WATER.
THERE'S WATER EVERY-WHERE.
AND I HAVE THE ORIGINAL WATER MEDAL IN MY POSSESSION.
FWIP

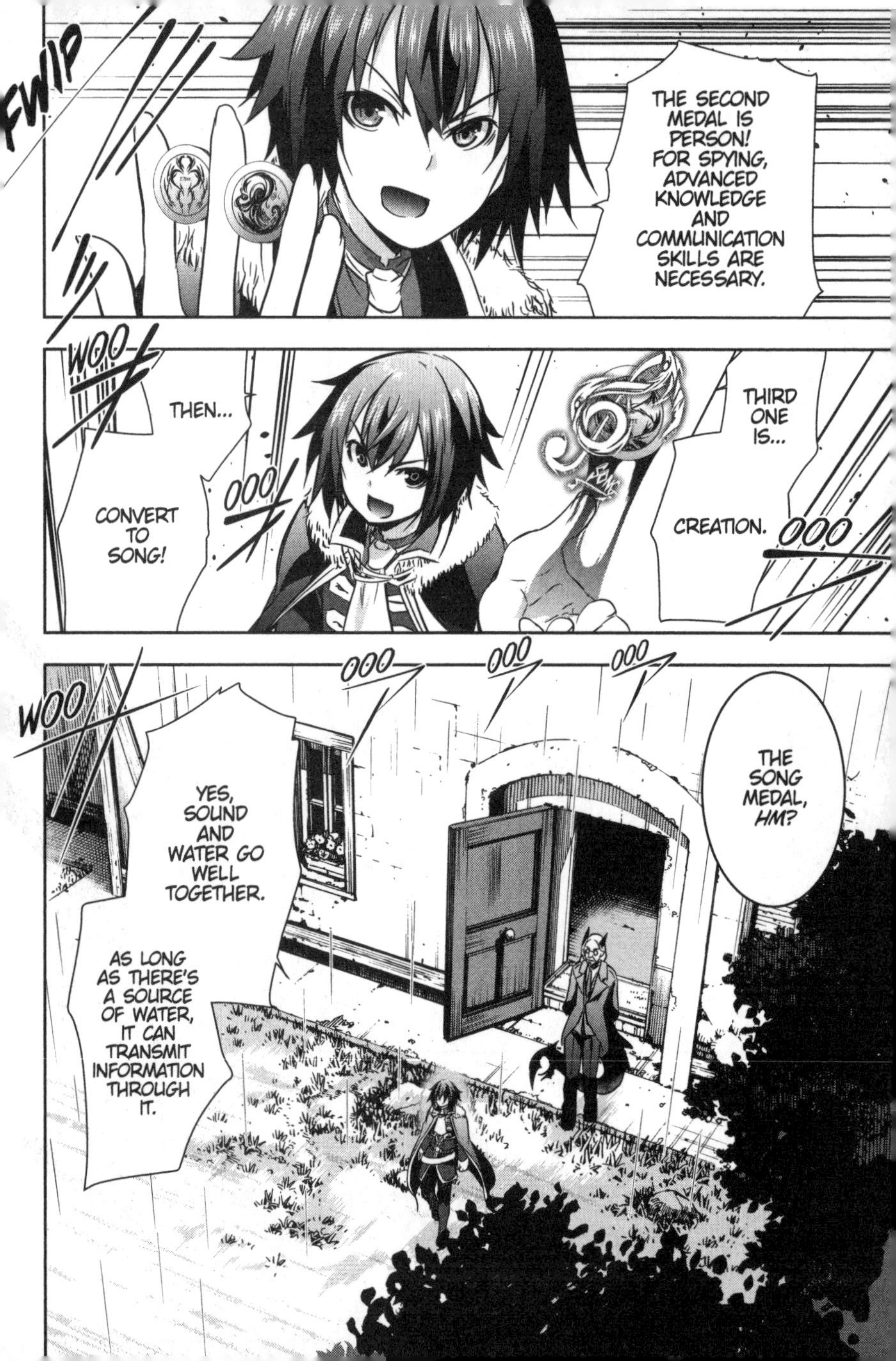
FWIP
THE SECOND MEDAL IS PERSON! FOR SPYING, ADVANCED KNOWLEDGE AND COMMUNICATION SKILLS ARE NECESSARY.
WOO
THIRD ONE IS...
CREATION.
OOO
THEN...
OOO
CONVERT TO SONG!
OOO
OOO
OOO
WOO
THE SONG MEDAL, HM?
YES, SOUND AND WATER GO WELL TOGETHER.
AS LONG AS THERE'S A SOURCE OF WATER, IT CAN TRANSMIT INFORMATION THROUGH IT.

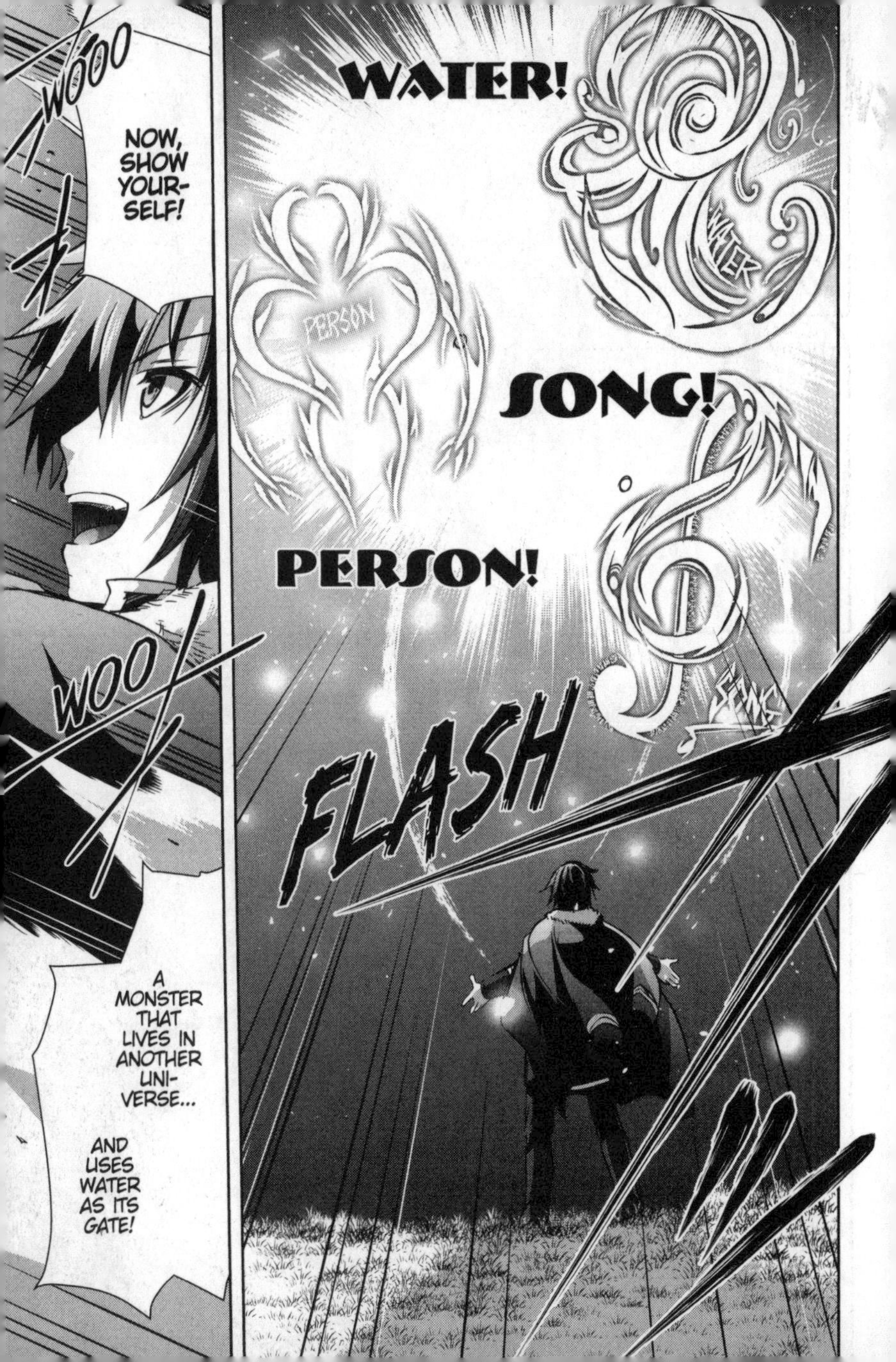

WATER!
WATER
SONG!
PERSON!
PERSON
SONG
FLASH
NOW, SHOW YOUR-SELF!
WOOO
WOO
A MONSTER THAT LIVES IN ANOTHER UNI-VERSE...
AND USES WATER AS ITS GATE!

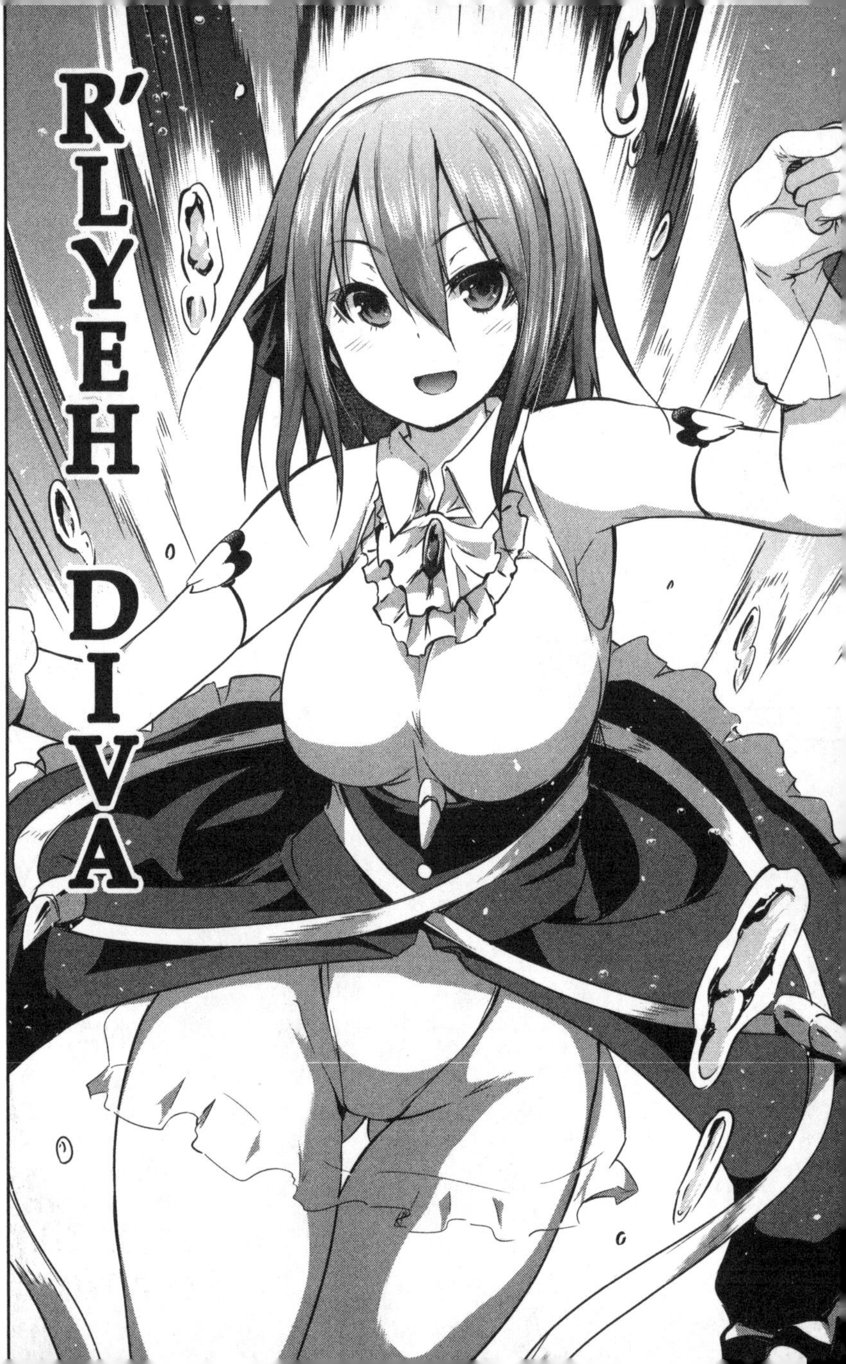
R'LYEH DIVA

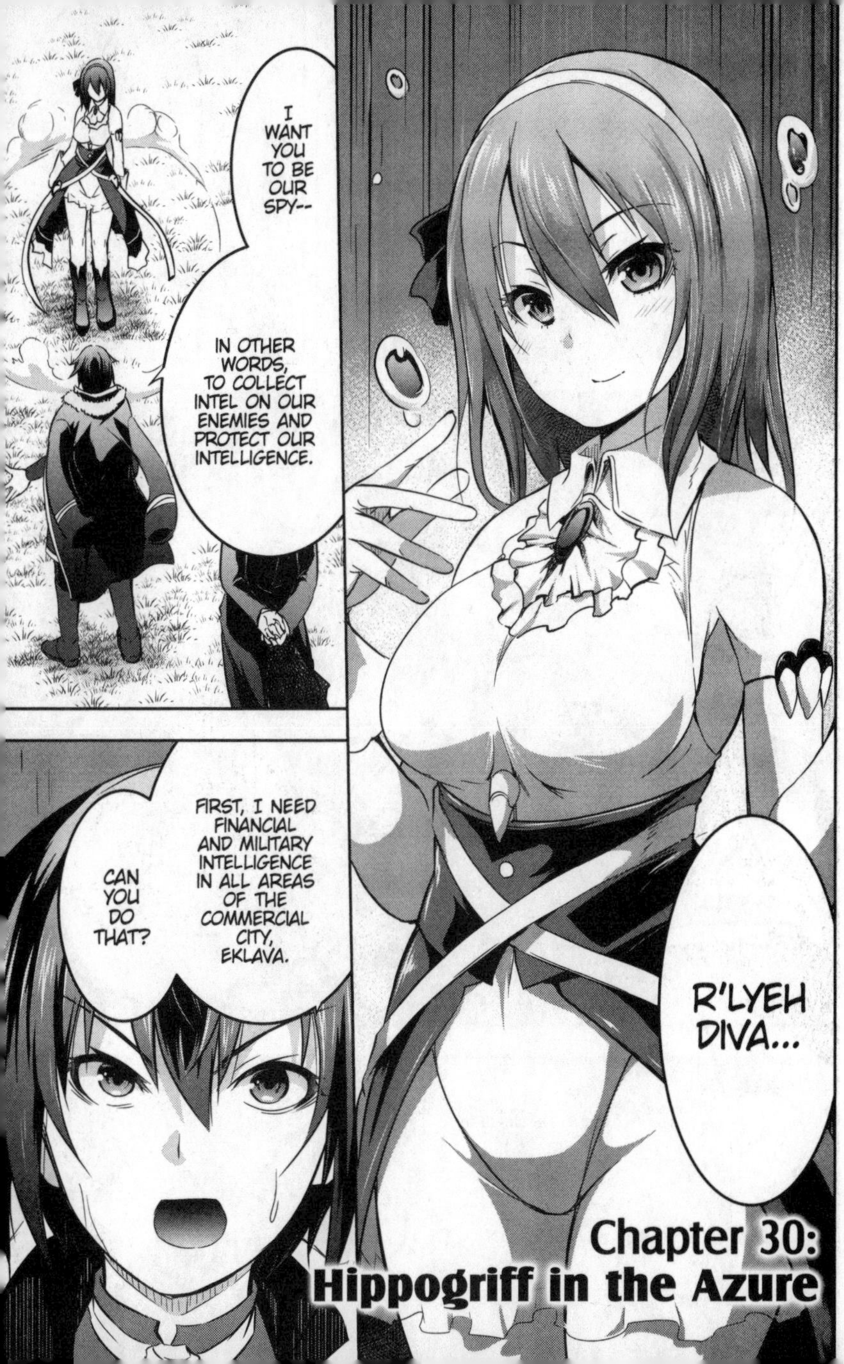
I WANT YOU TO BE OUR SPY--
IN OTHER WORDS, TO COLLECT INTEL ON OUR ENEMIES AND PROTECT OUR INTELLIGENCE.
FIRST, I NEED FINANCIAL AND MILITARY INTELLIGENCE IN ALL AREAS OF THE COMMERCIAL CITY, EKLAVA.
CAN YOU DO THAT?
R'LYEH DIVA...

Chapter 30: Hippogriff in the Azure

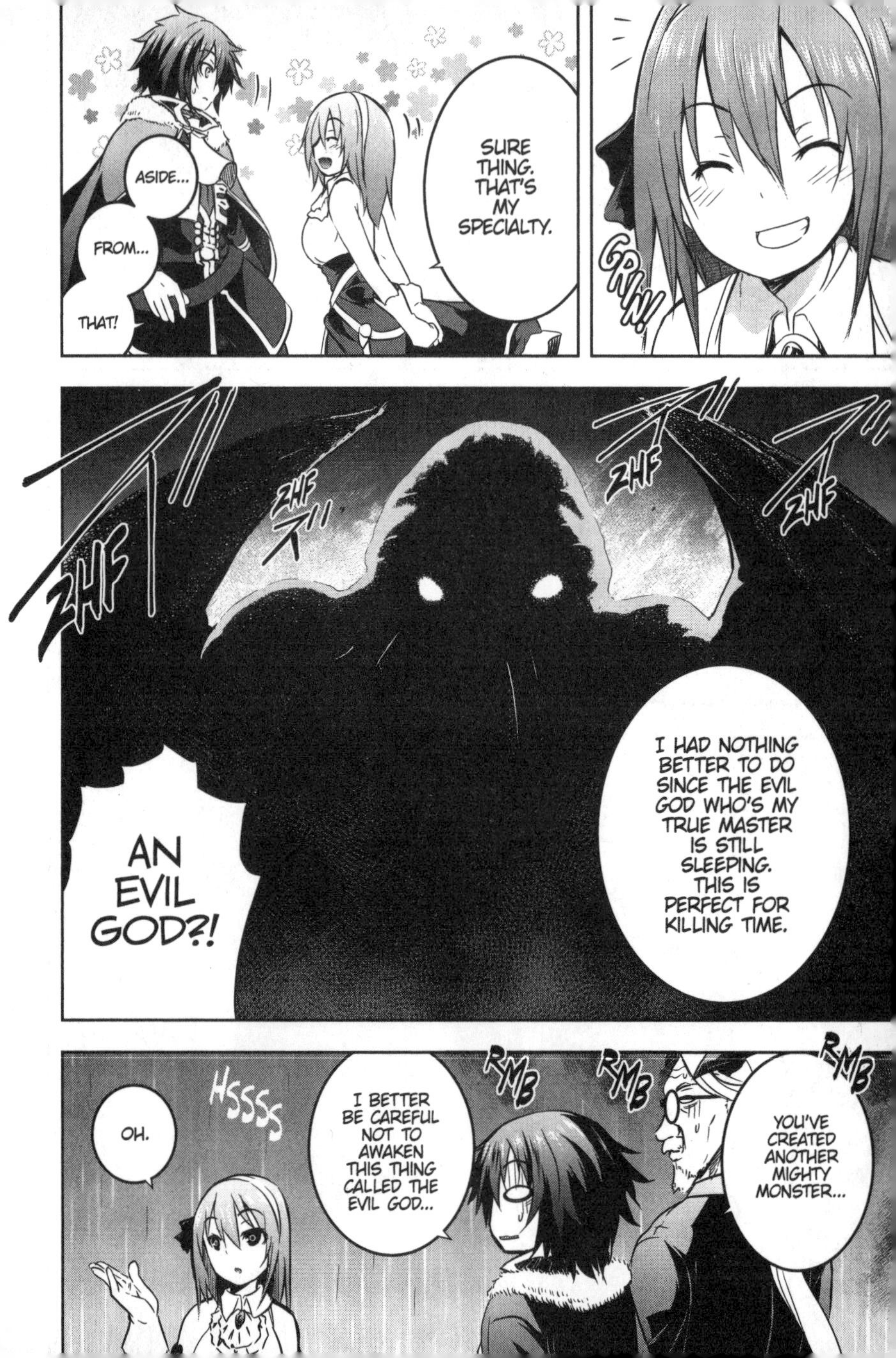
GRIN!
SURE THING. THAT'S MY SPECIALTY.
ASIDE...
FROM...
THAT!
ZHF
ZHF
ZHF
ZHF
I HAD NOTHING BETTER TO DO SINCE THE EVIL GOD WHO'S MY TRUE MASTER IS STILL SLEEPING. THIS IS PERFECT FOR KILLING TIME.
AN EVIL GOD?!
R-MB
YOU'VE CREATED ANOTHER MIGHTY MONSTER...
RMB
RMB
I BETTER BE CAREFUL NOT TO AWAKEN THIS THING CALLED THE EVIL GOD...
HSSSS
OH.

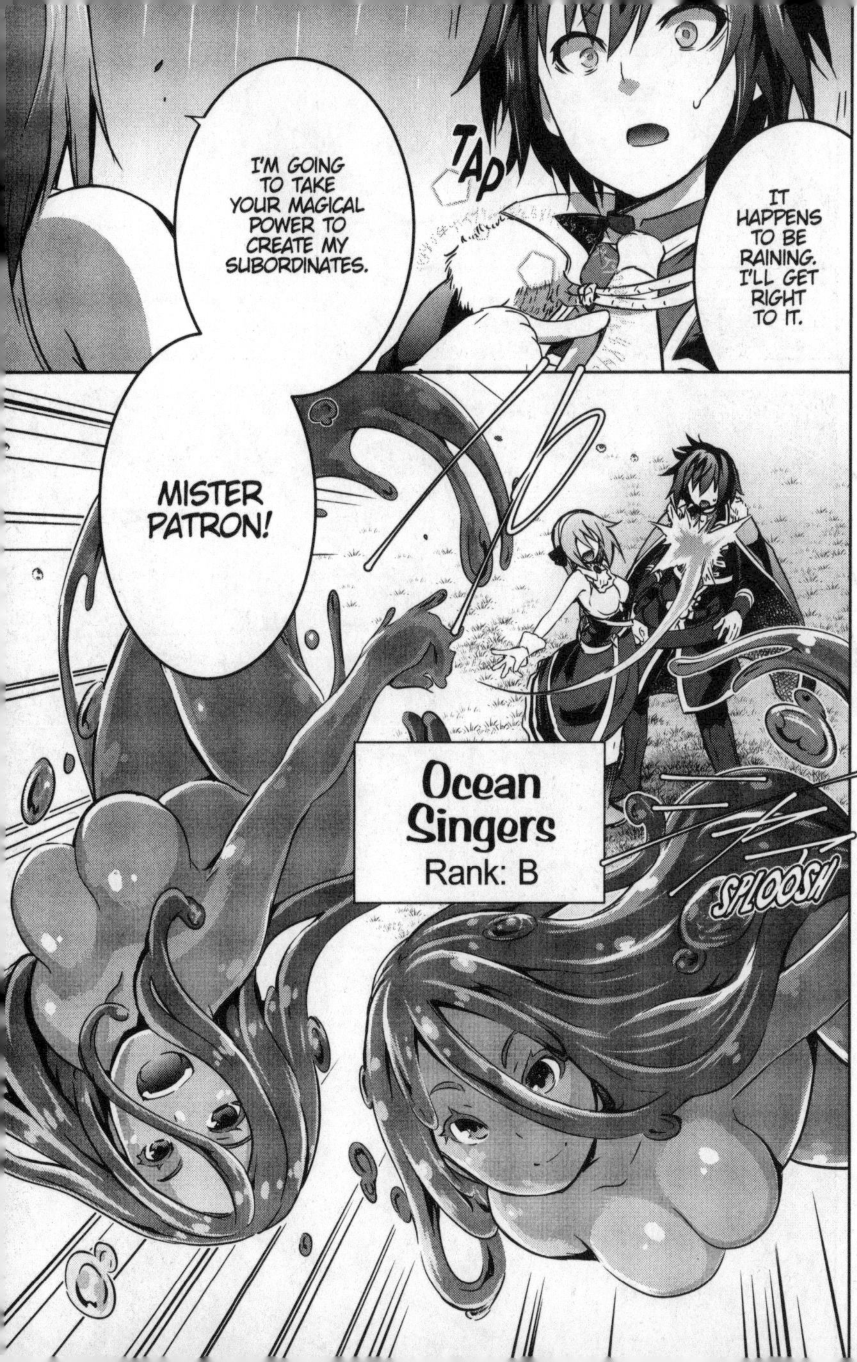
IT HAPPENS TO BE RAINING. I'LL GET RIGHT TO IT.
TAP
I'M GOING TO TAKE YOUR MAGICAL POWER TO CREATE MY SUBORDINATES.
MISTER PATRON!
Ocean Singers
Rank: B
SPLOOSH

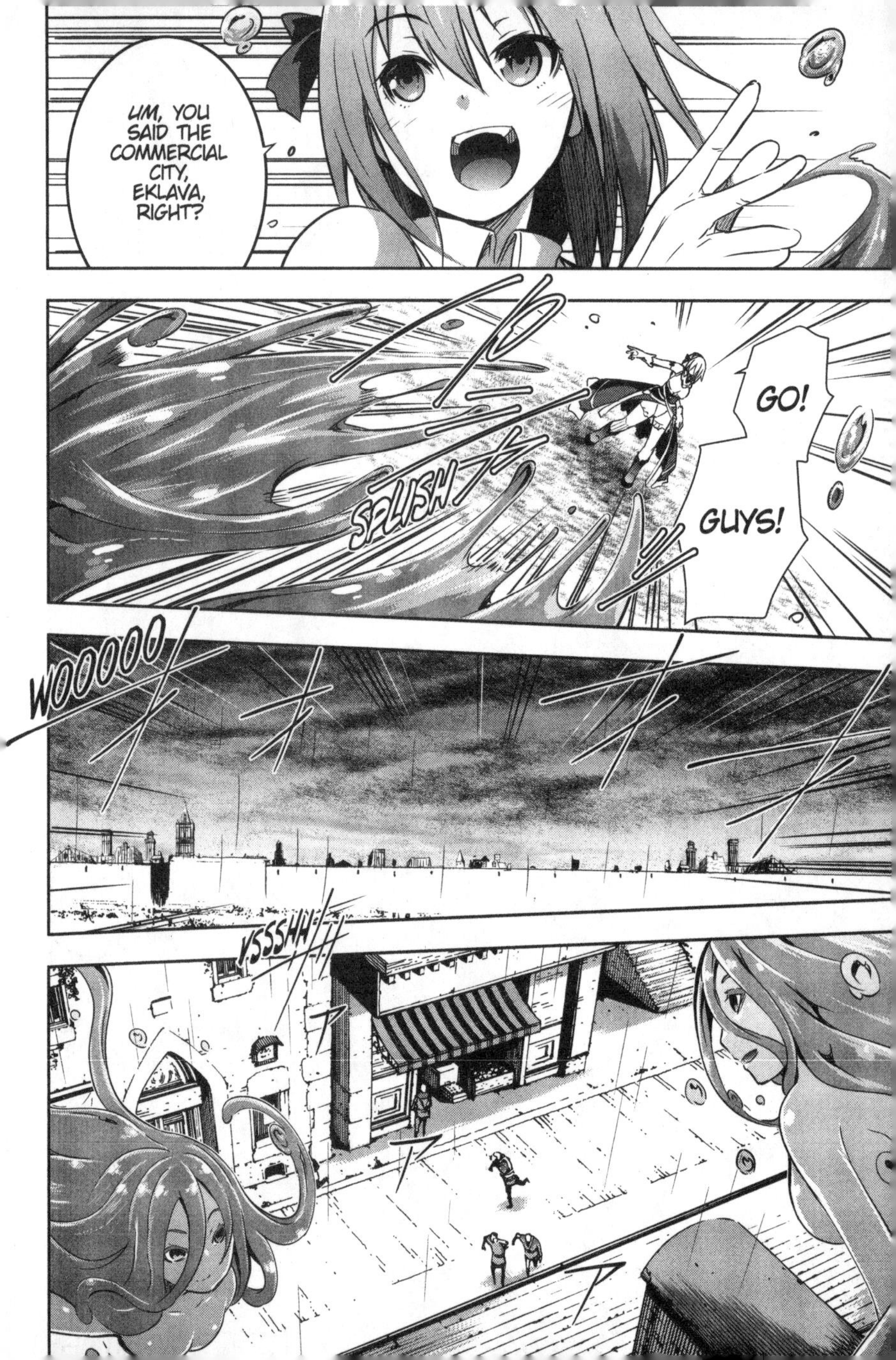
UM, YOU SAID THE COMMERCIAL CITY, EKLAVA, RIGHT?
GO!
GUYS!
SPLISH
WOOOOO
VSSSHH

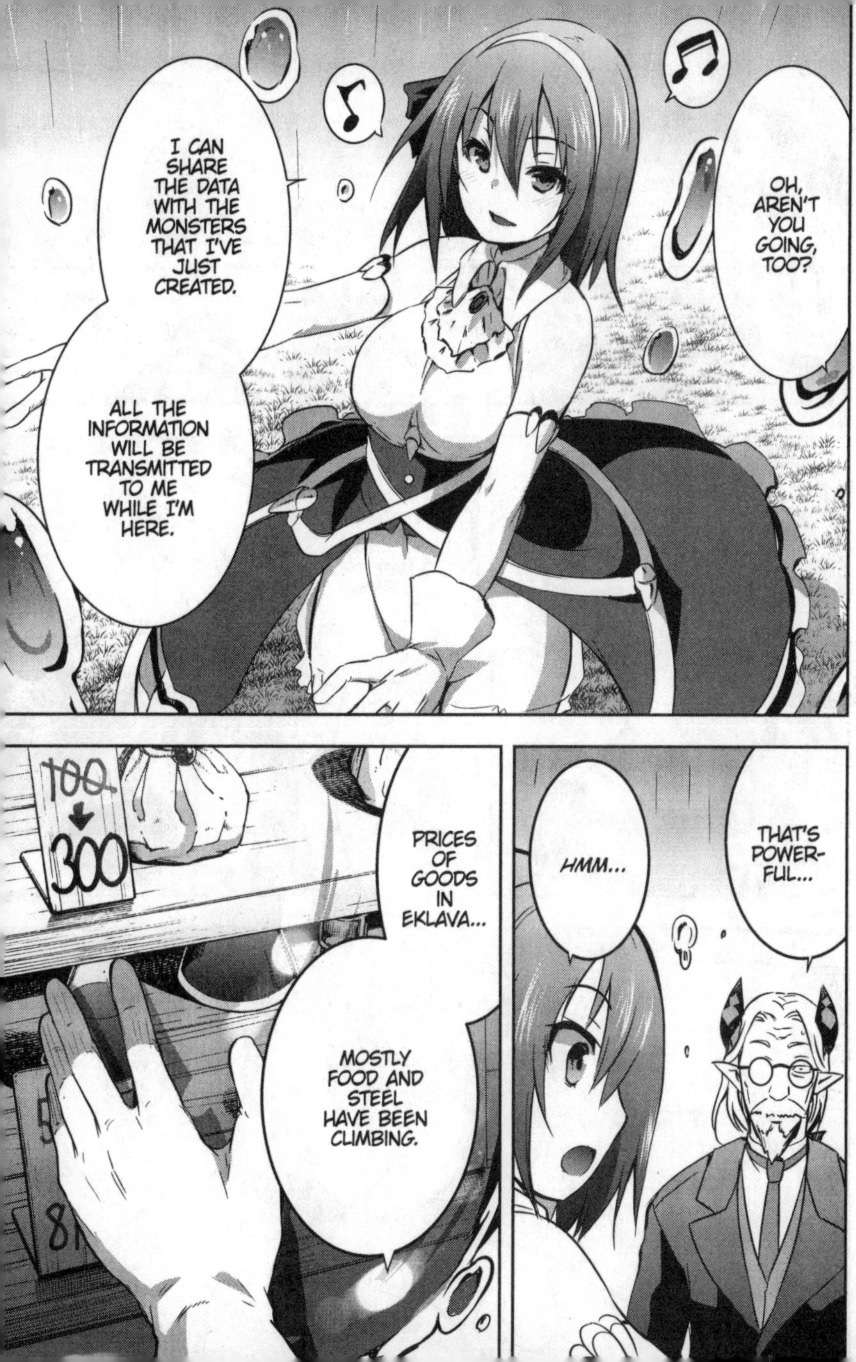
OH, AREN'T YOU GOING, TOO?
I CAN SHARE THE DATA WITH THE MONSTERS THAT I'VE JUST CREATED.
ALL THE INFORMATION WILL BE TRANSMITTED TO ME WHILE I'M HERE.
THAT'S POWER-FUL...
HMM...
PRICES OF GOODS IN EKLAVA...
100
300
MOSTLY FOOD AND STEEL HAVE BEEN CLIMBING.

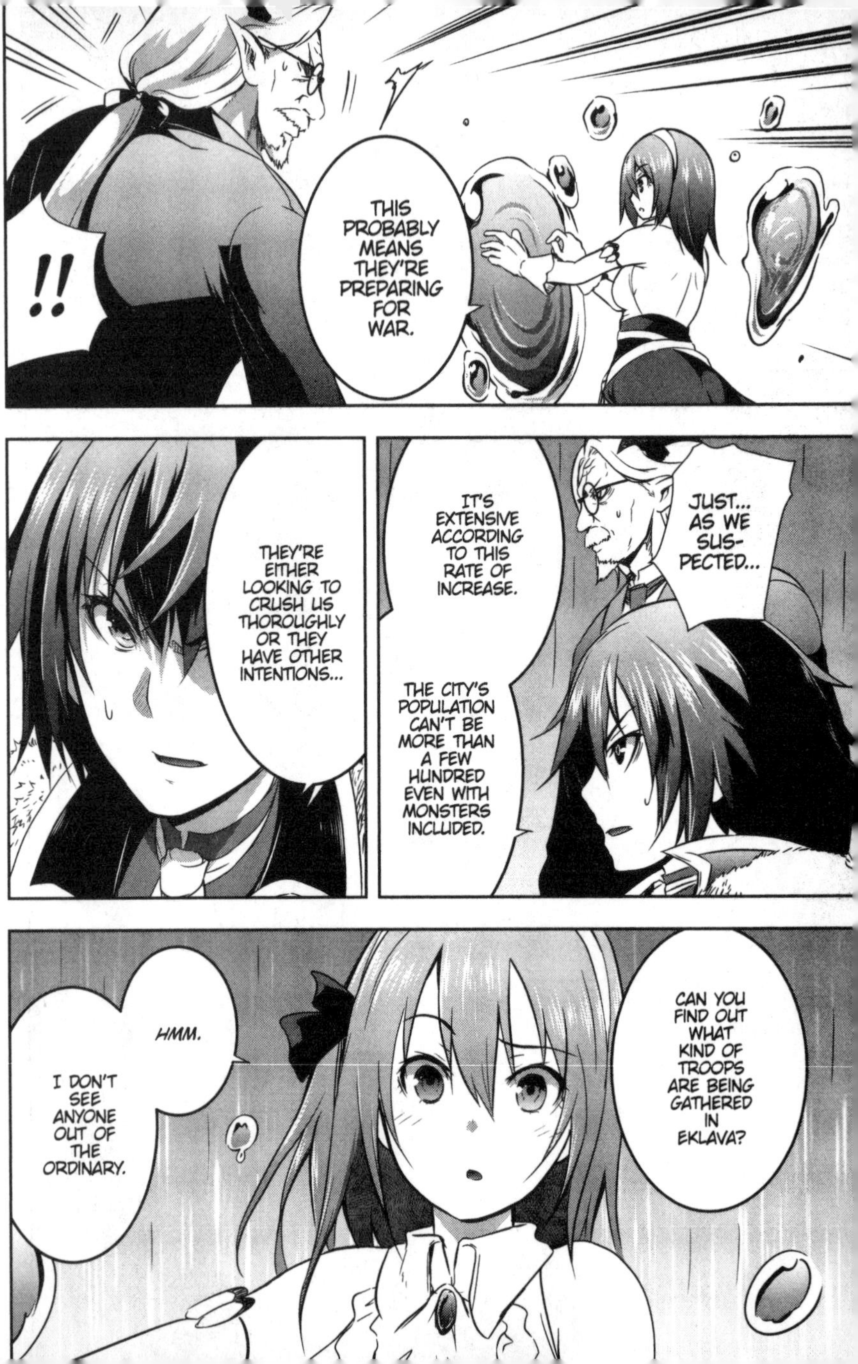
THIS PROBABLY MEANS THEY'RE PREPARING FOR WAR.
!!
JUST... AS WE SUSPECTED...
IT'S EXTENSIVE ACCORDING TO THIS RATE OF INCREASE.
THE CITY'S POPULATION CAN'T BE MORE THAN A FEW HUNDRED EVEN WITH MONSTERS INCLUDED.
THEY'RE EITHER LOOKING TO CRUSH US THOROUGHLY OR THEY HAVE OTHER INTENTIONS...
CAN YOU FIND OUT WHAT KIND OF TROOPS ARE BEING GATHERED IN EKLAVA?
HMM.
I DON'T SEE ANYONE OUT OF THE ORDINARY.

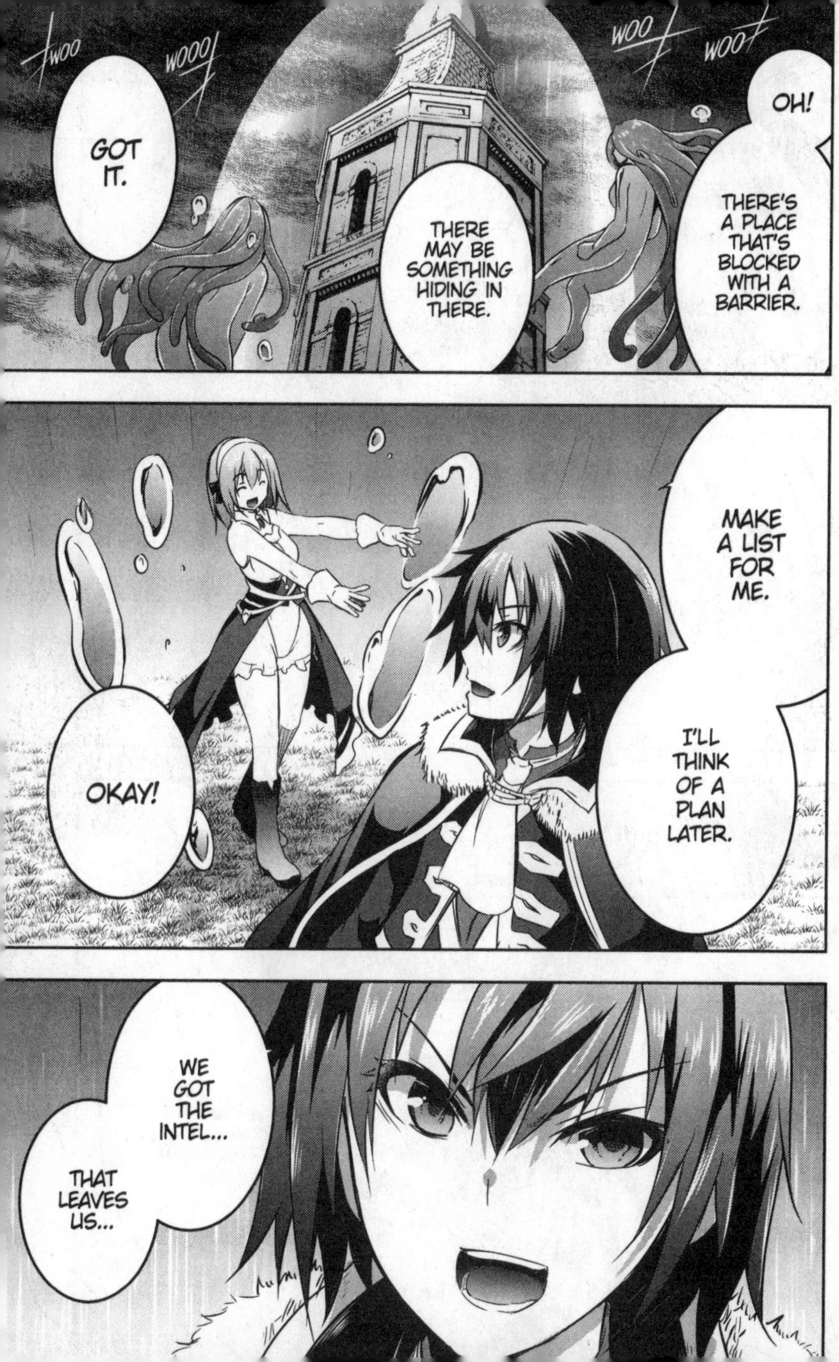
WOO WOO
OH!
THERE'S A PLACE THAT'S BLOCKED WITH A BARRIER.
THERE MAY BE SOMETHING HIDING IN THERE.
WOO WOOO
GOT IT.
MAKE A LIST FOR ME.
I'LL THINK OF A PLAN LATER.
OKAY!
WE GOT THE INTEL...
THAT LEAVES US...

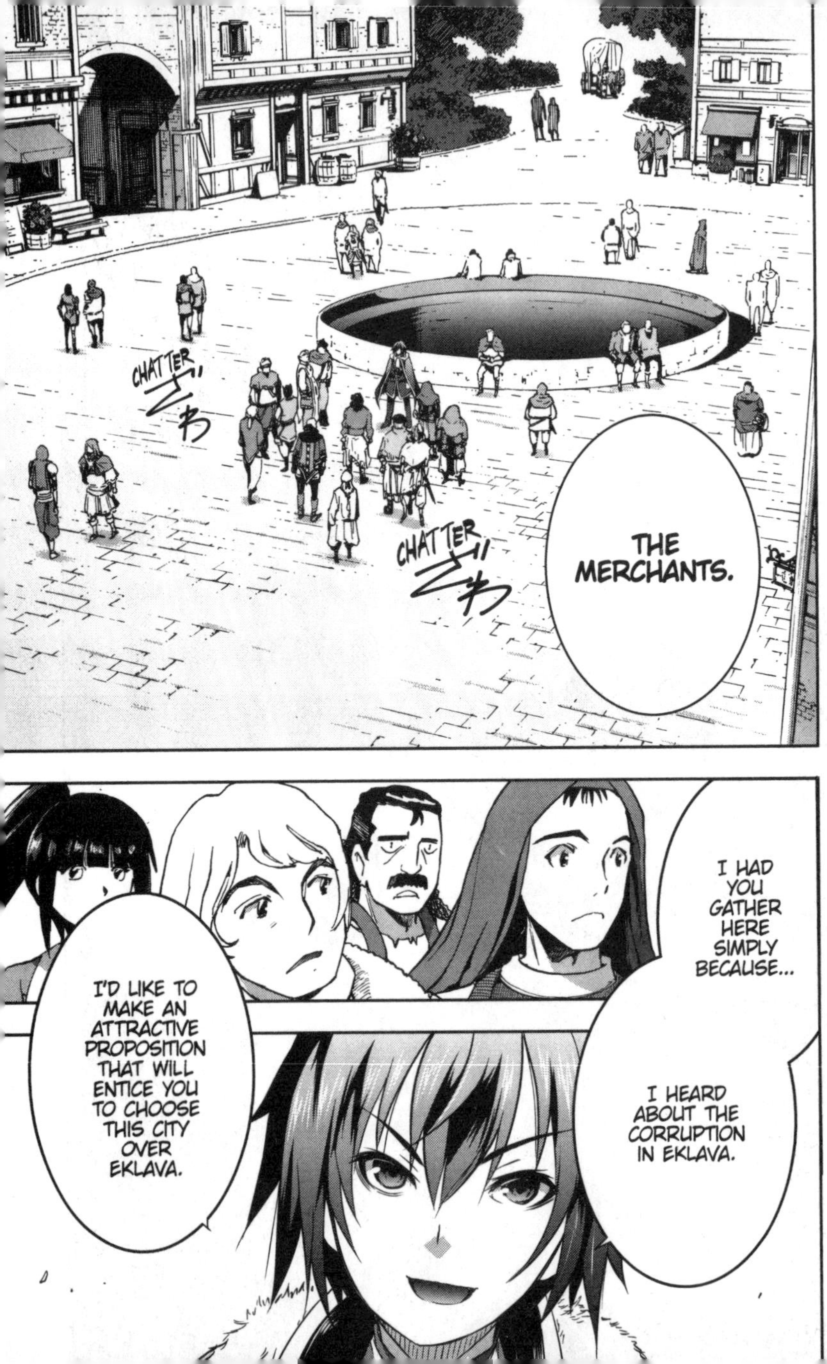
THE MERCHANTS.
CHATTER
CHATTER
I HAD YOU GATHER HERE SIMPLY BECAUSE...
I HEARD ABOUT THE CORRUPTION IN EKLAVA.
I'D LIKE TO MAKE AN ATTRACTIVE PROPOSITION THAT WILL ENTICE YOU TO CHOOSE THIS CITY OVER EKLAVA.

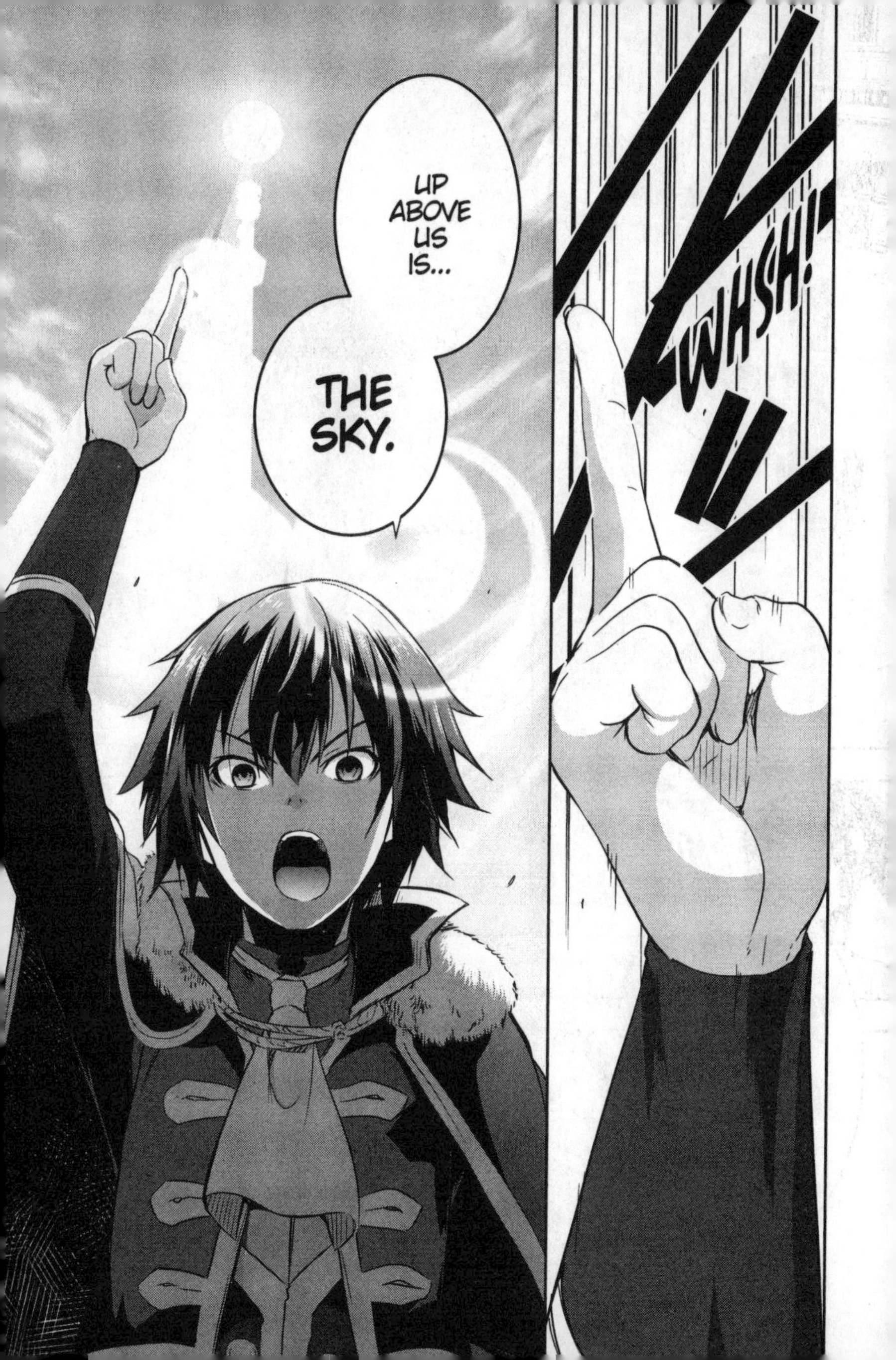
WHSH!
UP ABOVE US IS...
THE SKY.

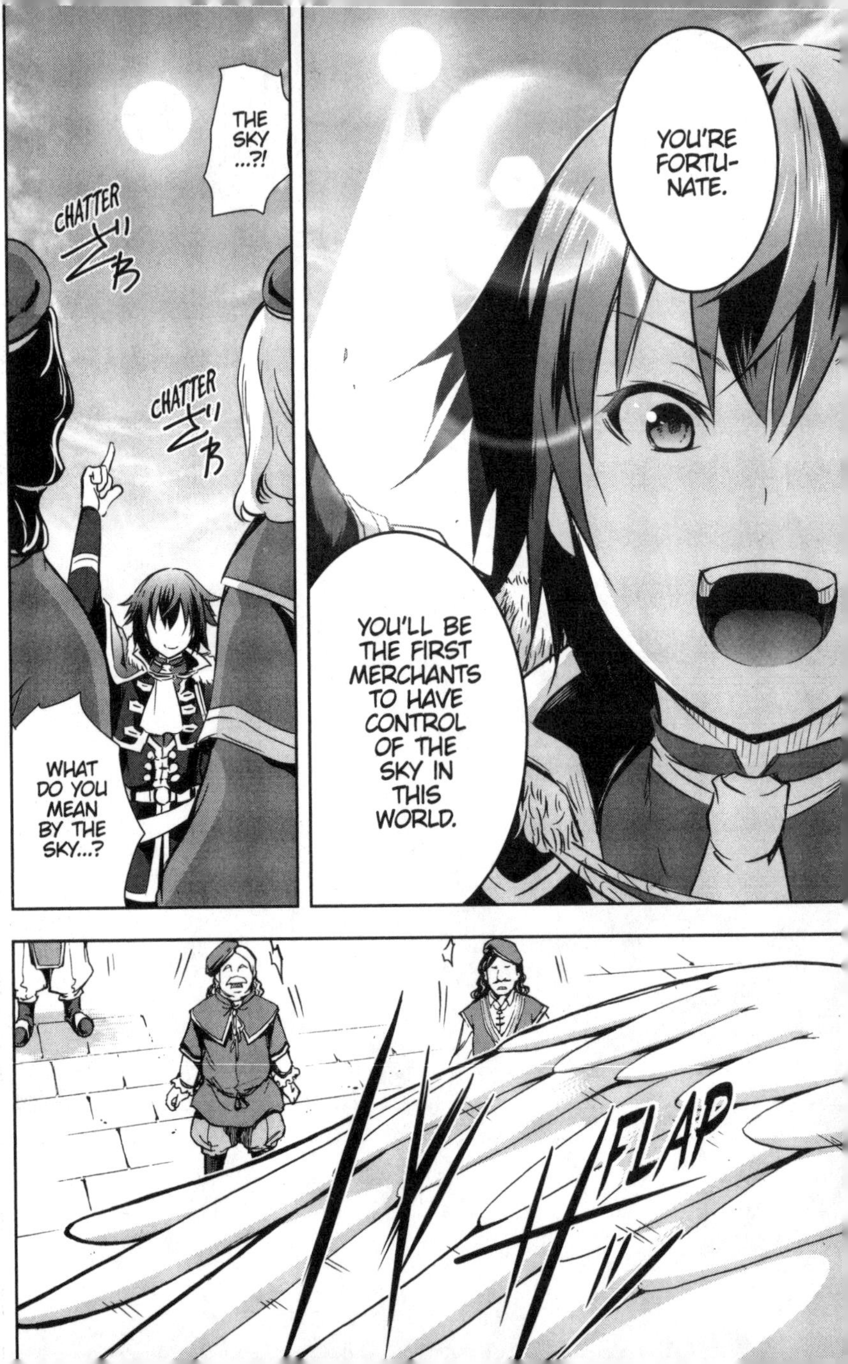
YOU'RE FORTUNATE.
YOU'LL BE THE FIRST MERCHANTS TO HAVE CONTROL OF THE SKY IN THIS WORLD.
THE SKY ...?!
CHATTER ざわ
CHATTER ざわ
WHAT DO YOU MEAN BY THE SKY...?
FLAP

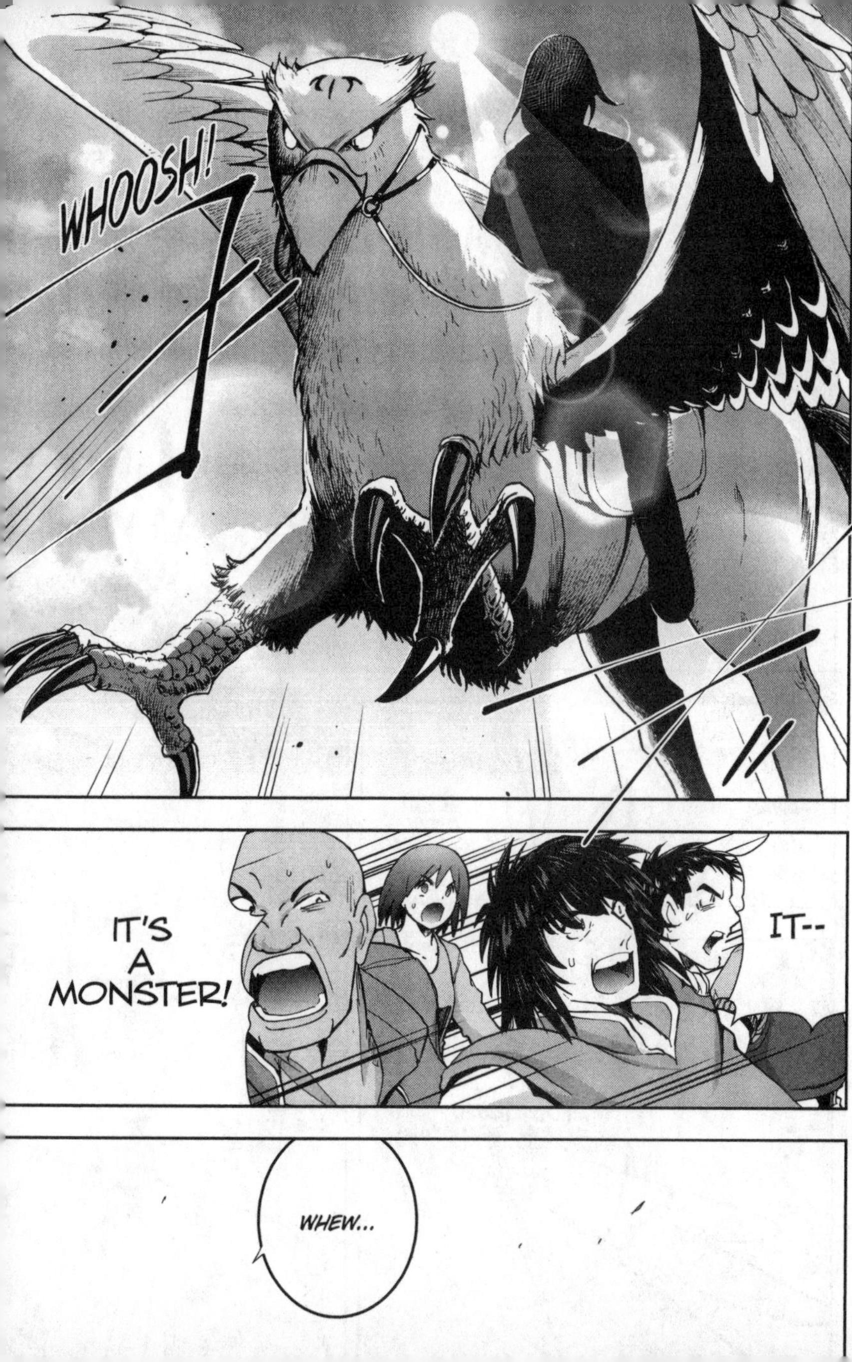
WHOOSH!
IT--
IT'S A MONSTER!
WHEW...

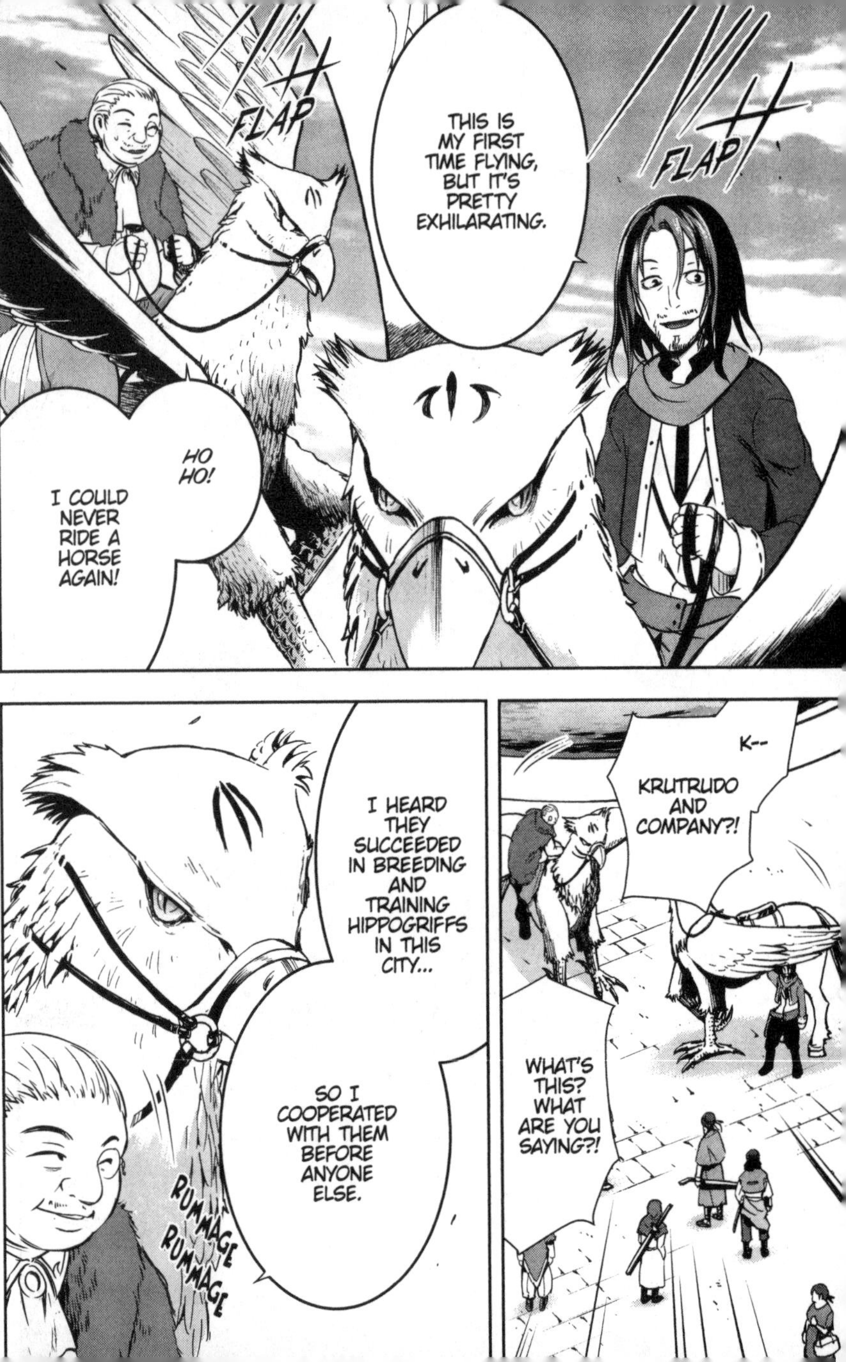
FLAP
FLAP
THIS IS MY FIRST TIME FLYING, BUT IT'S PRETTY EXHILARATING.
HO HO!
I COULD NEVER RIDE A HORSE AGAIN!
K--
KRUTRUDO AND COMPANY?!
WHAT'S THIS? WHAT ARE YOU SAYING?!
I HEARD THEY SUCCEEDED IN BREEDING AND TRAINING HIPPOGRIFFS IN THIS CITY...
SO I COOPERATED WITH THEM BEFORE ANYONE ELSE.
RUMMAGE RUMMAGE

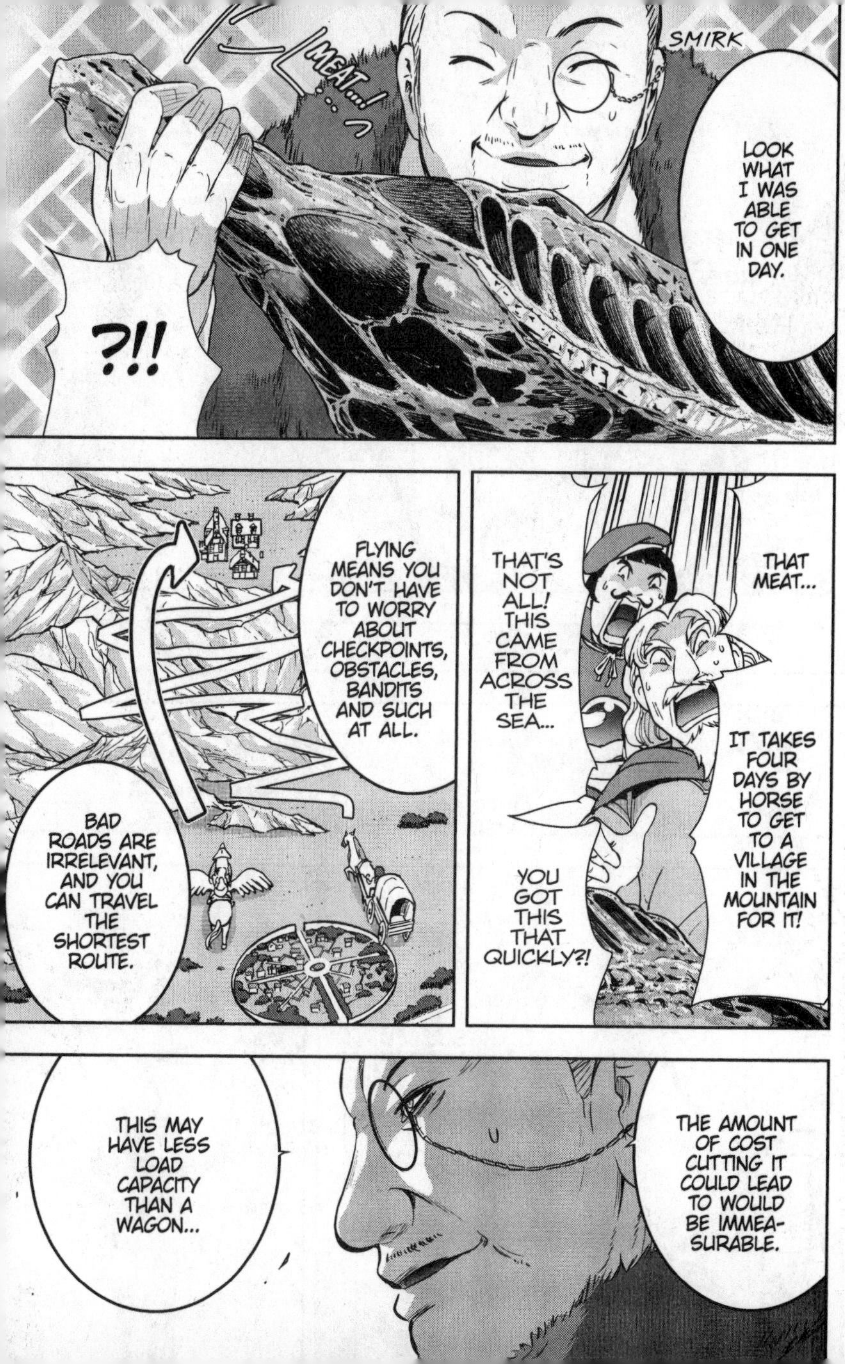

MEAT...!
SMIRK
LOOK WHAT I WAS ABLE TO GET IN ONE DAY.
?!!
THAT MEAT...
IT TAKES FOUR DAYS BY HORSE TO GET TO A VILLAGE IN THE MOUNTAIN FOR IT!
THAT'S NOT ALL! THIS CAME FROM ACROSS THE SEA...
YOU GOT THIS THAT QUICKLY?!
FLYING MEANS YOU DON'T HAVE TO WORRY ABOUT CHECKPOINTS, OBSTACLES, BANDITS AND SUCH AT ALL.
BAD ROADS ARE IRRELEVANT, AND YOU CAN TRAVEL THE SHORTEST ROUTE.
THE AMOUNT OF COST CUTTING IT COULD LEAD TO WOULD BE IMMEA-SURABLE.
THIS MAY HAVE LESS LOAD CAPACITY THAN A WAGON...

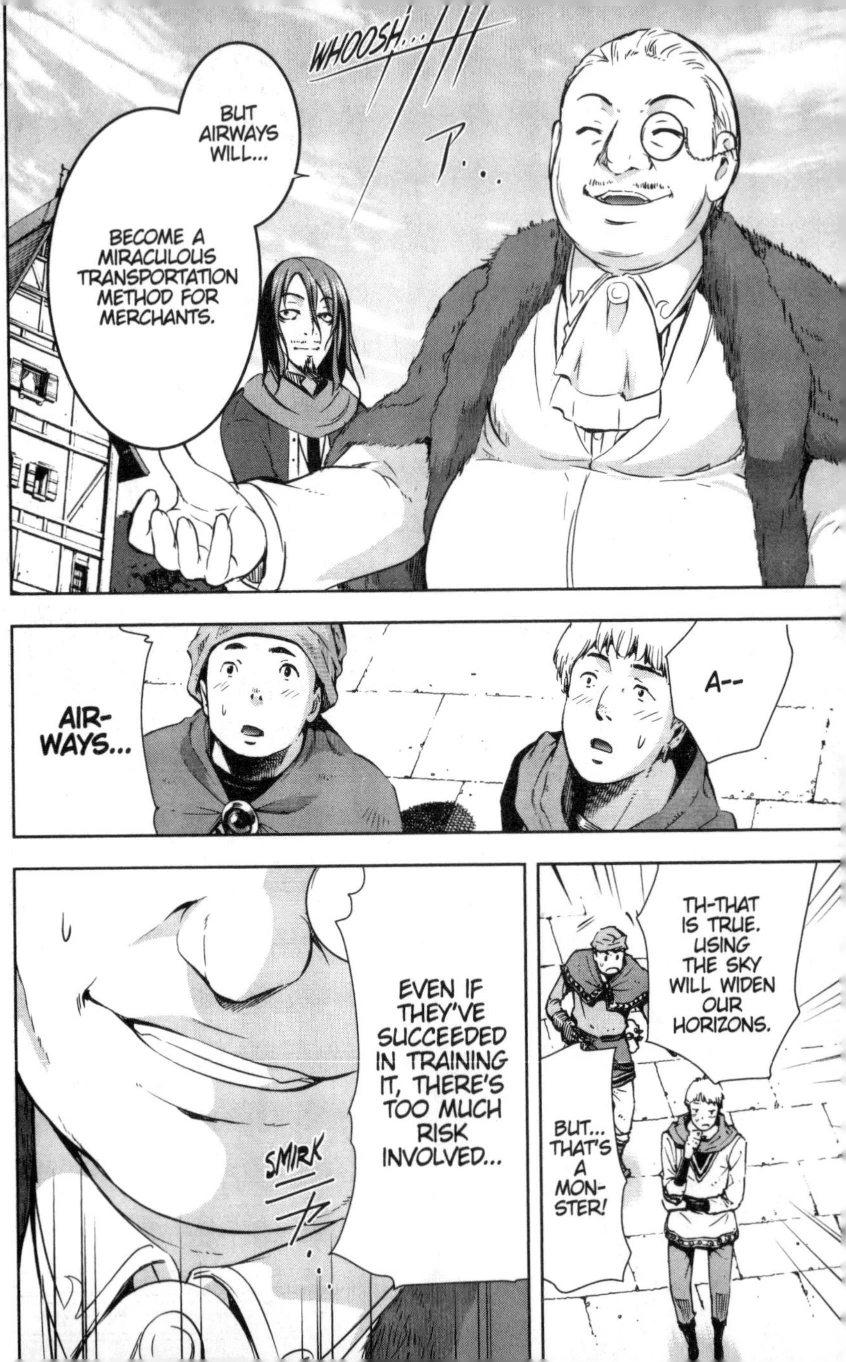
WHOOSH...
BUT AIRWAYS WILL...
BECOME A MIRACULOUS TRANSPORTATION METHOD FOR MERCHANTS.
A--
AIR-WAYS...
TH-THAT IS TRUE. USING THE SKY WILL WIDEN OUR HORIZONS.
BUT... THAT'S A MON-STER!
EVEN IF THEY'VE SUCCEEDED IN TRAINING IT, THERE'S TOO MUCH RISK INVOLVED...
SMIRK

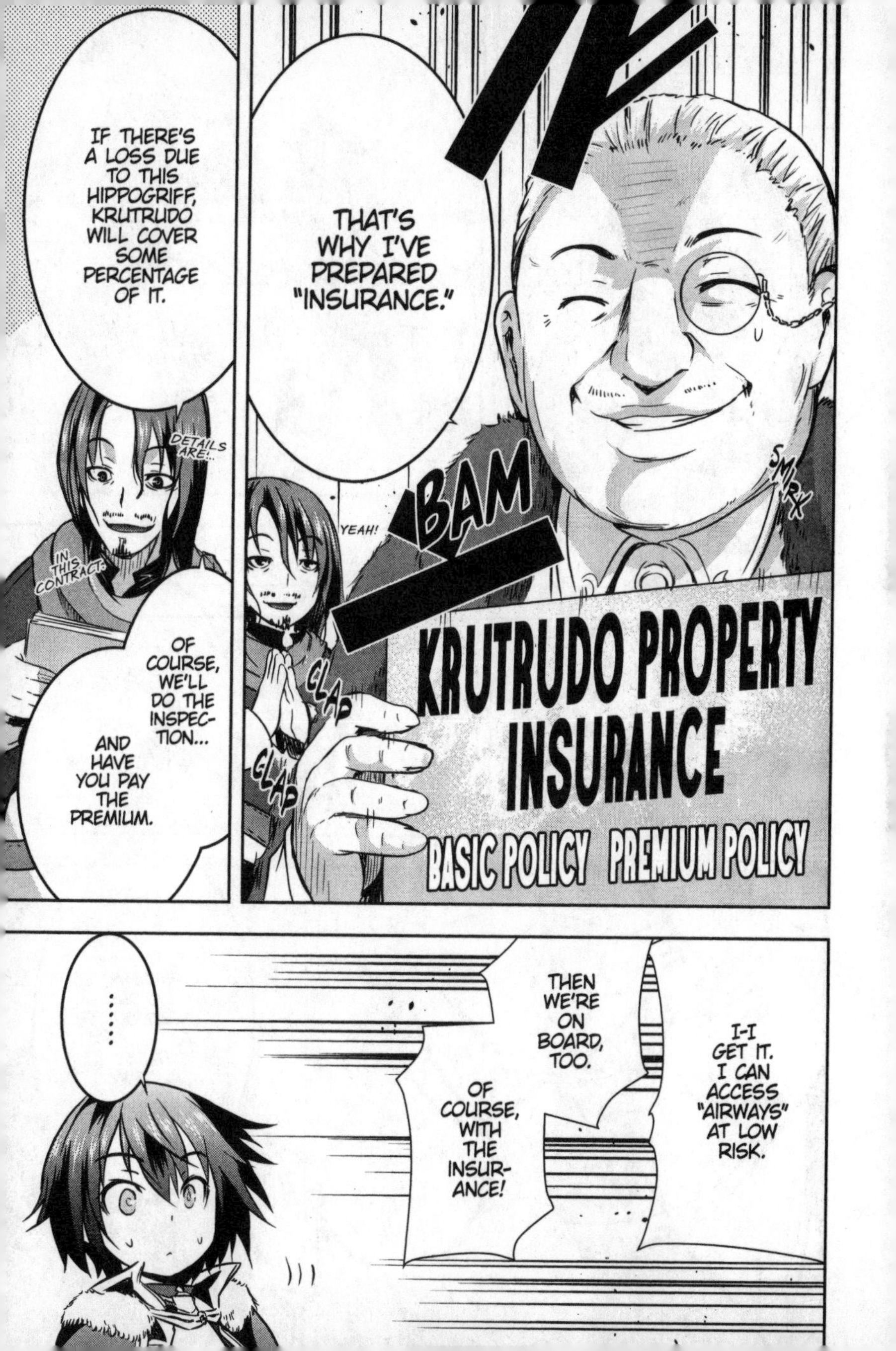
THAT'S WHY I'VE PREPARED "INSURANCE."
IF THERE'S A LOSS DUE TO THIS HIPPOGRIFF, KRUTRUDO WILL COVER SOME PERCENTAGE OF IT.
DETAILS ARE...
IN THIS CONTRACT.
BAM
SMIRK
YEAH!
CLAP
CLAP
KRUTRUDO PROPERTY INSURANCE
BASIC POLICY
PREMIUM POLICY
OF COURSE, WE'LL DO THE INSPECTION...
AND HAVE YOU PAY THE PREMIUM.
I-I GET IT. I CAN ACCESS "AIRWAYS" AT LOW RISK.
THEN WE'RE ON BOARD, TOO.
OF COURSE, WITH THE INSURANCE!
......

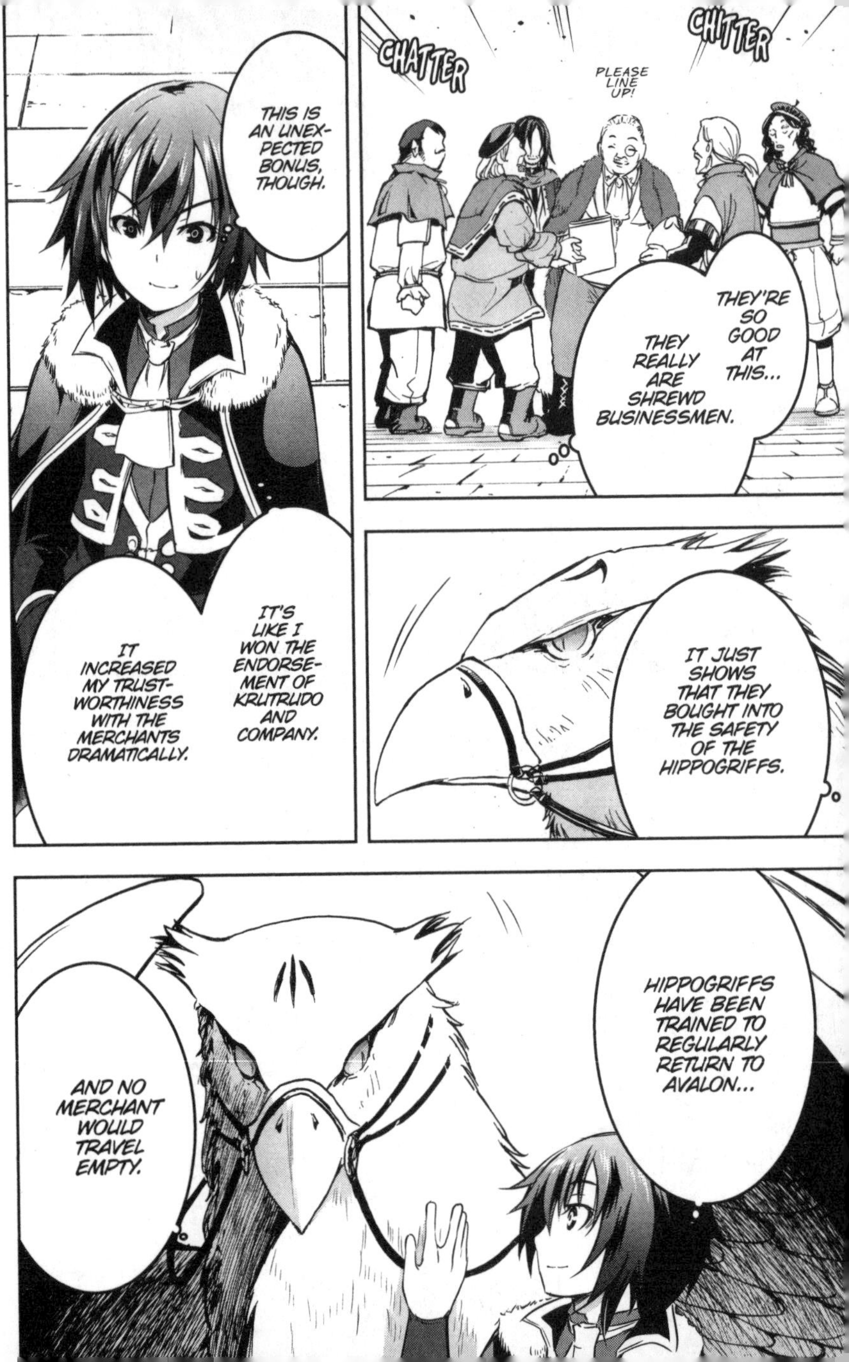
CHITTER
CHATTER
PLEASE LINE UP!
THEY'RE SO GOOD AT THIS...
THEY REALLY ARE SHREWD BUSINESSMEN.
IT JUST SHOWS THAT THEY BOUGHT INTO THE SAFETY OF THE HIPPOGRIFFS.
THIS IS AN UNEXPECTED BONUS, THOUGH.
IT'S LIKE I WON THE ENDORSEMENT OF KRUTRUDO AND COMPANY.
IT INCREASED MY TRUSTWORTHINESS WITH THE MERCHANTS DRAMATICALLY.
HIPPOGRIFFS HAVE BEEN TRAINED TO REGULARLY RETURN TO AVALON...
AND NO MERCHANT WOULD TRAVEL EMPTY.

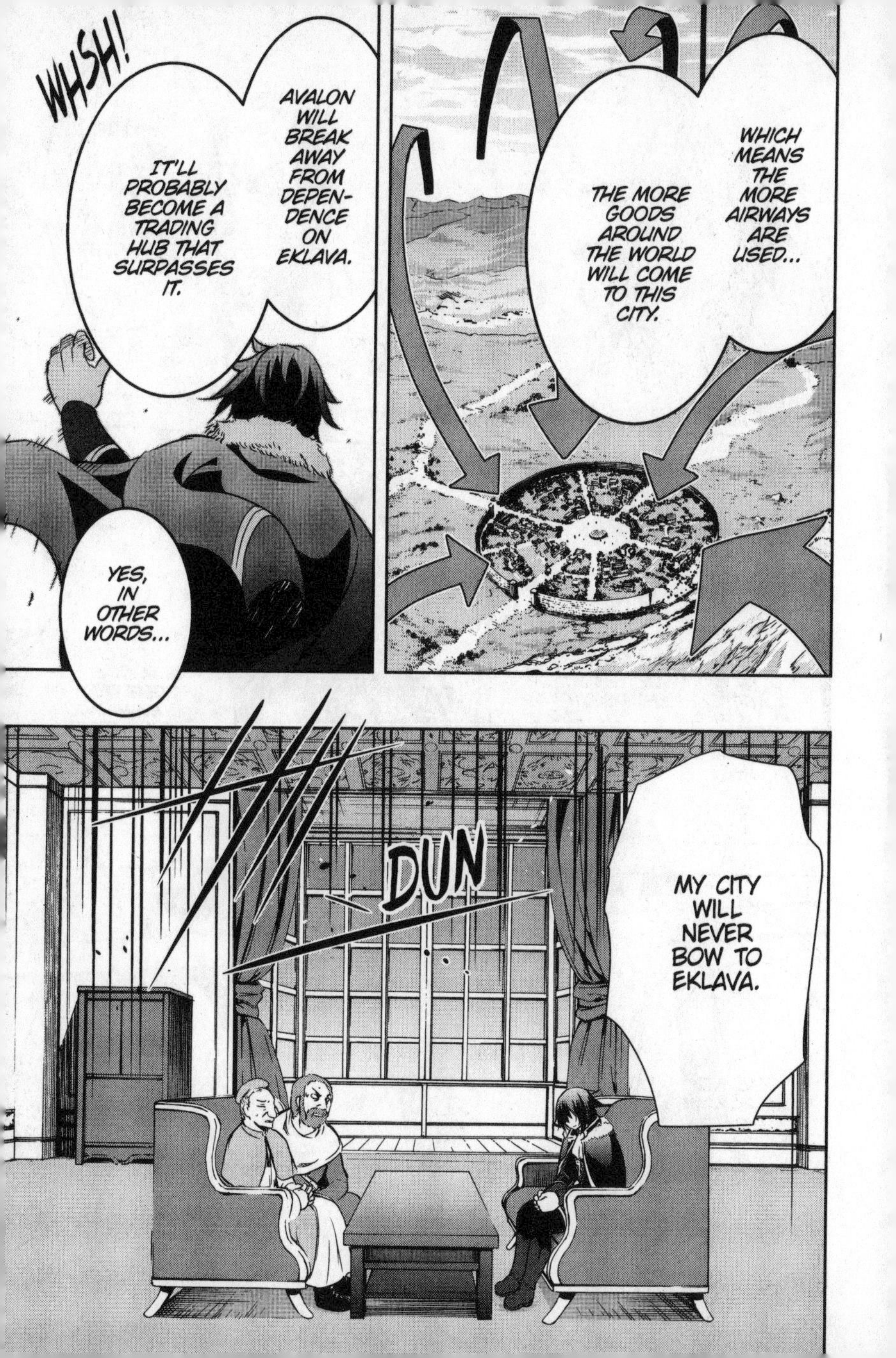

WHICH MEANS THE MORE AIRWAYS ARE USED...
THE MORE GOODS AROUND THE WORLD WILL COME TO THIS CITY.
WHSH!
AVALON WILL BREAK AWAY FROM DEPEN-DENCE ON EKLAVA.
IT'LL PROBABLY BECOME A TRADING HUB THAT SURPASSES IT.
YES, IN OTHER WORDS...
MY CITY WILL NEVER BOW TO EKLAVA.
DUN

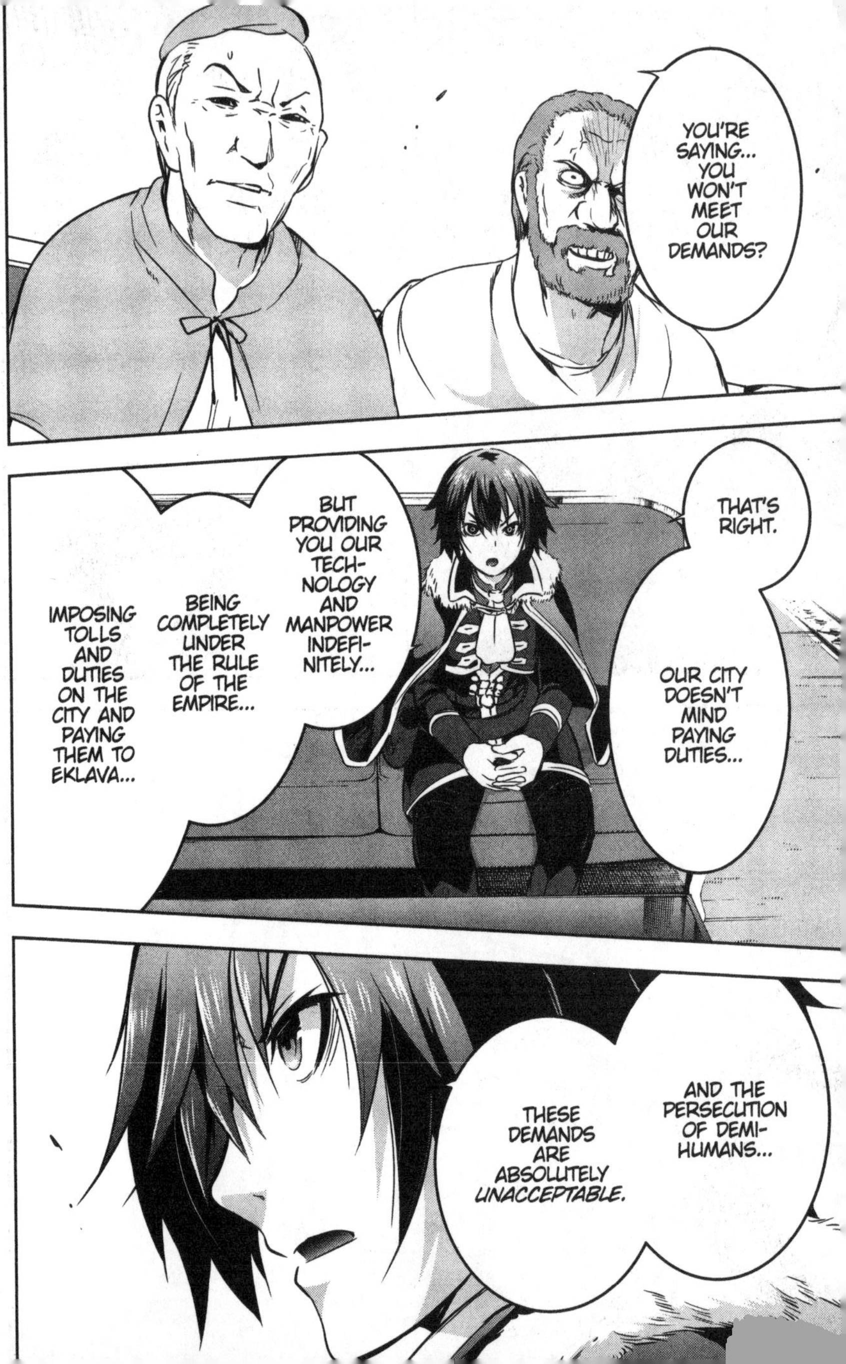

YOU'RE SAYING... YOU WON'T MEET OUR DEMANDS?
THAT'S RIGHT.
OUR CITY DOESN'T MIND PAYING DUTIES...
BUT PROVIDING YOU OUR TECH-NOLOGY AND MANPOWER INDEFI-NITELY...
BEING COMPLETELY UNDER THE RULE OF THE EMPIRE...
IMPOSING TOLLS AND DUTIES ON THE CITY AND PAYING THEM TO EKLAVA...
AND THE PERSECUTION OF DEMI-HUMANS...
THESE DEMANDS ARE ABSOLUTELY *UNACCEPTABLE.*

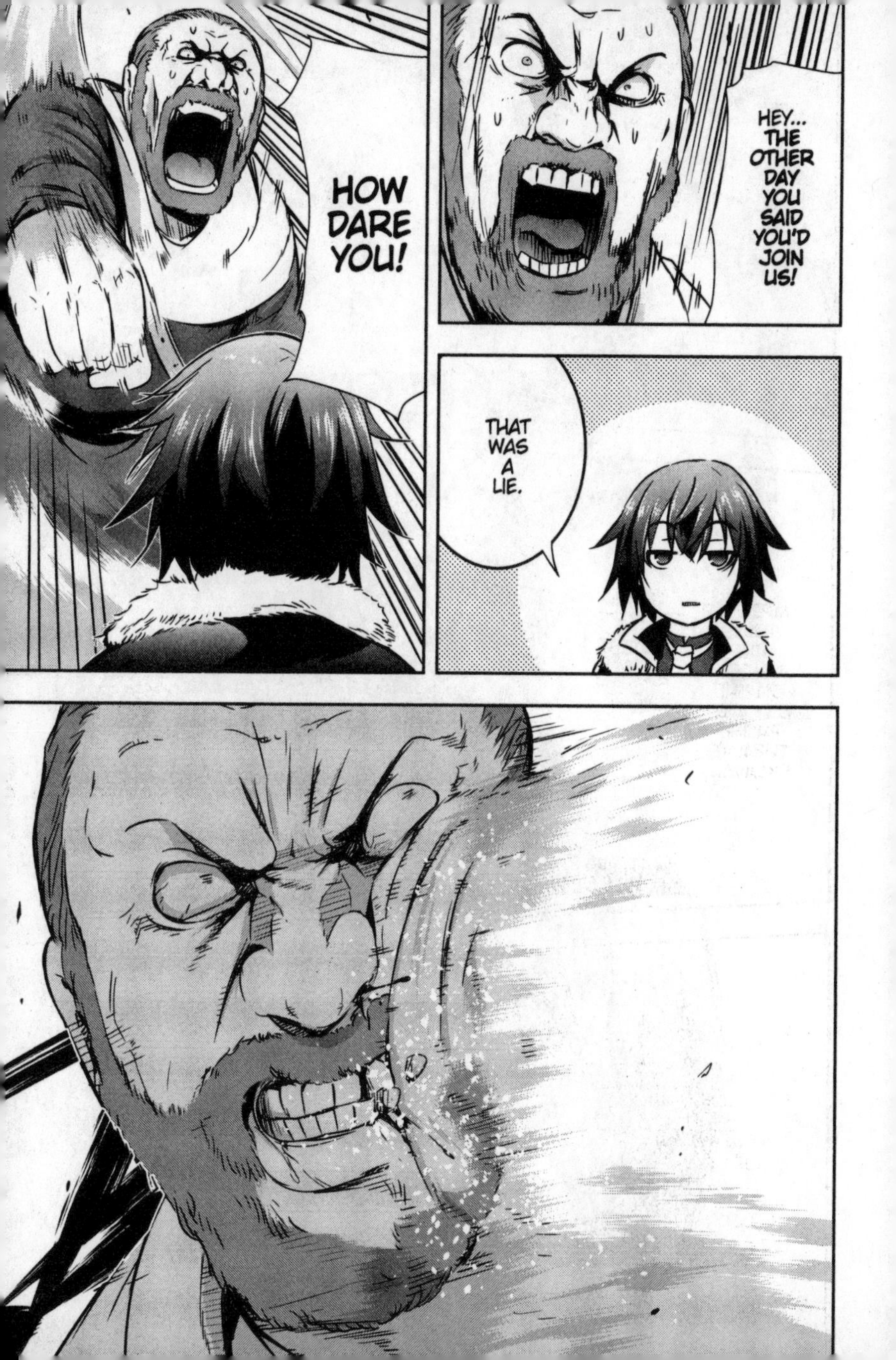

HEY... THE OTHER DAY YOU SAID YOU'D JOIN US!
HOW DARE YOU!
THAT WAS A LIE.

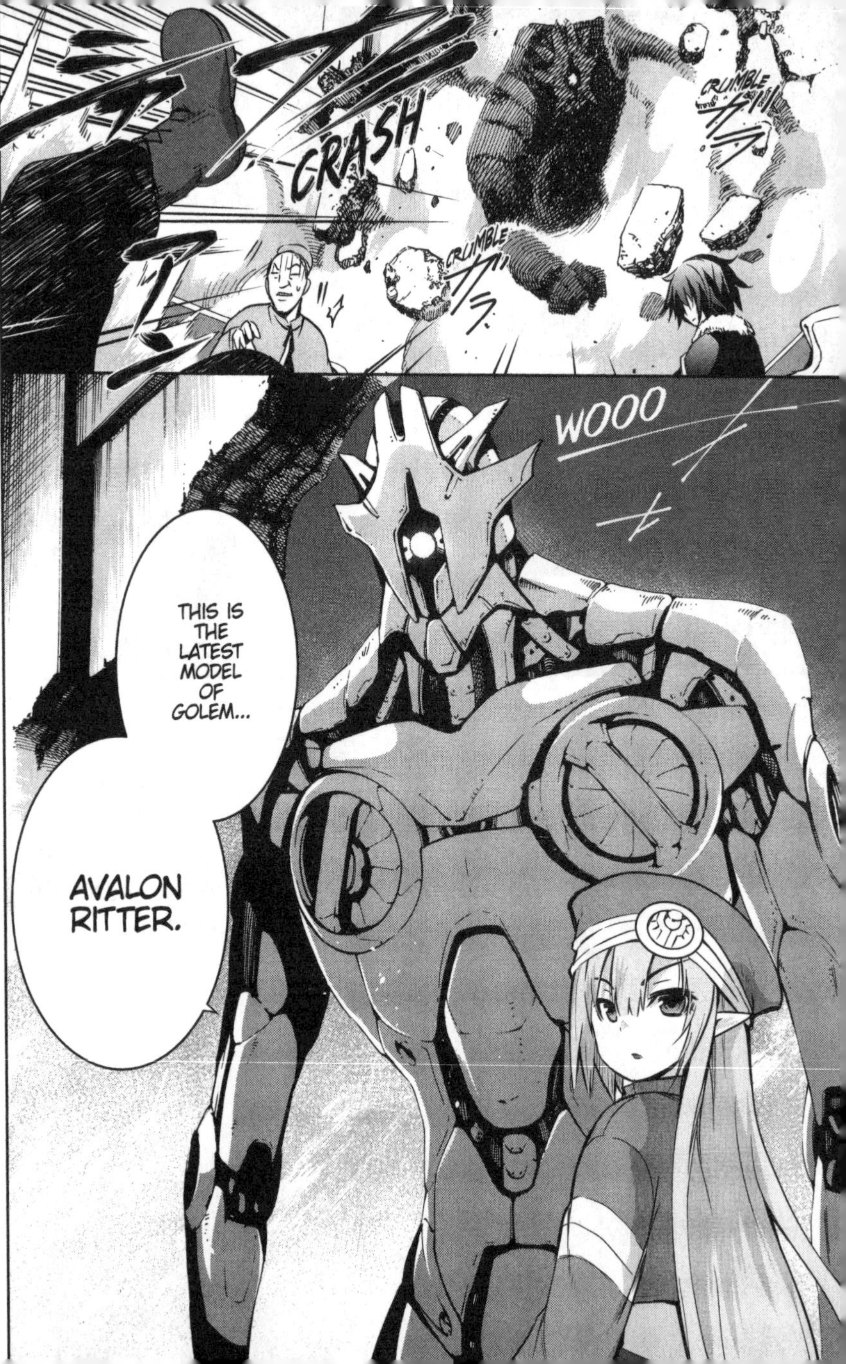

CRUMBLE
CRASH
CRUMBLE
WOOO
THIS IS THE LATEST MODEL OF GOLEM...
AVALON RITTER.

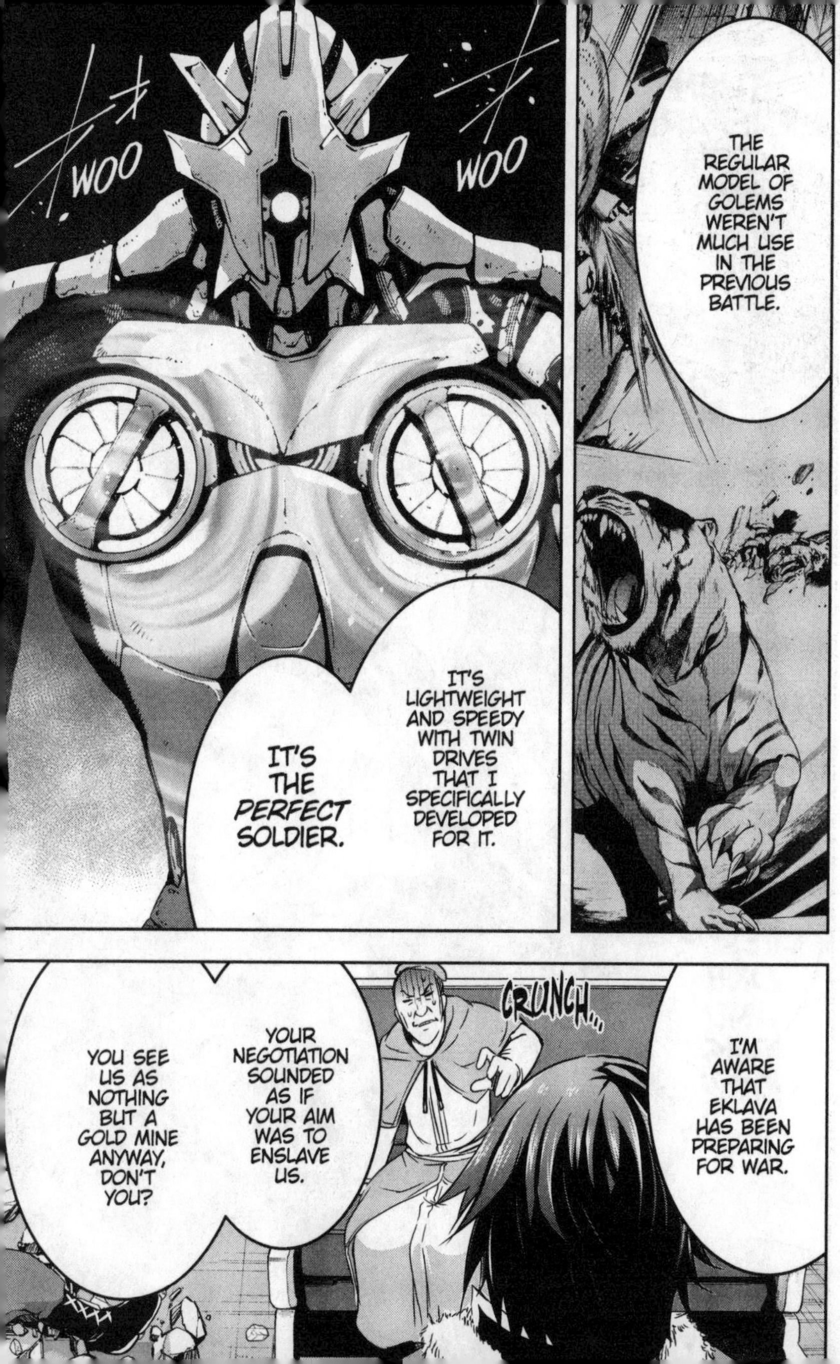
THE REGULAR MODEL OF GOLEMS WEREN'T MUCH USE IN THE PREVIOUS BATTLE.
WOO
WOO
IT'S LIGHTWEIGHT AND SPEEDY WITH TWIN DRIVES THAT I SPECIFICALLY DEVELOPED FOR IT.
IT'S THE *PERFECT* SOLDIER.
I'M AWARE THAT EKLAVA HAS BEEN PREPARING FOR WAR.
CRUNCH...
YOUR NEGOTIATION SOUNDED AS IF YOUR AIM WAS TO ENSLAVE US.
YOU SEE US AS NOTHING BUT A GOLD MINE ANYWAY, DON'T YOU?

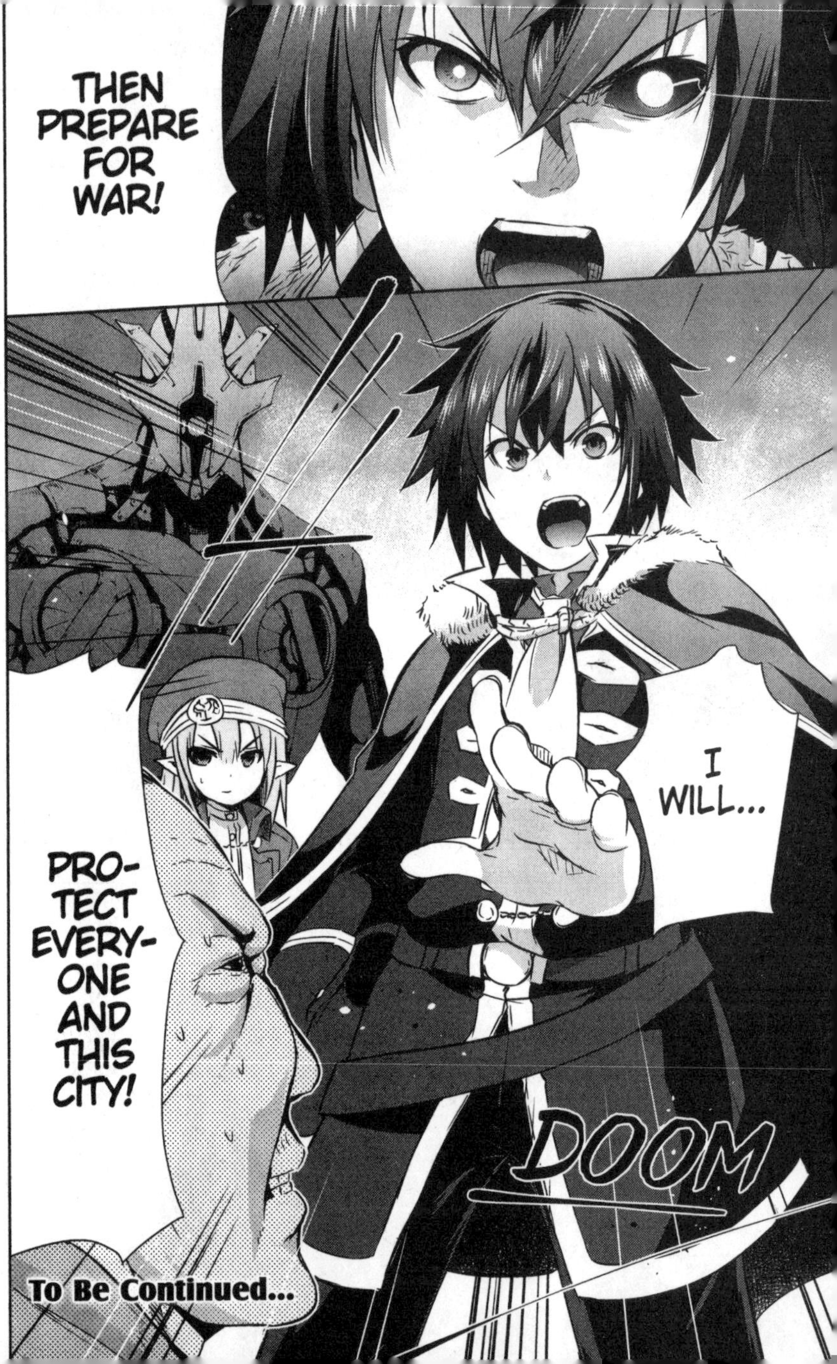
THEN PREPARE FOR WAR!
I WILL...
PROTECT EVERYONE AND THIS CITY!
DOOM
To Be Continued...

Bonus Manga: **Stolas' Trauma**

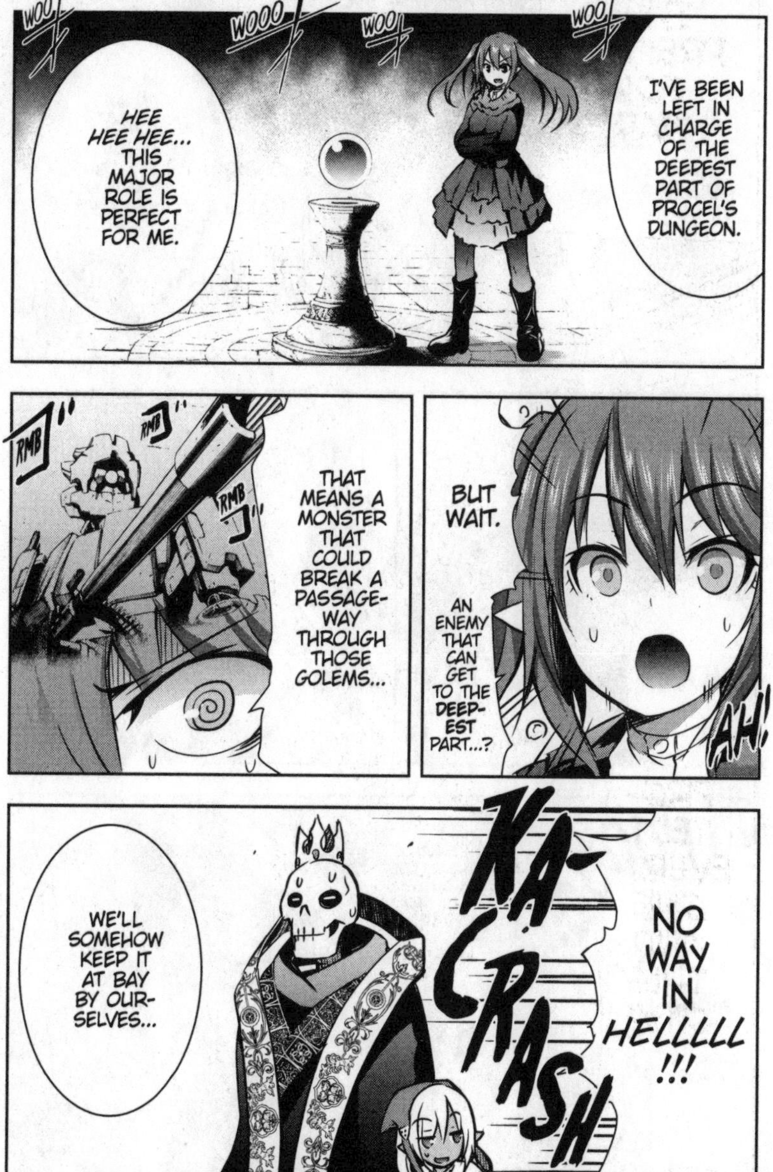
WOO
WOOO
WOO
WOO
I'VE BEEN LEFT IN CHARGE OF THE DEEPEST PART OF PROCEL'S DUNGEON.
HEE HEE HEE... THIS MAJOR ROLE IS PERFECT FOR ME.
AH!
BUT WAIT.
AN ENEMY THAT CAN GET TO THE DEEP-EST PART...?
THAT MEANS A MONSTER THAT COULD BREAK A PASSAGE-WAY THROUGH THOSE GOLEMS...
RMB
RMB
RMB
NO WAY IN HELLLLL!!!
KA-CRASH
WE'LL SOMEHOW KEEP IT AT BAY BY OUR-SELVES...

Bonus Manga: **Hang in There! Marcho!**

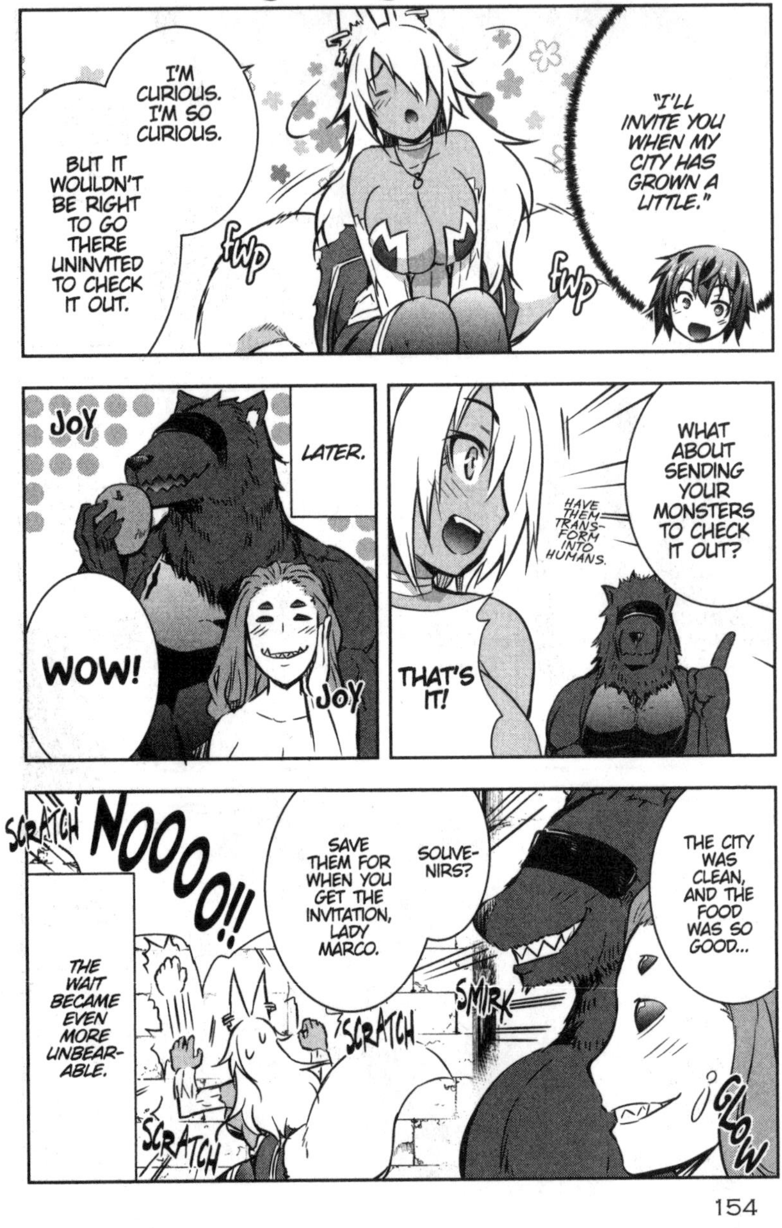
"I'LL INVITE YOU WHEN MY CITY HAS GROWN A LITTLE."
I'M CURIOUS. I'M SO CURIOUS.
BUT IT WOULDN'T BE RIGHT TO GO THERE UNINVITED TO CHECK IT OUT.
fwp
fwp
WHAT ABOUT SENDING YOUR MONSTERS TO CHECK IT OUT?
HAVE THEM TRANSFORM INTO HUMANS.
THAT'S IT!
LATER.
JOY
WOW!
JOY
THE CITY WAS CLEAN, AND THE FOOD WAS SO GOOD...
GLOW
SMIRK
SOUVENIRS?
SAVE THEM FOR WHEN YOU GET THE INVITATION, LADY MARCO.
NOOOO!!
SCRATCH
SCRATCH
SCRATCH
THE WAIT BECAME EVEN MORE UNBEARABLE.

Bonus Manga: **The Merchant Has His Needs, Too.**

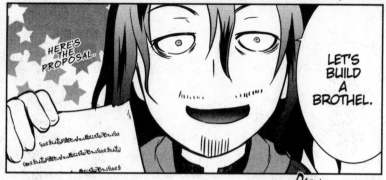

LET'S BUILD A BROTHEL.
HERE'S THE PROPOSAL.
DUN
NO... I DON'T WANT SUCH AN INAPPROPRIATE PLACE IN MY CITY.
PROCEL! MOST ADVENTURERS ARE YOUNG MEN AND WOMEN!
YOU WILL SEE A CRIME SPIKE IF THEY HAVE NO WAY TO RELEASE THEIR STRESS!
HUH?
LOOK WHAT COULD HAPPEN TO CUTE YOUNG DEMI-HUMANS WORKING IN THIS CITY, TOO!
HUH?
SO HE BUILT A BROTHEL.
OOHLALA
DAD, YOU PERVERT.
YOU'VE GOT IT WRONG!
IT WAS FOR EVERYONE ELSE!

I WAS SURPRISED IT WAS IMPLEMENTED EARLY ON IN THE ORIGINAL STORY.

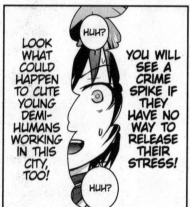

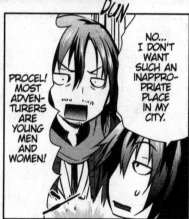

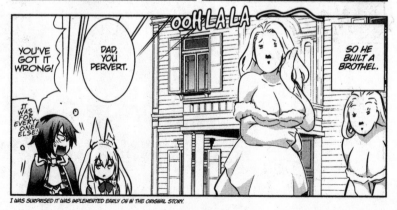

DUNGEON
BUILDER:
THE DEMON KING'S
LABYRINTH IS A
MODERN CITY!

BONUS SHORT STORY:
WIGHT'S COURT IN AVALON

Avalon is a city where monsters and humans coexist peacefully.

My three cohorts and I stood on a hill overlooking the city together.

"My feelings are spilling over and improving day by day."

"Quina and the others have been working hard, yah!" a young teenage, fox-eared girl with a fluffy tail said haughtily. She is Avalon's mightiest monster—Quina the tenko.

"Mm-hm, yes. We're turning it into a nice city. Being in the sixtieth percentile is solid, according to my data. This is based on my assessment and analysis of every city in the neighboring four countries," agreed the calm and cool, silver-haired girl about Quina's age, Rorono the elder dwarf. Her short height and flat chest are the characteristics of the dwarf race.

"It seems this land, the entire dungeon, increases its power as the demon lord experiences surges of power.

Delicious fruits and vegetables are growing abundantly!" This is Aura, a beautiful ancient elf with a voluptuous body. Besides giving the blessing of the elves to this land, she handles climate and flood control for us.

"That's great. A livable city will attract more people. More people means more goods, which in turn will attract even more people. I want to keep this flow going."

"Quina talks to lots of humans, but new people still get shocked at seeing monsters and humans living together, yah."

"Well, it can't be helped. Monsters are targets of fear to humans."

"Humans are afraid of monsters, but I personally feel humans are more frightening."

"Ah ha ha ha, that's because you have a shop, Rorono."

"Mm-hm. They make unreasonable demands, have no qualms about deceiving me, and steal. Monsters live more lawfully than they do." People blinded by greed are dirty and vulgar. An influx of those people come to her shop, where she's a mythic-level blacksmith.

"Rorono, tell Quina if there are any scumbags who get cocky with you! Leave them to Quina and the Avalon Police, yah!"

"Don't worry about that. My golems can handle them." Avalon has a system of thousands of golems that wander and automatically capture anyone breaking the law. However, they can only follow simple cases. Their self-purification capabilities don't work on non-violent crimes like scams, and many complaints and claims have been inundating me, the lord of this city. It's been a real headache. The problem grows bigger as the city grows, and I'm sick and tired of it.

"Hey, Dad looks worn out, yah."

"Yeah... I'm glad to see my city grow bigger, but it's been causing all kinds of trouble. I sure would like to know why humans become vulgar when it comes to money." To be honest, I'm annoyed at hearing "he said, she said" or "he deceived me, she deceived me" cases, which make me want to throw in the towel.

"Oh, about that. Wight is going to do something interesting."

"Something interesting?"

"Well, ahem. 'I can't allow my lord to be distressed over humans' ugly disputes. I'll do what needs to be done as his cohort.'"

"You're good at imitating Wight's voice."

"He-he-he, it's my special skill."

"I'm curious about what he's trying to do... I'm going to check it out."

"Hey, Quina wants to go too, yah!"

"Mm-hm, I'll go with you, too." So, the four of us decided to go to the basement. That's where Wight the King of Ghosts works.

In the basement, the skeleton crew was busily making bread. The view of over a hundred skeletons doing their perfectly delegated tasks in assembly is a spectacular one.

"Oh, my. What brings you here, my lord?" As I watched them work, Wight, who supervises the skeletons, approached. He exudes an atmosphere of an elderly gentleman with his sophisticated clothes and noble attitude despite his bony appearance.

"Well, Aura told me that you were doing something for me."

"I see. Lady Aura, I told you to keep this from my lord until it was completed."

"Oh, really? I'm sorry," Aura giggled and adorably stuck her tongue out.

"It's fine. Even though it happened over drinks, it was my fault for letting it slip."

"Wight... you can drink alcohol? You're all bones."

"No, I can't drink at all. However, I let myself feel the mood to get drunk. Not being able to enjoy physically allows me to appreciate it more emotionally."

"That's deep." Wight often impresses me. "So, what is it that you're trying to do?"

"I was considering the incorporation of a court."

"That system Murangara has just started adopting...but there's a lot of trouble involved in setting it up."

Murangara is a developed country, which has incorporated a court, and I visited it once with my monsters. I was impressed by this system, but it's very troublesome to set up and requires some expertise. I felt that it would be difficult to implement in Avalon at its current state.

"It would be a typical court. So, I've decided to cut some corners." Behind him, I faintly see a ghost floating.

It's a lower-level spiritual monster.

"Is that a wraith?"

"Yes. I became capable of generating wraiths in addition to skeletons ever since you gained more power. Having more people in the city is making it easier to obtain dead bodies as well as new souls. I have enough of them."

"I see. Is this wraith going to take the bench?"

"Oh, no, it won't. I'd like to show you a demo, but... Let's see. Lady Rorono, may I ask for your cooperation?"

"Mm-hm, sure."

"I'm going to have the wraith possess Lady Rorono. Please relax."

"Okay." When Rorono closed her eyes, the wraith entered her body, and she opened her eyes.

"Ahem! Well, Lady Rorono. Can you tell us how you feel about my lord?"

Rorono's usually cool and composed face changed. And then she broke into a smile and threw herself into my arms.

"Dad, I love you!" She rubbed her cheek against me. I've never seen Rorono like this before.

"I've always wanted to do this! I wanted to call you Dad like Quina does! But I was so embarrassed... I want to hug you whenever I can and have you be all mine." She continued to hug me. She's so adorable...

I actually knew that Rorono liked to be babied. Even when she wanted to be praised, she'd go out of her way to be in a good spot for me to pat her on her head or ostentatiously stare at my hand to get me to hold hers. Even when I do those things, she'd only break a slight smile. It's cute to see that modest side of her, but I like when she acts like this, too.

"Hey, Rorono. That's not fair, yah. Quina will hug him too, yah." Quina tried to jump in, but a giant golem that appeared from the ground repelled her with its hand.

"Uh-uh. It's my turn right now. Quina isn't fair. You always get spoiled by Dad, but you're trying to steal my turn. He's my Dad right now. Rub, rub, rub." When I praise Rorono, Quina would beg me like crazy to do the same for her. And then Rorono would look a little frustrated. Aha, what she really wants to say is Quina has to wait for her turn.

"That's enough." The spirit left Rorono's body, and Rorono collapsed to the ground.

"Is she all right?"

"Yes, she'll soon regain consciousness."

"Huh? What was I doing just now?"

"She doesn't have any memory from while she was being possessed, huh?" Rorono looked bewildered and glanced around.

"Did I do something?"

"No, nothing."

"Rorono, you were mean, yah. Mrr."

"No, nothing particular happened. Pfft!"

"It was just about what I expected." Rorono tilted her head. Quina looked at her with frustration, and Aura and Wight eyed her with a smile.

I won't tell Rorono what happened. Rorono actually wanted to be spoiled. I'll make a mental note of it.

"I understand. You're going to use the premise of court to have your wraiths possess people to make them obedient and fess up to everything they did."

"Yes, making them confess to everything will eliminate the need of collecting evidence or annoying procedures. And we can let the public instead of a judge decide cases."

"There are some issues, but I like the idea. Go right ahead with it."

"As you wish, my lord." I'm sure Wight, who's competent, will apply various measures to solve those issues.

A month later...

In conclusion, the court was a huge success. The court is in session again today, and a large crowd of townspeople have gathered there.

"You bum! I tricked your senile parents into signing the deed. It was to protect their store and their workers! There's no way a kid can run that store. Neither can the senile boss or his wife. This was the only way I could think of helping them...but you see! You can count on me to look after the store and your parents!"

"You scumbag! I don't give a damn about the store! I was gonna sell it and use the money to play with!" Both the plaintiff and the defendant were possessed by wraiths. In this case, the plaintiff claimed a head clerk has deceived his parents and taken over their store. When he came to me, he tearfully told me that he wanted to take care of the store all his life. But here was his true intention. Well, we learned that the store was wrongfully taken in court, but I honestly wanted to support the head clerk.

The other case was a divorce trial.

"Yeah, yeah. I cheated on you. But you don't work or do any housework, you have terrible spending habits, and you're rarely home. I needed to be loved! I'm fine with getting divorced, but what's this alimony for?! You were at fault!"

"Well, there you have it, guys. He admitted on cheating. You owe me alimony!!"

"Agghhh! But didn't you cheat on me, too? You were going out at night all the time. You had to be chasing after men."

"I was cheating on you left and right. I was flirting around every day. Those guys were hotter than you!"

"Then, I refuse to pay you alimony! Actually, you owe me alimony." The audience burst out laughing.

In both cases, learning the truth didn't tell us who was right or wrong. Humans are hard to understand. I'm glad that I left all the decisions to the people.

"Wight, was this good to do?"

"Yes, it was. Judgments are made by the people, which won't hold us responsible for them... And most of all..."

"Everyone is enjoying it." That's right. The court has become an entertainment for townspeople. Truth in the name of misfortune, screw-ups and the true feelings of people are very much worth watching. I can feel a tremendous amount of emotions flowing into me. Well, I won't think too deeply about this... The issue has been resolved and I've gotten my fill anyway.

"Good job, Wight. You're always saving my butt."

"I'm humbled by your words. I devote myself to my lord." His beautiful motion of thanks is as becoming of him as ever.

"Should we go out for a drink?"

"I'd love to. I think I will enjoy it with you, my lord." That must be how he truly feels. Wight respects me, but he won't try to suck up to me. This man is vital to me and Avalon. That's exactly why I care about him and I want to provide him a rightful place. I walked away as I thought of this. Wight feels the mood to get drunk, but I want to enjoy having an actual drink with him someday. I couldn't help but wish for this. It's just a hunch, but I think I'll make it come true someday. That's how I felt.

THE END

DUNGEON BUILDER:

THE DEMON KING'S LABYRINTH IS A MODERN CITY!

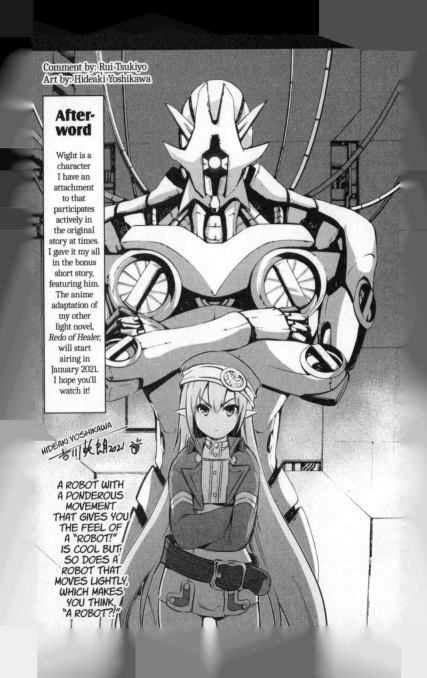

Comment by: Rui Tsukiyo
Art by: Hideaki Yoshikawa

After-word

Wight is a character I have an attachment to that participates actively in the original story at times. I gave it my all in the bonus short story, featuring him. The anime adaptation of my other light novel, *Redo of Healer,* will start airing in January 2021. I hope you'll watch it!

HIDEAKI YOSHIKAWA

A ROBOT WITH A PONDEROUS MOVEMENT THAT GIVES YOU THE FEEL OF A "ROBOT!" IS COOL BUT SO DOES A ROBOT THAT MOVES LIGHTLY, WHICH MAKES YOU THINK, "A ROBOT?!"

DUNGEON BUILDER:
THE DEMON KING'S LABYRINTH IS A MODERN CITY!